Children of the
American Jewish Ghetto

Also by Chaim M. Rosenberg
and from McFarland

The International Harvester Company: A History of the Founding Families and Their Machines (2019)

The Loyalist Conscience: Principled Opposition to the American Revolution (2018)

Losing America, Conquering India: Lord Cornwallis and the Remaking of the British Empire (2017)

Child Labor in America: A History (2013)

Children of the American Jewish Ghetto

Stories of Struggle and Achievement from 1881 through World War I

Chaim M. Rosenberg

McFarland & Company, Inc., Publishers
Jefferson, North Carolina

ISBN (print) 978-1-4766-9547-1
ISBN (ebook) 978-1-4766-5402-7

Library of Congress cataloging data are available

Library of Congress Control Number 2025000582

Front cover image: chicken vendors, Sixth St. Market, Cincinnati, 1912. Hyman Mormer, 9 years old, and brother Willie Mormer, age 12, of Kenyon Avenue and Rubenstein of West 6th Street, 12 years old (Library of Congress cph.3c15370).

Printed in the United States of America

McFarland & Company, Inc., Publishers
Box 611, Jefferson, North Carolina 28640
www.mcfarlandpub.com

To Dawn,
my wife and soulmate,
and to my dear friends,
Isaac Kalmanowitz (1935–2023),
Geoffrey Boner
and Laurence Geffen

Table of Contents

Introduction

"Remember, remember always, that all of us, you and I especially, are descended from immigrants and revolutionists.... We look for a younger generation that is going to be more American than we are."[1]

"America is God's Crucible, the great Melting-Pot where all the races of Europe are melting and reforming.... Germans and Frenchmen, Irishmen and Englishmen, Jews and Russians—into the Crucible with you all! God is making the American."[2]

Between 1881 and 1914, more than two million Jews came to America. Most were from the Russian Empire, coming from shtetls of the Pale of Settlements, steeped in Jewish tradition and religion, Yiddish-speaking, living separate lives and fearful of their Christian neighbors. A small percentage came from cities, had a secular education and absorbed Russian literature and culture. A number were members of the Jewish Bund, a socialist movement representing the small Jewish working class.

In this work I follow the Jews from their Russian shtetls and towns, to the ports of Hamburg and Bremen, to travel steerage on steamships across the Atlantic Ocean to the New World. In New York, Philadelphia, Boston and Chicago, they formed crowded Jewish ghettoes, living in cramped walk-up apartments and finding work in the clothing sweatshops or tobacco and cigarette factories. Government assistance was minimal. Pay was very low, perhaps $5 for 60 hours of work a week. Children as young as five years of age went out to earn extra money by selling newspapers, shining shoes, delivering telegraph messages, scavenging scrap metal, or working in the garment trade. They did not receive a warm welcome. Americans viewed the newcomers as uneducated, weighed down by religion, unskilled and weak in health and intelligence.

The small settled German-Jewish community was overwhelmed by the immensity of social problems that beset their Eastern European cousins. Many immigrant men abandoned their families, children were arrested for stealing and fighting. The newcomers faced unemployment, illness, or early death that robbed families of their main wage earner. The great blessing was the public schools where immigrant children learned the English language and American history, to become proud and patriotic citizens.

The early years were very difficult but over time the Russian Jews lifted themselves out of poverty. Many clung to the old ways centered on synagogues and religious schools, and establishing a vibrant Yiddish-language press and theater. But the desire, especially among the children, to become Americans was enormous. Within 15 years of arrival, most of the Russian Jewish immigrants had left the ghettoes for better neighborhoods and reached a standard of living equal to that of native-born Americans. Most aspired to a decent income, comfortable home and a nice neighborhood in which to raise a family. For a decade or two, they supported the Yiddish press and the Yiddish stage, but in their desire to fit in, they eagerly adopted American ways and dress, spoke and read English in preference to Yiddish and loosened their traditions and religious practices.

Many children of the Russian-Jewish immigrants had higher aspirations. From neighborhood elementary schools, the smart kids gained admission to elite high schools and acceptance into the nation's leading universities. Combining intelligence with hard work, they reached the top levels in their chosen fields: in the sciences, academia and the arts. Some 40 children of Russian Jews were Nobel laureates and many others Pulitzer Prize winners. During World War I, a quarter of a million Jews—many of them recent immigrants—fought for the United States against Germany.

The migration of Russian Jews 1881–1914 "to the New World broke the old patterns," wrote the philosopher Morris Raphael Cohen in 1949. "The old limitations on intellectual inquiry and discussion were removed." Arriving in America "many of the first generation, and many more of the second, despite the difficulties of the new environment and the strange language, brought to the tasks the New World presented a force … as if a great dam had broken and the force of water accumulated over many years had been let loose. A mighty force permeated every nook and corner of human endeavor.… The second generation had its boxers, gamblers and shyster lawyers, as well as great judges, teachers and scientists. Doctors, movie magnates, writers, merchants, philosophers, communists or defenders of corporate wealth, all showed an intensity that must have seemed a bit outlandish to the more comfortable and easy-going segments of the American population."[3]

At the close of World War I, the United States soured of immigration. Jews in America were accused of being unassimilable, fostering communism and anarchism, and taking too many places in the nation's elite colleges. America's open-door immigration policy ended soon after World War I. Stringent quotas drastically cut Jewish immigration. The nation's leading universities—Harvard, Yale, Princeton, Columbia—imposed quotas on Jewish admissions. In 1920, Henry Ford and his *Dearborn Independent* weekly newspaper claimed that the Jews of America were part of a secret but powerful conspiracy to gain control of the American and world economies. The anti–Semitic articles in the *Dearborn Independent* were gathered together into a book entitled *The International Jew: The World's Foremost Problem*. In America, claimed the Dearborn newspaper, "most of the big business, the trusts and the banks, the natural resources and the chief agricultural products, especially tobacco, cotton and sugar, are in the control of Jewish financiers or their agents. Jewish journalists are a large and powerful group here. Large numbers of department stores are held by Jewish firms, and Jews are the largest and most numerous landlords of residence property in the country. They are supreme in the theatrical world. They absolutely control the circulation of publications throughout the country" (pp. 10–11).

The *Dearborn Independent* alleged that America's theaters, motion picture industry, meat packing, shoemaking, jewelry, clothing industry, grain industry, newspapers and magazines were all Jewish owned and part of the conspiracy to dominate the world. Even trade union leaders like Samuel Gompers and Sidney Hillman were members of the secret cabal. "The Jew has succeeded in everything he has attempted in the United States, except farming" (p. 39). Inherently law-abiding and honest Gentiles are no match for the cunning and clever International Jew out to control the economy. The views expressed by Henry Ford's newspaper were based on *The Protocols of the Elders of Zion,* a fabricated text issued in 1903 in Imperial Russia. *The International Jew* and *The Protocols* were compulsory reading for teachers and students in Nazi Germany to justify their brutality and mass murder of European Jews.[4]

My research shows that there were very many *individual* Jews who grasped the opportunities offered by America to become eminent scientists, musicians, composers, actors, theater directors, movie directors, business owners, Nobel laureates and Pulitzer-prize winners, even leading boxers and basketball players, and a few leading mobsters. Far from being members of a secret international conspiracy, they identified individually closely with America and strove to be useful and patriotic citizens. American scientists of Russian-Jewish heritage discovered streptomycin for the treatment of tuberculosis, the vaccines that eliminated the scourge of poliomyelitis, as well as finding the fertility pill to prevent unwanted pregnancies. Aaron Copland, George Gershwin and Leonard Bernstein wrote wonderful and enduring American classical music. Irving Berlin gave us *God Bless America*, our unofficial national anthem. Jewish comedians and actors amused and entertained millions. Saul Bellow, Joseph Teller, Herman Wouk, Norman Mailer and Philip Roth wrote great American novels.

Russian Jews and their offspring were prominent in the movies and on Broadway. Arthur Miller was a leading playwright. Many of these high achieving Jews changed their names, attenuated their Jewish connections and married out of the faith. America gave each individual the chance to develop their talents, and very many Jews of Russian heritage excelled. Individual Jews offered their skills to benefit America by enriching its culture, building its industry, curing illness, improving the lot of working people, and offering laughs and deep thoughts. America was and is their Promised Land.

Each flow of immigrants—whether Irish, German, Polish, Scandinavian, Jewish, and more recently from Asia, Africa, South America and the Caribbean—evokes howls that the newcomers are inferior and are leading the nation into decay and ruin. It takes a generation for them to settle down, learn English and adapt to American ways. But, one can see how well the American-educated children find a comfortable and proud place in America. I offer the great Russian-Jewish immigration (1881–1914) as an example of an impoverished community that found a safe home in America. They succeeded, both for themselves and by making a significant contribution to the nation as a whole.

2

Immigration, 1881–1914

Before 1880, the United States was largely a rural agrarian society. Between 1880 and 1920 the nation was transformed into an industrial powerhouse based in the rapidly growing cities. The steel, silk, cotton and wool mills, clothing, footwear, glove, cigar and cigarette factories created a great demand for labor. Wages were low but mass production provided affordable goods.[1] Towns and cities across the nation were linked together by the telegram and a vast network of railroads. Employment opportunities attracting immigrants especially from southern and eastern Europe, largely southern Italians and Russian Jews. The United States at the time had an "open door" immigration policy. New arrivals needed only to pass a health test, and show they would not pose a danger or a burden on America; 98 percent of arrivals at Ellis Island were permitted entry.

During the years 1880 to 1914, around 21 million immigrants came to the United States, mostly Southern and Eastern Europeans. Among them were two million impoverished Yiddish-speaking Jews from Eastern Europe. The great majority came from the Polish, Lithuanian, Belarus, Ukrainian and Moldavian sections of the Russian Empire. In 1897, the region, known as the Pale of Settlements, had 42 million people of whom nearly five million were Jews, about 12 percent of the total population. Jews were long barred from many occupations, denied government jobs, and few admitted to universities. Most were shtetl Jews, steeped in tradition and religion. Their books were the Bible and the Talmud. They found work as storekeepers, innkeepers, tailors, shoemakers, lace workers, coachmen, and porters.

The rapid increase in the Jewish population of Russia during the second half of the 19th century added to the pressures of making a living wage. Chaim Weizmann, the future first president of the State of Israel, was born in the shtetl of Motol "in one of the darkest and most forlorn corners of the Pale of Settlements; that prison house created by czarist Russia for the largest part of its Jewish population."[2] A small number had been influenced by the Haskalah movement—Jewish enlightenment. They were educated in Russian schools, relatively well-to-do, living in the cities of Warsaw, Odessa, Vilna, Kishinev, Moscow, and St. Petersburg. They spoke Russian, French and German, read Russian novels and delighted in Russian music. A Russian maskil (enlightened Jew), Judah Leib Gordon, in his poem "Awake My People," proclaimed: "Be a Jew in your home and a man outside it." This catch-phrase appealed to those eager to enter Russian society. The assassination of Tsar Alexander II on March 13, 1881, at the Winter Palace, St. Petersburg, led to new restrictions and humiliations, and convinced both religious and enlightened Jews that Mother Russia did not want them.

Writing in 1898, Abraham Cahan describes the despair of Jews in Tsarist Russia

> We have striven to adopt the language and manners of our Christian fellow countrymen; we have brought ourselves up to an ardent love of their literature, of their culture, of their progress. We have tried to persuade ourselves that we are children of Mother Russia. Alas! we have been in error. The voice of the blood of our outraged brothers and sisters, cries unto us that we are only strangers in the land which we have been used to call our home; that we are only stepchildren here, waifs to be trampled upon and dishonored. There is no hope for Israel in Russia. The salvation of the downtrodden people lies in other parts,—in a land beyond the seas, which knows no distinction of race or faith, which is a mother to Jew and Gentile alike. In the great republic is our redemption from the brutalities and ignominies to which we are subjected in this our birthplace. In America we shall find rest; the stars and stripes will wave over the true home of our people. To America, brethren! To America![3]

Most migrants aimed for America. Smaller numbers of Russian Jews settled in France, Germany, Austria, Great Britain or South Africa.

The Russian-Jewish historian Simon Dubnow set out the causes of the economic collapse that afflicted Jews in Russia late in the 19th century. Following the assassination of Tsar Alexander II in March 1881, a wave of anti–Jewish pogroms swept the southern and western provinces of the Russian Empire. The notorious May Laws of 1882, sanctioned by Tsar Alexander III, forbade Jews from moving out of their villages and towns, and prevented them from operating their businesses on Sundays. The creation of a state liquor monopoly destroyed the livelihood of thousands of Jewish inn keepers, hostelries, bar-keepers and liquor store owners. Jews were forbidden to own land and were barred from entering the civil service. The state imposed a Jewish quota of 2 percent for students entering universities in Russia proper, and 7 percent of universities within the Pale of Settlements.

"An immense host of young men and women who found their way blocked to the higher educational institutions in Russia went abroad, flocking to foreign universities and higher professional schools.... A large number of these college youths returned home permeated with revolutionary ideas.... The reactionary Russian press, encouraged and stimulated by the official Jew-baiters, engaged in an increasingly ferocious campaign against the Jews.... Even the Russian stage was made subservient to the purposes of Jew-baiting." Pogroms convinced many Jews that they had no future in Russia. The "exodus of the Jews from Russia has helped create an important Jewish center in North America."[4]

During the years 1903–1906 rioters destroyed Jewish property and lives in the cities of Kiev, Odessa and Kishinev. "The anti–Jewish riots in Kishinev," reported *The New York Times* in 1903, "are worse than the censor will permit to publish. There was a well laid-out plan for the general massacre of Jews on the day following the Orthodox Easter. The mob was led by priests, and the general cry, 'Kill the Jews,' was taken up all over the city. The Jews were taken wholly unaware and were slaughtered like sheep. The dead numbered 120 and the injured about 500. The scenes of horror attending this massacre are beyond description. Babies were literally torn to pieces by the frenzied and bloodthirsty mob. The local police made no attempt to check the reign of terror. At sunset the streets were piled with corpses and the wounded. Those who could make their escape fled in terror, and the city is now practically deserted of Jews. Just as in 1881–1883, there was a popular belief among the Russian peasants that the Tsar decreed the slaughter of Jews."[5]

A burst of immigration followed the 1903–1906 pogroms. Low-cost rail journeys in Europe, steerage-class transatlantic steamship travel, and America's open-door policy encouraged many to migrate. Between 1881 and 1914, about one third of Russia's five million Jews emigrated.[6] For most it was a harrowing journey to the New World. In 1886 Morris Hillquit and his family "traveled for three weeks in the steerage.... The only food the family could afford to buy was potatoes."[7]

Morris Raphael Cohen's father went alone to America to raise the money to bring over the rest of the family. Enduring months of separation, the family left Minsk by train to Vilna and on to Kovno, where they were "distributed among a number of Jewish homes." From Kovno they traveled by wagon over gravel roads to Memel to cross into Germany. Traveling in a fourth-class railroad carriage without seats, the family reached the port city of Bremen to board ship and leave the Old World for the New. His mother brought a few loaves of kosher bread to sustain them over the journey.

> It took about 14 days to reach New York. We were huddled together in steerage like cattle. Naturally we could not eat the food on the ship, since it was not kosher. We only asked for hot water into which my mother used to put a little brandy and sugar to give it a taste. Towards the end of the trip when our bread was beginning to give out, we applied to the ship's steward for bread, but the kind he gave us was unbearably soggy.... It was with great joy one morning we heard the news that we were approaching America.[8]

Like so many other Jewish immigrants, the Cohen family settled into the grime of New York's Lower East Side. Within 12 years of his arrival in America, Morris Cohen had learned English, graduated from City College of New York (CCNY) and completed a Ph.D. at Harvard. At age 30, he was appointed a professor at CCNY to launch a brilliant career as philosopher and legal scholar.

From 1855 to 1892, Castle Garden located in the Bowery of Manhattan, served as the New York State immigration station. In 1892 the newly built station at Ellis Island began receiving immigrants. Between 1881 and 1924, about 12,000,000 immigrants, including 2.5 million Russian Jews, entered the United States via Ellis Island.

In her wonderful autobiography *The Promised Land*, Mary Antin describes the journey of her mother and four children from their shtetl Polotzk to join their father who had emigrated to Boston three years earlier. With steamship tickets in hand, the family bade an emotional farewell to family and friends and boarded the train to begin their journey. Antin wrote:

Our route lay over the German border, with Hamburg for our port. On the way to the frontier, we stopped for a farewell visit in Vilna, where my mother had a brother. On a grey wet morning in early April, we set out for the frontier. This was the real beginning of our journey, and all my faculties of observation were alert. I took note of everything; the weather, the trains, the bustle of railroad-stations, our fellow-passengers, and the family mood at every stage of our progress. The bags and bundles which composed our travelling outfit were much more bulky than valuable. A trifling sum of money, the steamer ticket, and the foreign passport were the magic agents by means of which we hoped to span the 5,000 miles of earth and water between us and my father.

At Versbolovo, the last station on the Russian side, we met the first of our troubles. A German physician and several gendarmes boarded the train and put us through a searching examination as to our health, destination, and financial resources. As a result of the inquisition, we were informed that we would not be allowed to cross the frontier unless we exchanged our third-class steamer ticket for second-class, which would require 200 rubles more than we possessed. Our passport was taken from us, and we were to be turned back on our journey.

Herr Schidorsky became the agent of our salvation. He procured my mother a pass to Eidtkuhnen, the German frontier station.... On the German side our course joined that of many other emigrant groups, on their way to Hamburg and other ports.... We emigrants were herded at the stations, packed in the cars, and driven from place to place like cattle.... We arrived in Hamburg early one morning, after a long night in the crowded cars. We were

In this 1904 illustration by Emil Flohri, an aged man labeled "Russian Jew" carries a large bundle labeled "Oppression" on his back; hanging from the bundle are weights labeled "Autocracy," "Robbery," "Cruelty," " Deception," and "Murder." In the background, a Jewish community burns, and Theodore Roosevelt chastises Tsar Nicholas II: "Why not remove his burden and have peace within your borders?" (Library of Congress, LC-DIG-ppmsca-05438).

Eastern European Jewish immigrants arriving in New York: "Welcome to the land of freedom—An ocean steamer passing the Statue of Liberty: Scene on the steerage deck" (*Frank Leslie's Illustrated Newspaper*, 2 July 1887, pp. 324–325).

> marched up to a strange vehicle, long and narrow and high, drawn by two horses and commanded by a mute driver. We were piled up on this wagon and our baggage was thrown in after us.

Along the way people attempted "to extort money from us.... My mother seeing her tiny hoard melting away." Reaching Hamburg, the family was placed in quarantine. "Two weeks within high brick walls, several hundreds of us herded in half a dozen rooms, sleeping in rows, like sick people in a hospital;

A Russian Jewess arrives at Ellis Island, 1905. Photograph by Lewis Hine (The Miriam and Ira D. Wallach Division of Art, Prints and Photographs: Photography Collection, The New York Public Library).

with roll-call morning and night, and short rations three times a day; with never a sign of the free world beyond our barred windows; with anxiety and longing and homesickness in our hearts." After further delays the Antin family "found ourselves on the deck of a great big steamship afloat on the strange big waters of the ocean. For 16 days the ship was our world." The journey across the Atlantic was rough

> when the ship pitched and rolled so that people were thrown from their berths; days and nights when we crawled through dense fogs, our foghorn drawing answering warnings from invisible ships. The perils of the sea were not minimized in the imaginations of us inexperienced voyagers.... All this while the seasickness lasted.... And so suffering, fearing, brooding, rejoicing, we crept nearer and nearer to the coveted shore, until, on a glorious May morning, six weeks after our departure from Polotzk, our eyes beheld the Promised Land, and my father received us in his arms.[9]

Immigrants traveled on the steamships of the White Star, Cunard, Red Star and Hamburg-American lines and entered America mainly through Ellis Island. Smaller numbers reached shore in Boston, Philadelphia and Baltimore. A small proportion of the Russian-Jewish immigrants came with funds but "by far the greater number needed assistance." In 1891 alone, Jewish charities in New York offered new arrivals more than 12,000 railway tickets to move to other cities.[10] Some 10,000 immigrants disembarked at Galveston, Texas, and dispersed to towns and villages along the Mississippi River, to the Rockies and as far north as Fargo, North Dakota.

In 1881, 8,000 Russian Jews came to America, followed during the next nine

Jewish Immigrants arriving on SS *Cassel* at Galveston, Texas, 1907 (Texas State Library and Archives).

years, by 500,000 more. From 1891 to 1914, over 1.5 million more Russian Jews arrived. Between the years 1881 and 1905, Jews comprised less than 5 percent of all immigrants to the United States. The peak years for Jewish immigration were 1906 with 147,209 and 1907, with 109,183 arriving. During these two years, Jewish immigration reached 11 percent of all immigrants. "They came here without means. They came with families, and the families were large."[11] World War I greatly reduced Jewish immigration to America. The 1917 Bolshevik Revolution slammed shut the path of immigration from Russia, but Jewish migration from newly independent Poland rose between 1919 and 1921. After 1924, strict immigration quotas reduced Jewish immigration into the United States to a trickle.

3

Jewish Ghettoes

The two million Russian-Jewish immigrants arrived mainly through Ellis Island, between 1881 and 1914. Having experienced centuries of persecution and separation in the Russian Empire, these immigrants huddled together and formed a vast ghetto in the Lower East Side of New York City, with smaller ghettoes in Chicago, Philadelphia, Boston, Baltimore and Cleveland. Here, the newcomers set up their *shtiebels,* houses of prayer, and their *landsmanshaftn,* mutual aid societies for people of the same village. They found work in the needle trades, cigar rolling, and as peddlers and shopkeepers. These ghettoes were packed with tenements and sweatshops. Desperate for any work, the Jewish newcomers accepted low wages, long hours and horrible working conditions.

The Lower East Side of New York City

In 1880, the Jewish population of New York City numbered 80,000—largely rapidly assimilating German Jews. The 1881–1914 migration made New York the world's most populous Jewish community. In 1910, the 1.45 square miles of the Lower East Side held 540,000 people (mostly Jews) with a population density of 375,000 per square mile; the most densely populated neighborhood on earth. Each six- or seven-story tenement buildings with rickety stairs, outside toilets, and tiny apartments, housed 300 people or more. The Yiddish-language and the traditions of the Russian Jews suffused the area. "It seemed at first that the Russian Jews could not be assimilated into American life; but soon practically all their children were rising into citizenship."[1]

In his 1890 book *How the Other Half Lives,* Danish-born Jacob A. Riis describes the squalor, overcrowding and despair of the Lower East Side. In the chapter labeled *Jewtown,* Riis writes:

> There is no need of asking here where we are. The jargon of the street, the signs of the sidewalk, the manner and dress of the people, their unmistakable physiognomy, betray their race at every step. Men with queer skull-caps, venerable beard, and the outlandish long-skirted kaftan of the Russian Jew, elbow the ugliest and the handsomest women in the land. The Eastern European Jewish immigrants pack sections of the Lower East Side through dark hallways and filthy cellars, crowded with dirty children.... Polish or Russian Jews deliberately starving themselves to the point of physical exhaustion, while working night and day at a tremendous pressure to save a little money.

> The homes of the Hebrew quarter are its workshops also. [On every street is heard] the whir of a thousand sewing-machines, worked at high pressure from earliest dawn till mind and muscle give out together. Every member of the family, from the youngest to the oldest, bears a hand, shut in rooms, where meals are cooked and clothing washed and dried, it is not unusual to find a dozen persons—men, women, and children—at work in a single small room. In a tenement building occupied by Russian Jews, Riis "found in three rooms father, mother, 12 children, and six boarders. They sleep on the half-made clothing for beds ... several people slept in a subcellar four feet by six, on a pile of clothing."[2]

In an 1896 article, Riis writes sympathetically of the struggles of the Russian-Jewish immigrants:

> Their customs are strange, their language unintelligible. ... The newcomers, struggling hand to hand with the dire realities of poverty; they brought boundless energy and industry to overcome it. Their slums are offensive, but unlike those of other less energetic races, they are not hopeless.... They do not rot in their slum, but rising pull it up after them. They show the resistless energy of people who will not rest content in poverty. Their slums on the East Side are dark mainly because of the constant influx of a new population ever beginning the old struggle over. The second generation is the last found in those tenements, if indeed it is not already on its way uptown to the Avenue.
>
> They brought temperate habits and a redeeming love of home. Their strange customs proved the strongest ally of the Gentile health officer in his warfare upon the slum.... The death-rate of poverty-stricken Jewtown, despite its crowding, is lower than that of the homes of the rich. The Jew's rule of life is his faith and it regulates his minutest action. His clannishness does not obstruct his citizenship. There is no more patriotic a people than these Jews, and with reason. They have no old allegiance to forget.
>
> The economic troubles of the East Side, their sweat shops and their starvation wages, are the faithful companions of their dire poverty.... Trade organization conquers the sweat shop, and the school drills the child not to be enslaved.... I verily believe these men would starve to death rather than bend their backs again under the yoke.[3]
>
> Riis had always been deeply touched by the miserable conditions under which the Jewish people lived in the East Side. He admired the way in which struggling fathers and mothers bent over their sweatshop machines day and night trying valiantly to earn a living and to pull themselves up by the boot straps. He paid a tribute to Jewish indomitability.[4]

Rose Cohen's father came first to America to earn enough money to send for his wife and children. Rose tells of her arrival in America in 1892: "From Castle Garden we drove to our new home in a market wagon filled with immigrants' bedding. Father tucked us in among the bundles, climbed up beside the driver himself and we rattled off over the cobbled stone pavement, with the noon sun beating down on our heads. As we drove along, I looked about in bewilderment. My thoughts were chasing each other. I felt a thrill: 'Am I really in America at last?' But the next moment it would be checked and I felt a little disappointed, a little homesick. Father was so changed. I hardly expected to find him in his black long tailed coat in which he left home. But, of course yet with his same full-grown beard and earlocks. Now instead I saw a young man with a closely cut beard and no sign of earlocks. As I looked at him, I could scarcely believe my eyes. Father had been the most pious Jew in our neighborhood. I wondered was it true that 'in America one at once became a libertine?'"[5]

Despite their poverty, the Jewish newcomers in New York established a vibrant

This 1909 picture, titled "The Ghetto," shows the Lower East Side with its tenement buildings and the pushcarts, vendors and customers that daily filled the streets (Library of Congress, LC-DIG-det-4a28391).

Yiddish-language culture with theaters, newspapers, magazines and books and literary clubs. The leading Yiddish newspaper was the *Forward*, established in 1897 with Abraham Cahan as editor. The socialist-leaning newspaper supported Jewish trade unions. By the 1920s its circulation reached 275,000. The *Forward* was the most prominent foreign-language newspaper in America. "Hundreds of educated young Hebrews earn their living, and often pay their way through college," wrote Cahan in 1898, "by giving private lessons in English in the tenement houses. ... The pupils of these private tutors are the same poor overworked sweatshop hands.... The poor laborer will pinch himself to keep his child at college, rather than send him to a factory that he may contribute to the family's income."[6] Cahan wrote in 1905: "The Russian Jews within the last 20 years have created a vast literature [to educate] thousands of ignorant tailors and peddlers, lift their intelligence, facilitate their study of English, and open to them the doors of the English library."[7]

The New York ghetto "was a huge collection of misery and poverty," wrote Edmund James, president of the University of Illinois, in 1907. Yet the children of the Russian Jewish immigrants "are, as a rule, bright, attentive and studious. They excel

Shoeshine for Rosh Hashanah, Lower East Side of New York, September 12, 1912 (Library of Congress, LC-B2-2425-1).

in mathematics, English and history.... The Jewish facility for adaptation and the progress of assimilation in this country are incontestable."[8]

The esteemed Yiddish writer Sholem Aleichem (born Solomon Rabinowitz in the Russian Empire) settled in New York in 1905 and remained to his death in 1916, at age 57 years. "A hundred thousand people of the east side, with sadness in their faces, lined the sidewalks yesterday when the funeral procession of Sholem Aleichem passed down Second Avenue and through East Houston. Eldridge, and Canal Streets, to the Educational Alliance, where services were held before the body was carried over the Williamsburg Bridge to Mount Carmel Cemetery in Cypress Hills."[9]

George and Ira Gershwin, Zero Mostel, George Burns, Eddie Cantor and Irving Berlin emerged from the teeming Jewish life of the Lower East Side. It also "called forth the Jewish prostitute, the Jewish gambler, as it called forth the Jewish criminal" in the likes of Benjamin "Bugsy" Siegel, Mayer Lansky and Louis "Lepke" Buchalter.[10]

Other Jewish-American Ghettoes

Smaller Jewish ghettoes were established in Brooklyn, the Upper East Side of the borough of Manhattan around 100th Street, as well as the New Jersey cities of

Funeral of the Yiddish author Sholem Aleichem, May 15, 1916, New York.

Jersey City and Newark. The Jewish Industrial Removal Office guided immigrants from New York to other American towns and cities. Large communities of Russian Jews settled in Chicago, Boston, Philadelphia, Detroit, Cleveland, Galveston, as well as in mill towns such as Lowell, Fall River and Lawrence.

In 1891, The *Chicago Daily Tribune* described the distinctive features of the Maxwell Street district:

> One can walk the streets for blocks and see none but Semitic features and hear nothing but the Hebrew patois of Russian Poland. In this restricted boundary, in narrow streets, ill-ventilated tenements and rickety cottages ... every Jew in this quarter who can speak a word of English is engaged in business of some sort ... everyone is looking for a bargain, and everyone has something to sell. ... The principal streets in the quarter are lined with stores of every description.... In a room of a small cottage, 40 small boys all with hats on, sit crowded into a space 10 × 10 feet in size, presided over by a stout middle-aged man with a long, curling, matted beard, who also retains his hat, a battered rusty derby of ancient style. All the old or middle-aged men in the quarter affect this peculiar head gear.

The Russian Jews who came to Chicago were "little affected by modern culture, ignorant of our language and culture ... and domiciled in wretched dwelling houses in the worst part of our city, where they have created their own ghetto.... Persecution abroad developed a hereditary tendency to trading [leaving them fit] only for making a livelihood by peddling or by unskilled labor." They settled on the West Side of Chicago "in a district bounded by 16th Street on the south and Polk Street on the north and the Chicago River, and Halsted Street on the east." One can walk the streets for blocks and see none but Semitic features.[11] With its Yiddish-speaking, bearded peddlers, pushcarts, sweatshops, large families, the Maxwell Street area had "a teeming, transplanted Eastern European shtetl atmosphere."[12]

"The physical characteristics of the Chicago Ghetto do not differ materially from the surrounding districts," wrote an observer in 1907, "The streets may be a trifle narrower; the alleys are no filthier. There is only one saloon to 10 in the other districts.... It is the religious distinction which everyone notices, the synagogues, the Talmud schools, the kosher signs on the meat markets.... On bright days, groups of adults join the multitude, especially on Saturday and Sunday, or on Jewish holidays."[13]

Most worked in the needle or cigar trades but, as early as 1905, Chicago had Jewish

> iron molders, machinists, locomotive engineers, sailors, farm helpers, boiler makers, butchers at the stock yards, street sweepers, section hands on railroads, motormen and conductors on the street cars; bricklayers, carpenters, steam fitters, plumbers; in bicycle plating shops; in manufactories of electrical appliances, of iron beds and springs, of shoes, of wood work, and of upholstery; in tin, mattress and picture frame factories; and in bakeries.... Very few wage-workers among Russian Jewish people who settled in Chicago regarded it as their permanent lot in life to remain laborers for wage. Almost all are bending their energies to get into business or to acquire an education so that they may fit themselves for some other calling than that of the wage-earner. More of our boys and girls who have attended the public schools enter stores and offices than shops and factories.[14]

"The Jewish ghetto of Philadelphia extending from Spruce Street in the north to Christian Street in the South and from 3rd Street to 6th Street east to west, and south of Lombard Street, where foreign Jews are crowding in, and being very poor, the Hebrew charities are drawn upon heavily."[15] South 4th Street was the Jewish marketplace in Philadelphia with kosher butcher shops, fish shops, grocery stores and tailoring shops, and peddlers alongside the trolley tracks, selling fruits and vegetables and dry goods loaded on their pushcarts.

The Russian Jews in Philadelphia were concentrated largely in the needle trades, making shirts, skirts, cloaks, wrappers, pants, overalls and underwear. "In the manufacture of clothing in Philadelphia the majority of the employees are Russian Jews. Jews were also employed as peddlers, cigar makers, clerks and small shopkeepers. As early as 1905, there was clear evidence of upward mobility 'with a number of young men studying for the professions, so that within the near future the list of the latter will be largely increased.'"[16]

East European Jews came to Boston to seek work in the clothing sweatshops and shoe and boot factories. They settled first in the historic, but rundown, North End and West End where street peddlers plied their trade. In 1875, only 3,000 Jews lived in Boston. By 1900, the migration of Russian Jews created a community of 40,000

The Jewish ghetto of Chicago. Russian Jews settled on the west side of the city, in a district bounded by 16th Street on the south and Polk Street on the north and the Chicago River and Halsted Street on the east. In 1910, the ghetto held 50,000 (Library of Congress, Jews. LC-DIG-stereo-1s12667).

and by 1914, 90,000 Jews. Many moved on to the shoe and boot towns of Haverhill, Lynn, and Brockton, or to the textile towns of Lowell, Lawrence and Fall River. Early in the 20th century, one-third of the shoemakers of Lynn were Jewish immigrants, working long hours for low wages. There were also Jewish carpenters, plumbers, tin workers, textile mill workers and glass cutters.

In Cleveland, Russian Jews with their kosher grocery shops, stores and synagogues lined E. 105th Street. The Jewish quarter of Detroit was formed by Monroe, Watson, Bush and Orleans Streets, with Hastings Street its commercial center. Russian Jews settled in East Baltimore. In Cincinnati, the Russian Jews established

North End, the Jewish Quarter of Boston. Pen and ink drawing by William Allen Rogers, 1899 (Library of Congress, LC-DIG-ppmsca-05435).

a ghetto in the West End, north of Court Street and up to Liberty Street. In 1915 a Jewish cultural center at 15th Street and Central Avenue opened, offering live theater, movies, classes in English and civics, a swimming pool and exercise room.[17] In Syracuse, New York, Jewish immigrants clustered in the 7th Ward, the East Side of downtown. In the 1920s and 1930s the Boyle Heights district of Los Angeles attracted many Yiddish-speaking immigrants, with Jewish delis and shops and synagogues.

The Russian Jewish ghetto in the Lower East Side was by far the largest, followed by Chicago, Philadelphia and Boston. The occupants of these ghettoes were similar as were their patterns of growth and decline. Soon after their arrival in the ghettoes, the Russian Jews overcame despair and poverty, and found their footing. The humble needle workers became clothing contractors or opened their own sweatshops and clothing factories. The street peddlers established clothing and food stores, the ragmen formed cotton-waste, scrap metal and paper businesses, carpenters became builders and contractors, hiring others to do the manual work. As they became successful, they moved out of the ghettoes, and their places were taken—until 1914—by newly arrived Jews fleeing the Russian Empire.

Jews began leaving the slums of the Lower East Side of New York early in the 20th century. The opening of the Brooklyn Bridge in 1903 helped their move to Williamsburg and Brownsville in Brooklyn, Washington Heights; and to East and South Bronx, and especially the Grand Concourse. In Chicago, Jews left the Maxwell Street district and moved to Lawndale in the Far West Side. By 1940s they were moving to Hyde Park in the south Chicago or north to Rogers Park and then Skokie and Evanston, and further into the tree-lined wealthy towns of Wilmette, Glencoe, Deerfield and Highland Park.

By the 1920s, Jews of Boston left the North End for Roxbury, Dorchester and Mattapan to the south, and Chelsea and Malden to the north. Later still, their children, college graduates and newly established doctors, lawyers and businessmen, moved to the affluent suburbs of Brookline, Newton, Swampscott and Marblehead. The Philadelphia Jewish ghetto began to empty, with Jews moving south of Washington Avenue and east of Broad Street. Others moved to West Philadelphia and Strawberry Mansion. In Detroit the Jews moved to Oak Park, Southfield and West Bloomfield. By 1921, quota restrictions virtually dried up the immigration into America of Eastern European Jews.

The Lower East Side of New York and Maxwell Street of Chicago were increasingly home to Puerto Ricans and African Americans. "After World War I and during the Twenties, the modest prosperity of the immigrant generation was reflected in a phenomenally rapid desertion of the old congested centers of settlement. In 1916, the Lower East Side of New York held, it was believed, 353,000 Jews; in 1930 it held 121,000. Between 1914 and 1920, the number of Russian-born Jewish immigrants in the old ghetto area of Chicago was more than halved."[18]

By the 1950s the Jewish ghettoes of America with their crowded tenements, outdoor toilets, public baths, street peddlers, kosher food stores, synagogues and sweatshops were a nostalgic memory.

In their 1961 book *Children of the Gilded Ghetto*, Judith R. Miller and Seymour Leventman described how Russian-Jewish immigrants, their children and their grandchildren adjusted to life in America. For the immigrants who arrived between 1881 and 1914, the ghetto was "a complete, albeit narrow, social world organized around traditional religious values that permeated even the smallest detail of existence.... Religious orthodoxy constituted a way of life for immigrants aware of few alternatives. [Their children] wished not merely to survive in an alien land, but to better themselves and become 'real Americans' [to assume] the values of the dominant society [and] adapt to a middle-class American-style of life" by moving to the suburbs, to join "the gilded ghetto, whose social life was carried on exclusively with Jews of appropriate status." "They entered the professions, established Reform and Conservative temples and joined country clubs. Few rejected their Jewish identity."

The Miller-Leventman study was conducted in Minneapolis, Minnesota, then with a Jewish population of some 20,000. Grandchildren (third generation) entered even more deeply into American life by intermarriage and establishing "a way of life that renders them indistinguishable from their non–Jewish neighbors.... The conflict between the first and second generation was between the values of the traditional ghetto and the values of an acculturated ethnic community. The conflict between the second and third generation is a conflict between the values of an acculturated but separate ethnic community and the values of a general status community."[19]

The 1961 Miller-Leventman study would suggest that Jewry in America was rapidly shedding its identity and moving to assimilation. Now entering the sixth and seventh generations since the great migration of Russian Jews between the years 1881 and 1914, American Jewry in 2024 still remains vibrant. The twin cities of Minneapolis–St. Paul hold some 65,000 Jews, supported by a wide range of religious and Jewish social services.

4

Jewish Newsies

> "We have an army of children at large and alone upon our avenues and alleys. Its members are engaged in newspaper selling, in boot-blacking, in delivering messages and goods: they are peddlers and venders and barkers at street stands.... The young street toilers in many cities have been left almost un-befriended and undefended. The need of money at home is the general plea of the boys."[1]

Israel "Izzy" Beilin, born in 1889 in the shtetl of Tolochin in Tsarist Russia, was the youngest of eight children of Moshe Beilin, a synagogue cantor and his wife Lena. When Izzy was four years old the family left Russia and arrived at the Bowery in New York. Their first home in America was a small basement apartment in a tenement on Monroe Street in New York's Lower East Side. After Moshe found irregular work certifying kosher meat in butcher shops, the family moved to a slightly larger apartment at 330 Cherry Street. "Eight or nine of us in four rooms." To get away from the stifling heat of summer "we slept on the fire escape or on the roof.... I was born with poor parents."[2]

To add to the meager family income, the four younger girls Rebecca, Sarah, Chasse and Sifre found work rolling cigars. Izzy's older brother Benjamin worked in a sweatshop, sewing shirts. Like his father, Izzy had a fine voice and appeared destined to follow his father's career as a cantor. Izzy paid little attention to public school or afternoon religious classes, but he enjoyed singing in the synagogue. "I suppose it was singing in *shul* that gave me my musical background," he recalled. "It was in my blood."[3] Moshe died when Izzy was eight years old, compelling the little boy to join his siblings earning money to support the family. Izzy soon learned that he could collect extra pennies by singing songs while selling copies of the *Evening Journal*, published by the Hearst Company. When the children returned home, "they would deposit the coins that they had earned that day into [mother] Leah's apron."[4]

Izzy left school at age 14, to spend his teen years moving from one dismal lodging house to another. He subsisted by singing songs in the saloons of the Bowery, hoping that the customers—sailors, prostitutes, laborers—would reward him with a few pennies. He was determined to make his way in the music business. His big break came at age 23 with *Alexander's Ragtime Band*. He changed his name to Irving Berlin. So began his illustrious career as singer, composer and lyricist. Drafted during

World War I, Berlin wrote the words and the lyrics for the musical *Yip Yip Yaphank*, which included the songs "Oh, How I Hate to Get Up in the Morning," and "The Girl I Left Behind." He left out "God Bless America" but used it 20 years later for the World War II hit musical, *This Is the Army*.

Song writer Irving Berlin in uniform, 1919 (Library of Congress, LC-DIG-ppmsca-5056).

At the close of the 19th century, the United States offered few social programs such as health care, sick leave, vacations or higher educational opportunities. Wages were low and families large. The sickness or death of a wage-earner would rapidly plunge the family into abject poverty and homelessness. To help support their families, more than two million children under age 16—some as young as five—were working across the length and breadth of America on farms, canneries, bottle companies, mattress companies, collecting scrap metal, in the fisheries, textile mills, slaughter houses, mines, offices, in the tenement sweatshops, working as messenger boys, fruit and vegetable peddlers, or selling newspapers and chewing gum on city streets. Wherever Russian Jews settled, "the pay was often too small to support the large family even in the poorest style, it became necessary for his wife and children to join in work," wrote Charles Bernheimer in 1905.[5] Like the Italian, Irish and other immigrants, many Jewish kids went to work to help sustain the family.

Born 1874 in Oshkosh, Wisconsin, Lewis Wickes Hine made his mark in 1905 taking pictures of recently arrived immigrants at Ellis Island. In 1908, he was hired by the National Child Labor Committee (NCLC) to travel across the United States to take pictures of working children. The NCLC believed that children selling newspapers led to truancy, fighting, gambling, stealing and health problems. Lugging his 5-by-7-inch box camera that made glass-plate negatives, between the years 1908 and 1924, he traveled from Maine to the Gulf States and from New York to California, taking over 5,000 pictures of laboring children. The crystal-clear images, over a century old, remain the principal record of the harrowing story of American child labor. The names of most of the children are not known. In some cases, Hine jotted down the child's name, ethnic group and address. I have assembled about 60 of the Hine pictures of children with clearly Jewish names. There probably were many more Jewish youngsters among Hine's subjects. The Russian Jewish immigrants settled largely in America's large cities and towns. Working Jewish children were largely newsboys and newsgirls, messenger boys, or employed making clothing, rolling cigars, or collecting and selling scrap metal.

At the close of the 19th century, the newspaper magnates Joseph Pulitzer and William Randolph Hearst engaged in sensationalist journalism to build circulation. Both companies called for Cuban independence from colonial Spain. In February 1898, after the U.S. battleship *Maine* exploded and sank in Havana's harbor, these newspapers raised patriotic rage by demanding an American war against Spain. Hearst further escalated his battle against Pulitzer by lowering the price of his New York newspaper to one penny a copy. Many Jewish kids hawked the English-language newspapers but also the Yiddish-language papers. Founded in 1897, and edited by Abraham Cahan, the *Forward* (*Forverts*) became America's leading Yiddish-language newspaper, with a circulation that reached 300,000. The socialist *Di Vahrheit* (*The Truth*) was founded in 1903 by Louis F. Miller, but it folded in 1919.

In New York City, 10,000 newsboys (and a small number of newsgirls) were on the streets, mornings, evenings and on weekends. Each newsboy bought his daily allotment. Selling all his papers would yield a small profit, but if left with even a few unsold copies, the result was a loss. In 1899, the Joseph Pulitzer's *New York Evening World* and William Randolph Hearst's *New York Evening Journal* raised the price to newsboys from 50 cents a hundred copies to 60 cents. In protest the newsboys organized a strike. Pinned to their hats or jacket was the notice: "Please don't buy the Journal or World because the newsboys have striked."[6] Louis "Kid Blink" Baletti was the charismatic leader of the strike. When he stepped down, Morris Cohen was elected president of the newsboys' union. On July 27, Pulitzer received a report that "A young fellow named Morris Cohen, who sells about 300 Worlds a day in City Hall Park got ahold of the boys and got them to strike." Other Jewish boys who lead the union were Myer Cohen, treasurer, and Barney "Peanuts" Cohen, delegate. The newsboys strike spread to other cities. The strike ended after two weeks when the newspapers agreed to give the boys more money and re-imburse them for unsold papers. These events inspired *Newsies*, the 2012 hit Broadway show.

Newsboys and newsgirls were the most publicly visible form of child labor. In cities and towns across the nation, many Jewish kids were newsies. In 1911 Milwaukee, Wisconsin, published a study of 80 Jewish newsboys from that city. The boys were age 6 to 13 years, with an average age of 10 years. Most had been out selling newspapers for a year or more, with average earnings of $1.80 a week, of which $1.50

went to help support the family. The Jewish homes were small, often shared by two or more families. Most children came from homes with a father and mother present. Half of the fathers were peddlers or scrap metal dealers. Eight were tailors and eight were Hebrew school teachers; a few were clerks or laborers. Most of the fathers had seasonal, irregular incomes and the boys' regular earnings, though small, helped pay the rent and put food on the table. Most parents wanted their children to go out to work and most of the boys did so willingly.

The parents spoke Yiddish, while the children responded in English. Street work had its benefits and risks. The boys learned how to transact business, and get along with adults. Some of the boys got into gambling, smoking, going into saloons, staying out late, getting into fights, and causing conflict at home. Selling newspapers "did not prevent the boys from being attentive and staying awake in the classroom." The teachers were often unaware that the children were out late selling newspapers. The teachers estimated that in "about a third of the cases the boy was injured by selling newspapers."[7]

> "The street trades of Washington employ one-fourth of the total number of children engaged in all occupations," announced the Washington Post in 1908. "It is a surprising fact that of the number of children under 15 who have come within the arm of the law, more than two-thirds are from the ranks of children in these trades. The boys selling papers are especially subjected to temptations. These youngsters, some of them seven and eight years old, quickly learn that it is much easier to make money by failing to have the correct change than to be content with the legitimate profit on the sale. Knowledge of sharp practice when acquired is hard to eradicate. The tendency is for the child to learn to believe that through begging or questionable means he can reap a larger harvest than is possible legitimately."[8]

"Night after night hundreds of boys and men hung around the newspaper offices, fought their way to the distributing counters and out into the street. I found them wandering about ... hanging onto the job until one or two in the morning, simply to make a record sale, perhaps, or to unload the heavy bunch of papers in which they had unwisely invested."[9] In the early days of the newspaper, "the Irish boy held absolute possession," wrote Jane Addams of Hull House fame, in 1903. "The Jewish boy came next. He would not fight the Irish [but] every day he was at his post, in winter and summer, in good weather and bad; the customer could depend on his appearance with the paper. So, his trade increased and at last he gained a monopoly at the corner." By 1900, there were 4,000 newsboys and newsgirls in Chicago, with Jewish kids competing against Italian, Scandinavian, German, Black and Irish kids. Few earned more than $1 a day, but a busy corner, like Clark and Madison in Chicago, could bring in $5 a day. Working long hours, newsboys missed parts of their schooling, suffered ill health and some of them picked up the bad habits of smoking and gambling. After only two years in public schools the immigrant child "in all intents and purposes has become an American, while his parents remain European peasants." Jane Addams estimated that in 1903, 5 percent of the Chicago newsboys were Jewish.[10]

In a 1917 Cincinnati survey, Jews comprised about 6 percent of the population but Jewish children made up a quarter of the newsboys out on the streets, reflecting "the large proportion of Jewish newsboys wherever in America."[11] Vincent DiGirolamo writes that in 1892 most of Cleveland's licensed newsboys were Jews. In a 1931 survey of Omaha newsboys, one in four was a Jewish kid.[12] In a 1914 Kansas City study, half the newsboys were Jewish, one-third Italians and the rest of English, Irish, and German extraction.[13] In 1905, about 80 percent of the Denver newsboys were Jewish.[14] A 1928 government survey of children in street work reported that a high percentage of newsboys in Atlanta, Cleveland, Cincinnati, Toledo, Omaha and Wilkes-Barre were children of Russian Jews.[15]

At 2:00 a.m. on April 12, 1908, Abe Bloom of Eldridge Street, Lower East Side, was still out in the streets of Tenderloin, New York City, selling newspapers. Tenderloin was then the center of New York's entertainment and red-light district with many nightclubs, gambling halls, saloons, dancehalls, and crime. Joseph Lehman, a 7-year-old New York newsboy regularly entered barrooms to sell newspapers. When questioned about the newsboy's badge he was wearing, issued only to boys over age 14, he responded: "Oh! Dat's me brudder's."

Hersh Baraznik was born in 1890 in a Ukrainian shtetl. At age 12 he came alone to the United States. "On my very first day in Boston, I began selling newspapers because I had to support myself.... Thus, I found myself in the world of working children with all the hardships and problems that work on the streets involved," wrote Hersh in 1944, under his new name Harry Ernest Burroughs.

> I was—and am—that boy: that newsboy, that bootblack, that messenger boy, that street peddler, shivering in the cold of winter, sweltering in the heat of summer; that hard-working, ambitious, bewildered boy.... Many of us graduated from the streets to become lawyers, doctors, educators, businessmen.... Not a few of them found their way into crime of one sort or another. Others took menial jobs from which they have never escaped. A few are still selling newspapers.... Newsboys are more ambitious, energetic, industrious, independent, and persevering, and they have a greater sense of responsibility. They support themselves.... They share in providing and sometimes earn the bulk of the family income. They stick to a hard, uninteresting job through fair weather and foul. They have to be alert to win and keep customers, to secure and retain favorable stands or corners.[16]

Bright and ambitious, Hersh won a scholarship to attend law school, passing the bar examination in 1912. After serving in World War I, he established a law practice in Boston. His practice thrived and he rose to become chairman of the board of the Massachusetts Law Society. He never forgot his humble origins and in 1927, at a cost of $500,000 (about $8.5 million in 2024), he established the Burroughs Newsboys Foundation at 10 Somerset Street on Boston's Beacon Hill. The foundation provided a second home to many of Boston's 4,000 newsboys. Over the years the foundation provided health care, education, training in the trades, scholarships, recreation and cultural opportunities to thousands of Boston's boys working in the trades. Using the in-house printing press, the boys issued their own weekly newspaper.[17] Harry Burroughs died in 1946, aged 56 years. His efforts on behalf of poor working children "brought him national renown."[18]

Six-year-old Hyman selling newspapers on Massachusetts Avenue, Lawrence, Massachusetts, 1911 (Library of Congress, LC-DIG-nclc-03748).

Nathan R. Miller was one of the many Boston newsboys who came regularly to the Burroughs Foundation. Born in 1919 to a poor Jewish family, Nathan trained in accountancy. During World War II he enlisted in the U.S. Army. Returning to Boston he established an accounting office, branched into real estate, and acquired many properties. In 2005, he gave $2 million to Suffolk University to buy the Burroughs Newsboy Foundation site on which the Nathan R. Miller Residence Hall was built.

In 1845, Abbott Lawrence established the Essex Company to build large textile mills, powered by the flow of the Merrimack River. The Lawrence mills attracted immigrant families, including Jews who were sent directly from Ellis Island by the Industrial Removal Office of the United Hebrew Charities of New York to work in the Massachusetts mill towns of Lowell and Lawrence. In 1911, Hyman, a bare-footed six-year-old newsboy, sold papers until 6:00 p.m. on Massachusetts Street, Lawrence, Massachusetts. The next year, Lawrence was the site of the bitter Bread and Roses Strike for more pay and better working conditions.

Until 1880, Hartford, Connecticut, had a 1,500-person German-Jewish community. The arrival of Russian-Jews swelled the Jewish population to 20,000 by 1920. They found work as peddlers, tailors, cabinet makers, and bakers, and opened clothing stores and kosher butcheries. Hartford had a dozen Orthodox synagogues, Jewish old-age home, orphanage, benevolent society and a burial society. Opened in 1923, Mt. Sinai Hospital employed Jewish doctors and provided kosher food to its patients. Jewish children like Bessie Goldman, Alice Goldman, 12-year-old Rebecca Cohen and Hyman Alpert were out early in the morning and late in the afternoon selling newspapers. In 1909, Hartford newsboys formed a union led by Morris Zelkowitz, Michael Levy and Nathan Feinstein, demanding that newspaper owners buy back unsold copies.[19]

Eight-year-old Bessie Brownstein was one of 10 children of Yiddish-speaking immigrants, Meyer and Jenny Brownstein. Meyer was a fruit and vegetable peddler. In 1918, Bessie married Harry Rosenthal, and raised two children. During World War II, she worked for the Red Cross blood bank. Abraham and Anna Navinsky, from Grodno, Russia, had four daughters. In 1905, Abraham arrived alone and settled in Hartford, Connecticut, working as a carpenter. Two years later, his wife and daughters joined him. The children went to work to help support the family. Dora Navinsky married Frank Basch, and was the mother of four children. Dora Basch died in 1984, aged 85 years.

Joseph and Mayer Bishop (formerly Bischoff) went into saloons to sell papers. Joseph said: "Drunks are my best customers. I sell more than my brother does. They buy me out so I can go home." The brothers sold newspapers every afternoon and night, and were out again at 6 a.m. Sundays. Their father Jacob Bischoff came alone to Hartford to raise money working as a fruit and vegetable peddler. His wife Yetta

Yedda Welled (age 11), Rebecca Cohen (age 12) and Rebecca Kirwin (age 14) selling newspapers on the streets of Hartford, Connecticut, March 1909 (Library of Congress, LC-DIG-nclc-03239).

On a Sunday morning in March 1909, 10-year-old Morris Horowitz sells newspapers in Hartford, Connecticut. Starting at seven in the morning, he sells around 25. Lewis Hine described Morris as "a bright business-like chap, but shows signs of nervousness" (Library of Congress, LC-DIG-nclc-03245).

and their young sons arrived in Hartford in 1907. Meyer and Joseph were soon put to work to help the family. In adult life Meyer and Joseph moved to Los Angeles and found work in the fast-growing movie business. Joseph served in the U.S. Army during World War I and World War II.

By the start of World War I, Eastern European immigrants swelled the Jewish population of New Haven, Connecticut, to 20,000. The New Haven Boys Club was a popular meeting place for Hyman Alpert and other Jewish boys. Established in 1871, the club offered a pool room, gymnasium, basketball court and a swimming pool. In 1970, it opened its doors to girls to become the Boys and Girls Club of New Haven.

Beginning in 1677, a small Sephardi Jewish community was established in Newport, Rhode Island. The Jeshuat Israel synagogue (also known as the Touro synagogue) was built in 1763. Arriving between 1881 and 1914, some 20,000 Eastern European Jews settled in Rhode Island, finding work in the jewelry industry, and as peddlers, shopkeepers, tailors and shoemakers.

Charles Rome emigrated alone from Kovno (Kaunas, now in Lithuania) and settled in Burlington, Vermont. Two years later, he had saved enough money working as a junk peddler to send for his wife and two children. Son Meyer was born in Burlington. The family lived in the North End of Burlington, known as Little

Morris Levine, shown here in December 1916 at 11 years old, sold papers every day on Park Street in Burlington, Vermont, for several years. He earned 50 cents on Sundays and 30 cents on other days (Library of Congress, LC-DIG-nclc-03979).

Jerusalem, and joined Ohavei Zedek synagogue. In 1916, Charles died and Meyer, at age 8, was sent out to work to help support the family. Meyer Rome died in 1918 from the Spanish flu, aged 10 years. Louis and Fanny Levine emigrated from Russia, arriving at Ellis Island in 1904. They settled in Brooklyn, where Morris was born in 1905, the third of 12 children. In 1907, the Levine family moved to Burlington, Vermont, where Louis found work as a tailor in a men's store. Young Morris sold newspapers. In 1928, Morris married Kathryn Lucier from a French-Canadian family. They raised six children with both Catholic and Jewish values. Morris and his family left Vermont for New York where he worked as a chef in a restaurant. Upon retirement Morris and Kathryn moved to Florida and then Los Vegas, where he died in 1996, aged 90.

At the start of the 20th century, Prince Street was the center of Jewish life in Newark, New Jersey, with kosher food shops, pushcarts, vendors and peddlers. The Eastern European Jewish immigrants lived in cramped, cold-water apartments above the stores, and used the Montgomery Street bathhouse. The Baron Maurice de Hirsch agricultural school opened in 1894 in Woodbine, New Jersey, with the aim of taking young Jewish immigrants out of the cities and training them in farming.

Newsboys Max and Jacob Schwartz lived on Howard Street, close to Prince Street in Newark. The brothers Joe, Jacob, Benny, and Levi sold newspapers in

Newark. Teachers said in 1912: "Joe doesn't know anything, not even enough to be bad. He is always drowsy in class. Jacob is awful in school work and conduct. He gets sleepy in class. Benny is good in school work and conduct." Fourteen-year-old Harry Schertzer, 12-year-old Sam Tumin and 12-year-old Abel Schertzer were out on the streets of Newark, until 10:00 p.m., selling pretzels and chewing gum to hungry newsboys. "Newsies are good customers."

A textile industry was established in Paterson, New Jersey, powered by the 77-foot Great Falls of the Passaic River. Nathan Barnett (1848–1925) came to Paterson from Poznan, Poland, to become the leading silk manufacturer in the city. Twice mayor of Paterson, he funded the Barnett Hospital, the Hebrew Free School, the Barnett Memorial Temple (Reform), as well as homes for the aged and for orphans. Between 1880 and 1920, some 5,000 Jewish immigrants arrived in Paterson, mainly from Lodz and Bialystok, and found employment in the silk factories. The Jewish workers joined the 1913 Silk Strike. Albert Sabin, of oral poliomyelitis vaccine fame, attended high school in Paterson, New Jersey.

With the influx of Eastern European immigrants, the Jewish population of Wilmington, Delaware, rose to 4,000 by 1920. Many found work in the leather and shoe factories. They established the Young Men's Hebrew Association, charity organizations, a society to help the sick and the aged and built several synagogues. Harry Silverstein's father worked in a leather and shoe company in the city, earning $18 a week. Young Harry sold newspapers on the streets of Wilmington.

Jewish life in Philadelphia began during the Colonial Period. In 1765, Jewish businessmen like Benjamin Levy, David Franks and Nathan and Bernard Gratz were signers of the Non-Importation Resolutions, promising not to import or sell British-made goods. The Congregation Shearith Israel served the 300 Jews of Philadelphia. The Jewish population of the city was boosted by the arrival of German Jews during the middle of the 19th century. The great expansion came with the arrival of Russian Jews between 1880 and 1920. They settled in an area between Christian and Spruce Streets and 2nd to 6th Streets and developed an active community with synagogues, sweatshops, Yiddish theater, grocery shops, delicatessens, as well as literary societies and social organizations. Willie Cohen and Mac Rafalowitz attended the John Hay School, built 1904 at the corner of Sixth and Wharton Streets, South Philadelphia, the school was named for John Hay, secretary to Abraham Lincoln during the Civil War.

During the Civil War, the Jewish population of Washington numbered 1,500. Gustav Lansburgh, Samuel Hecht and brothers Louis, Solomon and Ludwig Kann established large department stores in greater Washington. Eastern European Jews, arriving between 1880 and 1914, boosted Washington's Jewish population. At that time, 7th Street NW was at the center of Jewish immigrant life. Jews opened small shops and grocery stores. They established the Hebrew Relief Society, Hebrew Free Loan Society, Hebrew Home for the Aged, as well as several synagogues. The immigration of poor Yiddish-speaking and largely Orthodox Eastern Europeans raised Washington's Jewish population to 10,000 by 1920. In 1925, President Calvin Coolidge spoke at the laying of the cornerstone of the Jewish Community Center. Washington's Jewish population grew to 165,000 by 1997, and 300,000 by 2020.

David Marks arrived in New York from Russia in 1892. Dealing in scrap metal, he raised enough money to bring his wife Rachel to America. Sons Eli and Morris were born in Brooklyn, two of the seven Marks children. After David was killed in a work accident, Rachel moved her family to Washington, D.C., where she had relatives. The family was very poor and the children went out to work. Eli and Morris worked afternoons and nights selling chewing gum and newspapers. Despite long hours on the streets, both boys graduated from high school. Morris went to law school and made his career in real estate. Eli died in 1984 and Morris in 1993.

Born in Galicia in 1908, Harry Weinberg was the son of immigrant parents who settled in Baltimore, Maryland. He left school at age 12, worked in his father's automotive repair shop and sold newspapers. Barely out of his teenage years, he began buying depressed properties, fixing them up and selling at a profit. He expanded into large real estate deals and into mass transit, that brought him enormous wealth.

Nine-year-old Israel "Izzy" April of I Street, SW, selling newspapers near the Willard Hotel, Washington, D.C., 1912. Lewis Hine described him as "quite a pugnacious little chap." With his brothers Samuel and David, Israel was daily out on the streets earning small amounts of money for the family. They claimed a large clientele among ambassadors and senators, and even the president. Their father was a fruit and vegetable peddler and later operated a grocery store in Washington, D.C. The luxury Willard Hotel on Pennsylvania Avenue NW opened in 1901 and was known as "The Hotel of Presidents" (Library of Congress, LC-DIG-nclc-03780).

In 1959, he established the Harry and Jeanette Weinberg Charitable Foundation. He moved to Honolulu in 1968, and rapidly became "the biggest individual landowner in Hawaii."[20] At his death in 1990, Harry Weinberg left $1 billion to his foundation to benefit the poor.

Despite the hardships and the squalor, Chicago's Maxwell Street ghetto produced clarinetist Benny Goodman, U.S. Supreme Court justice Arthur Goldman, the father of the U.S. atomic-powered submarine Hyman Rickover, the boxer Barney Ross, and the actor Paul Muni. By 1910, there were 50,000 poor Russian Jews huddled together in the Chicago ghetto. The urge to move ahead was strong. By 1927, the ghetto still contained some 60,000 Jews, with another 300,000 scattered throughout metropolitan Chicago.

Amongst the sharpest of the Chicago newsboys were Max and his younger brother Moses (Moe); two of eight surviving children of Tobias and Sheva Annenberg, Orthodox Jews, who fled the village of Kalvishken in 1885. The family passed through New York to settle in the Jewish ghetto around Maxwell Street. From his pushcart and going door-to-door, Tobias sold scarves, mirrors, combs and thimbles. A few years later, Tobias opened a grocery store at 1255 South State Street, with the family living in rooms behind the store. Max and Moe briefly attended the Haven School at 15th Street and Wabash Avenue, but with Max at around 11 years of age, were sent out to work to help support the family. Impulsive and with a fiery temper, Moe sold newspapers on Chicago streets and worked as a messenger boy for American District Telegraph. Later, Max and Moe worked in the circulation department of the Chicago Tribune. From this modest beginning, Moe Annenberg established his own newspaper-circulation agency, and expanded into restaurants, bowling alleys, taxicabs and real estate. He bought the *Daily Racing Forum*, *New York Morning Telegraph*, *The Racing Guide*, and in 1936, paying $15 million, he purchased the venerable *Philadelphia Inquirer.* In 1939, Moe Annenberg was indicted for income tax evasion and sentenced to three years in the Lewisburg Federal Penitentiary, in Pennsylvania. He died in 1942 at age 64.

Walter Annenberg, only son of Moses, was determined to restore the family's good name. Unlike his father, Walter was raised with great privilege and wealth. He expanded his late father's publishing empire, purchased the *TV Guide* and bought radio stations. After selling his businesses at great profit, Walter formed an outstanding collection of Impressionist paintings, which he later gave to the Metropolitan Museum in New York City. He was the friend of presidents and served as United States ambassador to Great Britain. Walter Annenberg died in 2002 at age 94.

Sandor Herz was born in 1870 in the village of Szklabinya, then part of the Austria-Hungarian empire. When he was five, the family migrated to Chicago. Determined to fit into American life, he changed his name to John Daniel Hertz. His formal education ended in the fifth grade and he began selling newspaper at street corners. After an argument with his father, he ran away and lived in a waif's home. Despite his limited education, Hertz was employed as a newspaper reporter.

Possessing an enterprising spirit, he got into the taxicab business and in 1915 formed the Yellow Cab Company. Nine years later he established the nationwide Hertz-Drive-Ur-Self Company. He became a partner in Lehman Brothers. His Hertz Foundation grants scholarships in the sciences. John Hertz died at age 94 in 1961. Raised in great luxury, his son John D. Hertz, Jr., enjoyed racing his 72-foot ketch *Ticonderoga* and set the time record for the St. Petersburg to Havana race. In 1943, John D. married the actress Myrna Loy but they divorced two years later.

Joseph Rosenberg (1848–1891) was the son of Jacob Rosenberg, co-founder of the Michael Reese Hospital and of Chicago's first Jewish congregation, Kehilat Anshei Maarav (KAM). While working as a Chicago newsboy, the local merchants repeatedly refused him a drink of water. He made his fortune in San Francisco real estate. On his death in 1891, Joseph fulfilled his early vow to build a fountain in Chicago where newsboys could quench their thirst. In 1893 the Rosenberg Fountain was built, at a cost of $10,000 [about $350,000 in 2024], at East 11th Street, Grant Park, near his childhood home. The fountain has since been restored and moved to the Lincoln Park Conservatory.

Small numbers of Jews settled in Texas early in the 19th century. In 1868, German-speaking Jews in Galveston established the Reform Congregation B'nai Israel. Sensitive to rising anti–Semitism, German-born banker Jacob Schiff

Philip Weinstein, eight years old, and an older boy who uses him as a decoy, on Broadway, Nashville, Tennessee, November 1910. Many young truants were on the street during school hours (Library of Congress, LC-DIG-nclc-03711).

established the Jewish Immigration Bureau to send some of the Jewish immigrants to the South instead of arriving at Ellis Island. Between 1907 and 1914, 10,000 Russian Jews entered the United States through the port of Galveston, Texas, to settle in Texas, Colorado, and Kansas. Max and Rebecca Shuman and their children entered the United States in 1907 at Galveston. Max was a fruit and vegetable peddler and later opened a grocery store. At an early age, sons Morris and Louis went to work to help support the family. Later, Louis worked as an automobile mechanic. During World War II, he served in the U.S. Navy.

German-speaking Jews were among the early settlers of the frontier trading town of Dallas. After 1880, Yiddish-speaking Russian Jews arrived, opened pawn shops, grocery stores, dry goods businesses, tobacco stores and tailoring shops. In 1907 Abraham Lincoln Neiman formed a partnership with Hebert Marcus to establish the high-end Neiman-Marcus department store. The small Jewish communities in southern cities like Nashville and New Orleans were weakened by the Civil War. They recovered after 1880 by the arrival of Yiddish-speaking Russian Jews. Many of their children were out on the streets selling newspapers or delivering telegram messages.

5

Messenger Boys, Scrap Metal, Factory Workers and Trades

> "Most parents could entertain no hope of seeing their children through high school. Very often they had to take them out of grammar school and put them to work to help the family budget. Children of 10 and 12 years of age spent many long hours in shops. Young boys and girls were employed in large factories under unhealthy conditions."[1]

Earning money for the immigrant Jewish families took Jewish kids into a wide range of jobs, before school, after school, weekends, or in place of school. Selling newspapers was most common. (See Chapter 4.) Jewish kids also worked as messenger boys, in stores and factories, collecting and selling rags, old clothes, and scrap metal, selling poultry and vegetables, making gloves, purses and shoes, cracking nuts, making artificial flowers, and working in the sweatshops.

David Sarnoff was nine years old in 1900 when his Russian-Jewish family settled on the fourth-floor walkup of a tenement on Monroe Street in New York's Lower East Side. His father Abraham was ill with tuberculosis. David was

> never to know that childhood could be bright and joyful.... Within weeks after his disillusioning arrival, David was handing over to his mother little fistfuls of pennies each night, gathered by hawking Yiddish newspapers on those hostile ghetto streets against the competition of older and more experienced boys. At the age of 10 and 11, his small earnings would frequently make the difference between eating and not eating, between gaslight and candlelight. Before he was 13, two more children were added to the brood, his brother Irving and his sister, Ede, while their father's earning power was swiftly dwindling toward zero. David faced up to the cruel fact that he was the main breadwinner, at that tender age, for a family of seven. ... Peddling papers was a competitive enterprise, in which victory went to the fleetest and the strongest. From school you rushed to East Broadway, which was Yiddish newspaper row, to grab a bundle, then ran through the streets crying "Extra!" The sooner you got your papers the more easily you sold them. There were no returns, and an unsold surplus could spell a wasted day. Fifty papers meant a profit of 25 cents and if you were quick and lucky you might dispose of a hundred in an afternoon. After a time, David also worked up a route, delivering papers to homes. That meant running up and down many stairs six days a week, and again on the seventh to collect.[2]

At age 15 years David found work as an office boy in the Commercial Cable Company. After his boss refused to grant him time off on Rosh Hashanah, David moved to the Marconi Wireless Telegraph Company. Telegraph communication then was person to person. Rising up through the ranks at Marconi, Sarnoff saw the vast potential of one person's reaching out to many others at the same time. After Marconi merged into the Radio Corporation of America (RCA), Sarnoff developed the technology to bring speech and music into the home. In 1921, RCA broadcasted the Jack Dempsey–Georges Carpentier heavyweight boxing match, heard by an audience of 300,000. After the broadcast of the fight, the demand for home radios boomed. In 1925, RCA established the National Broadcasting Company (NBC) spreading radio broadcasting nationwide.

Four years later, at age 38, Sarnoff became president of RCA-NBC. He saw the potential of combining electronic transmission and motion pictures, and introduced television, with a screen size of 7 to 12 inches, at the 1939 World's Fair in New York. During World War II, Sarnoff set up radio communications between the Allied armies. He oversaw the building of the radio transmission for Radio Free Europe, for which he received the brigadier general star and awarded the Legion of Merit. At his death in 1971, the immigrant boy from the shtetl of Uzhyany, near Minsk, was entombed in a mausoleum in Kensico Cemetery, Valhalla, New York, wearing his military star.

David Sarnoff, messenger boy who became president of RCA and chairman of the board of NBC, 1939 (Library of Congress, LC-DIG-hec-25961).

Many Jewish children from poor families found work delivering telegraph messages, working in offices, department stores, making purses, selling poultry, collecting scrap metal, serving as bootblacks, or rolling cigarettes and cigars. Smaller numbers found work in the great textile mills of Lawrence, Lowell, Fall River and other cities.

The electric telegraph greatly speeded up the transmission of printed information. Companies like Western Union, Mackay, Metropolitan Messenger & Mailing, and the American District Telegraph (ADT) set up thousands of offices in towns and cities across America where the dots and dashes of the telegraph were decoded into English. Messenger boys with their bicycles at the ready, worked long hours, day and night, ready to hand-deliver the telegraphs, and speedily come back to the office with the reply. In 1886, messenger boys went on strike, demanding an increase in pay from $4 to $5 a week.[3] In 1903, the boys refused to work until their pay increased from 90 cents to $1.25 a day.[4]

Among the many thousands of American telegram messengers were sizeable numbers of Jewish boys, especially in the main centers of Jewish life—New York, Philadelphia, Boston and Chicago. Solly Hamber and Harry Friedman delivered telegrams for the Metropolitan Mailing and Telegraph Company of Tremont Street, Boston. David Caplan of Monroe Street, New York, worked from 11:00 p.m. to 8:00 a.m. the following day, delivering telegrams. The family of Samuel Weinstein and other Russian Jews settled around Columbia Street and Second Street, Fall River, Massachusetts, and found work in the textile mills. Others were peddlers and, in time, opened shops. At its peak, the Fall River Jewish community numbered 4,000, served by synagogues, Hebrew schools, and social service agencies.

Jacob William Black was born in 1897 in the Russian Empire, the son of Morris and Bessie Black. The family arrived at Ellis Island in 1907 and settled in Lawrence, Massachusetts, where Morris found work as a peddler. Still in his early teens Jacob started work in the mills. After the 1912 Bread and Roses Strike in Lawrence, the Black family moved to Manchester, New Hampshire, to operate a newsstand. In 1918, Jacob registered for the military draft. Later, he found work in a photography store and then as an electrician. In 1926, Jacob married Emily Schwartz, moved to Boston and started a family. Jacob operated a number of furniture stores. During World War II he served as an air raid warden. Jacob Black died of lung disease in 1972, aged 74. His wife Emily died in 1999 at age 95.

In the 17th century, the Dutch city of Amsterdam became a major center for importing and processing tobacco into snuff. Most of the factory workers were Sephardi and Ashkenazi Jews. Many Jewish children and adults found work in the cigar and cigarette-rolling factories in Europe and then America. "Like all children of the poor," wrote Samuel Gompers in his autobiography, "we early found our way to the city streets...." It is the education of the street that produces that early shrewdness in the children of those "who have not" that often leaves an ineradicable difference between them and the children of those "who have." "...When I was 10 years and

Group of Metropolitan Messenger and Mailing Company messenger boys on Tremont Street, Boston, 1917 (Library of Congress, LC-DIG-nclc-03984).

three months, I had to go to work.... The teacher told father that it was wrong to rob me of an education. But father could not do otherwise. I left school at an early age to help earn a living.... My father found it extremely difficult to support a family of six children on his scanty wages earned at the cigarmaking trade, so I was placed to learn the trade of shoemaking. After I had been at work for eight weeks the boss gave me six cents a week as wages."

Hoping to improve their lot, the Gompers family moved from London to New York's Lower East Side. "We found a home on Houston Street. Those four rooms signified progress from the little London home. I was then 13 years, six months, and two days old. Father began making cigars at home and I helped him."[5] Samuel Gompers was born in 1850 into a Sephardi family living in London. He rose to president of the Cigar Makers' International Union, Local 144. Later, he founded the American Federation of Labor (AFL) and served as its president from 1886 to his death in 1924. Gompers set an example for Russian Jewish tobacco workers employed in New York at Kinney Brothers and the Goodwin Tobacco Factories to form branch unions and strike for better pay and conditions.

In 1881, the tobacco mogul James Buchanan Duke of Durham, North Carolina, started a new business of cigarette rolling. Duke traveled to New York City and recruited 19-year-old Moses Gladstein and Joseph Siegel, recently dismissed for organizing a strike, to assemble a team of skilled but unemployed Jewish rollers to move to the South. Other Durham tobacco firms also hired Jewish rollers from New York. By 1885, about 125 Russian Jewish rollers with their families had moved to Durham to work in the cigarette companies. They formed a small Jewish ghetto around Pine Street. Duke offered his Jewish workers 70 cents per 1000 rolled cigarettes. The highly skilled Jewish workers were able to roll 2,500 cigarettes a day, earning $10 a week. The happy arrangement lasted a couple of years, with Duke's factory producing 250,000 hand-rolled cigarettes a day. Not able to satisfy the fast-growing demand for cigarettes, Duke turned to technology and in 1885, purchased the Bonsack cigarette rolling and cutting machine, capable of producing 240,000 cigarettes a day. James A. Bonsack's invention was the "curse of labor." "The Jews with their experience in labor and socialist movements" organized a union and threatened to smash the machines.

Telegraph delivery boys Samuel Weinstein (left) of Spring Street and William Locke of West King Phillip Street, Fall River, Massachusetts, 1910 (Library of Congress, LC-DIG-nclc-0337).

The Durham cigarette companies responded by easing out their Jewish workers and replacing them with a local and more compliant labor force. "We never had any trouble in the help," said the Duke Tobacco Company, "except when 125 Polish Jews were hired to come to Durham to work in the factory. They gave us no end of trouble. We now employ our own people." Nearly all the Jewish workers returned to New York. The few who remained opened stores in Durham.[6]

Lazar Meir was born in 1884 in a shtetl near Minsk in the Russian Empire. His parents Jacob and Sarah were Yiddish-speaking and religious. Coming to the New World, Jacob eked out a living, collecting and selling scrap metal.

At age 12, Lazar dropped out of school and joined his father as J. Meir & Son, junk dealers. Father and son roamed the streets collecting discarded locks, nails,

Boys working in the textile mills of Lawrence, Massachusetts, 1911. Jacob William Black of Union Street is the boy front row center, wearing suspenders. Other boys in Lewis Hine's picture are John Gopen, Joseph Stonge, Billie Welch, Tim Carroll, Michael Devine and John Gopen. The great textile mills of Lowell and Lawrence, Massachusetts, attracted Irish and French-Canadian as well as Jewish workers (Library of Congress, LC-DIG-nclc-02331).

copper trimmings, and scrap metal. Young Lazar learned to dive into the ocean to salvage bits of metal from ship wrecks, and drag them to shore. Moving to Boston he set up as a scrap metal dealer. Changing his name to Louis B. Mayer, he entered the nascent movie business. Mayer joined with fellow Russian-born Jew, Samuel Goldwyn, to form Metro-Goldwyn-Mayer (MGM), Hollywood's most prestigious movie studio.[7] An early tycoon in the movie business, Goldwyn (born Samuel Gelbfisz, the son of a peddler) began his career sweeping floors in a Gloversville, New York, glove factory and worked his way to vice-president of sales, and on to Hollywood.

Kirk Douglas was a "member of the pantheon of leading men ... of the golden age of Hollywood movies. He was instantly recognizable: the jutting jaw, the dimpled chin, the piercing gaze and the breaking voice." He played the role of Vincent van Gogh in *Lust for Life* (1956), a World War I French colonel in *Paths of Glory* (1957) and the leader of a slave rebellion in the epic *Spartacus* (1960). "He was born Issur Danielovitch in 1916, in Amsterdam, New York, a small city about 35 miles northwest of Albany." As he put it in his autobiography, he was "the son of illiterate Russian Jewish immigrants in the WASP town of Amsterdam," one of seven children, six of them sisters. By the time he began attending school, the family name had been changed to Demsky, and Issur had become Isadore, earning him the nickname Izzy. The town's mills did not hire Jews, so his father, Herschel, known as Harry,

Louis B. Mayer, head of Metro-Goldwyn-Mayer Corporation, calls at the White House with his family, 1925. From left: Edith Mayer, Mr. and Mrs. Mayer, Irene Mayer, and Mabel W. Willebrant, assistant attorney general, who introduced them to President Calvin Coolidge (Library of Congress, LC-USZ62-124530).

became a ragman, a collector and seller of discarded goods. "Even on Eagle Street, in the poorest section of town, where all the families were struggling, the ragman was on the lowest rung on the ladder," Mr. Douglas wrote. "And I was the ragman's son."[8]

Collecting scrap metal, copper wiring, rags and discarded household goods was a common source of work and income for poor, newly arrived Russian Jews. They began with a horse and cart, roaming the streets and picking up items of some value. Over time, many established large junk yards to crush automobile frames and metal cans. These were melted down and recycled into the American economy. In 2020, the Maryland Jewish Museum staged the exhibition, "Scrap Yard: Innovators of Recycling," tracing the history of scrap yards and the prominent role of the Jewish immigrants in the metal recycling industry.

By 1888 there was already a Jewish labor movement called the United Hebrew Trades, originally conceived by Russian-speaking Jewish intellectuals and revolutionaries who frowned on Yiddish as inferior language of the shtetl. As committed anarchists and socialists, they sought to organize the Jewish working class, but in order to do so, they first had to master Yiddish.[9]

Getting shoes polished for Rosh Hashanah, Lower East Side of New York, 1910 (Library of Congress, LC-DIG-ggbain-1989).

> The Purse Makers' Union joined the United Hebrew Trades. In 1890, almost half of the members of the union were children of school age from 12 to 14. Some of them had already left school to help support their families. The younger ones among these workers would arrive in the factory after school hours and work until 10 at night. On Sundays they worked all day. At that time New York did not yet have the law forbidding children under 16 to work in the factories. In the purse trade of those days there were many contractors who had their shops along Henry, Orchard, and Broome Streets of the East Side. At the union meeting both English and Yiddish were used. The meetings were more often than not disturbed by the youngsters. Under the influence of these talks, the youngsters became quite revolutionary, and were prepared to go far to help the union.... The Purse Makers' Union lasted until 1894 when it dissolved. Many of the youngsters had grown up and had left the union for other trades. New youngsters, together with "green" Jewish immigrants, came into the industry. All in all, however, there were not enough to make a strong union.[10]

Here are some case studies from a U.S. Children's Bureau study published in 1928: "A Russian-Jewish family had been known to the Hebrew charities since 1912, when the parents and three children were living in one room." The father bought and sold old clothes for a living. Three boys, 10, 13, and 14 years of age, sold papers, but the mother complained that they spent their money on motion pictures. The oldest boy made as much as $14 a week selling papers but was too lazy to continue doing so. The family received from charities $50 for rent and $25 for coal. The boys made from $7 to $9.50 each, selling papers 17 to 33 hours a week. All three said that their earnings were used for food and clothes (pp. 83–84).

A 14-year-old Russian-Jewish newsboy, who had begun to sell papers at age 7,

Chicken vendors, Sixth St. Market, Cincinnati, 1912. From left: Hyman Mormer (9 years old), and brother Willie Mormer (12 years old), of Kenyon Avenue and Rubenstein of W. 6th Street (Library of Congress, LOC cph.3c15370).

was brought before the court when 10 for selling papers under age and without a permit. Two years later, he was arrested for disorderly conduct and selling papers without a permit, and put on probation. His parents were determined that the boy should sell papers, though the probation officer tried to keep him off the streets. The Hebrew charities reported that the family income was small and the boy's money was needed in the home. The boy said he had begun to sell because he wanted extra spending money, and he spent part of his earnings on violin lessons. He sold only on Saturday nights from 6:30 to 11:30 p.m. (p. 91).

A 13-year-old Jewish boy ran an outdoor fruit stand. Four boys and two girls worked six days a week, four were hired and two ran their own business. Several stand-tenders worked after 6 p.m. and until 8 p.m. on school days and until 11 p.m. on weekends (a 13-hour day) (p. 119).

A 10-year-old Jewish newsboy used to drag himself off to sell, and come home tired. His parents objected to the work, but the boy went out saying: "I will work because other boys do" (p. 141). A boy of Russian-Jewish parentage, sold papers for five years, beginning at the age of 10, was brought to court in January 1921, for truancy, and stealing from other newsboys (p. 148). A 13-year-old Russian-Jewish boy earned $7 a week selling newspapers. He contributed none of his earnings toward the support of the family but bought his own clothes, put $5 a week in the bank, and had 75 cents a week for spending money. The 14-year-old son of a Russian-Jewish hotel keeper earned $13.75 a week. He spent his money on clothes and shows (p. 196). Aiming to abolish work for children under 16 years, the U.S. Children's Bureau published many such stories.[11]

6

Sweatshops

In the Russian Empire, many Jews earned their living knitting and sewing clothes for men, women and children. During the period of their immigration to America the garment industry was rapidly growing. "As early as 1890 almost 80 percent of New York's garment industry was located below 14th Street, and more than 90 percent of these factories were owned by German Jews. Lower New York, therefore, was a powerful magnet for Eastern Europeans throughout the period of mass immigration. Immigrants were attracted by jobs and by Jewish employers who could provide a familiar milieu. ... By 1897 approximately 60 percent of the New York Jewish labor force was employed in the apparel field, and 75 percent of the workers in the industry were Jewish."[1]

Much of the work was done in large factories, but also in cramped and unhealthy apartments (sweatshops) where parents and children worked side by side. "An unscrupulous contractor," wrote Jane Addams of Hull House, Chicago, "regards no basement as too dark, no stable loft too foul, no rear shanty too provisional, no tenement room too small for his workroom.... There is a constant tendency to employ schoolchildren, as much of the work in the house and in the shop can easily be done by children."[2]

In 1895, Florence Kelley described the appalling conditions in the Chicago sweatshops in which "large numbers of young girls are employed 13 hours a day throughout the week, and 15 hours on Saturday. They are paid by the piece, the pay is just enough to attract the most ignorant and helpless children in the city.... Benny Kelman, a Russian Jew, was found running a heavy sewing machine. He had been put to work when just 13 years old."[3]

In 1904, Florence Kelley's Consumer Union described a typical sweatshop in the Lower East Side of New York City:

> On the top floor of a Mott Street tenement, up five flights of stairs it is so dark that the women who drag up great bundles of clothing to be finished cannot see the stairs before them. In one corner of the 10 by 10-foot room, lay a man in bed, racked with the consumptive's cough.... His wife and sister sat sewing beside him, finishing men's coats and trousers at five cents per piece. The remaining room was taken up by a larger bed, upon which a child tossed in fever, the first stage of some serious disease. This bed too was covered with unfinished garments, upon which the grandmother, the fifth member of the family, was sewing boys' knee-pants, ready to carry the germs of measles or scarlet fever from the sick child of the tenements to

their more prosperous little wearers.... The combined work of the whole family amounted to about 60 cents a day.... The whole tenement house swarms with these workers. Hardly a floor without some room doing service as workshop, or workshop and home combined. How many people are working without licenses no one knows.... The children of the sweatshops have absolutely no legal protection. No hours are too long for them to be worked by parents or employers; no age too young for them to begin work.[4]

In 1901 there were 20,000 sweatshops in New York involving some 50,000 people. The sweatshops were operated by immigrants who had arrived in America a few years earlier. They were sub-contractors who picked up pre-cut but unsown garments from larger manufacturers and brought the bundles up the stairs of the tenements and into their living rooms. Working under the thinnest of profit margins, they hired newly arrived immigrants, "greeners" working long hours for little pay. Parents and children labored together as pressers, button-hole makers, pocket finishers, making garters, neckties or tags. In the small apartment of Adolph Weiss, family and neighbors worked until late at night making garters. This happens several nights in the week when there is plenty of work.

The youngest children, 7-year-old Sarah and Mary and 10-year-old Sam work until 9 p.m. The older children and the adults work until 11:00 or later. The neighbor's children come regularly to work. "It's better than running the streets," said the father Adolph Weiss, of East 3rd St., New York. He was a grocery clerk but was unemployed for months and worked at home on the garters. Mrs. Rothenberg and her family of Allen Street, New York, spend their afternoons and evenings making neckties. Her 11-year-old daughter and 13-year-old son worked on the ties every day after school. In the little inner bed-room the father worked at his sewing machine. Mrs. Goodman of Framingham, Massachusetts, and her sons, 14 and 10 years old, made tags for the nearby Dennison factory. Another son, 12 years old, was sick in bed in next room. Father worked as an umbrella mender. This family earned $25 to $35 a month.

The teenage Rose Cohen and her father worked in Lower East Side sweatshops, trying to save enough money to bring over mother and the other children from Russia. "Father worked very hard," wrote Rose. "He never comes home before 11 and leaves at five in the morning." Rose did piece-work and felt pressure from the boss. Arriving at work at seven, the boss snarled and said: "If you want to work here, you better come in early. No office hours here." Rose felt "the boss was hurrying the life out of me" but she needed the work. Even a dollar more a week would help bring the Cohen family together sooner.[5]

Mr. Schneider of 87 Ridge Street and Mr. Silberberg of 30 Suffolk Street, New York City, set up small sweatshops in their tenement apartments, hiring a few men, women and children seated cramped together at small tables near the windows to sew and stitch. Boston, Chicago, Philadelphia and other cities also had tenement sweatshops.

Jewish family working on garters in kitchen of New York tenement home, 1912 (Library of Congress, LOC cph.3a38584).

A sweatshop in the Jewish ghetto near Maxwell Street, Chicago, 1910.

Jews and the Garment Trade Unions

Lacking a country of their own, Jews were permanent foreigners in the Russian empire. They faced discrimination, poverty and pogroms. Many young Jews—male and female—found a home in the leftist movements, including anarchism, socialism and communism, that opposed the Tsar and his government. The Marxist-oriented General Union of Jewish Workers, known as the Bund, was founded in 1897 in Vilna to organize working-class Jews enduring terrible conditions in the emerging industries of Tsarist Russia. Using Yiddish, the secular Bund hoped to secure an equal place for Jews in the Russian Empire. By 1906, the Bund had 40,000 members, of whom one-third were women.

The Russian government cracked down on the Bund and imprisoned its leadership. Many Jews despaired that Russia would change and sought to emigrate. Members of the Bund, like David Dubinsky and Sidney Hillman, who came to the United States, brought their socialist convictions with them.[6] The conditions of work in the Lower East Side were hardly better than what they left behind in Russia. "The typical working day in New York City's large mercantile establishments is 8 a.m. to 6 p.m., with 30 to 45 minutes for lunch Monday through Saturday, though in some stores employees work later on Saturdays, often until 9 or 10 p.m. Large numbers of girls 14 to 16 years of age are employed at $1.50 a week."[7]

At the close of the 19th century and well into the 20th century, Russian-Jewish immigrants emerged as leaders of Jewish and national trade unions, especially in the needle trades. Exploited by the owners of the sweatshops and the large textile companies, these firebrands rallied the Jewish proletariat with petitions and strikes for better pay and work conditions. Arriving penniless, they took the first job they could find, typically in a sweatshop, where they earned "only a few dollars a week, working 15 to 18 hours a day, sewing shirts, children's pants, cheap dresses." A sweatshop was "both an apartment and a workshop. The boss would be there with his family. The front room and the kitchen were used as a workshop, while the whole family slept in another room. Near the windows, the operators worked the sewing machines. The middle of the workshop were big bundles of material, covered with dust."

Born in Odessa, Bernard Weinstein came to the United States in 1882, at age 16. He describes "the troubles and suffering of the Jewish immigrants during their first years in America." Young Bernard found work in a cigar factory in the Lower East Side, and joined the Cigar Workers Union and the Socialist Party. In 1888, he founded the Hebrew Trades of New York. A decade later, he joined forces with Abraham Cahan and Morris Hillquit to establish the Yiddish-language *Daily Forward* as the newspaper for the New York Jewish working classes. Socialism and unionism were in the air. Weinstein dedicated his life to improving the lot of Jewish workers. In his book *The Jewish Unions of America*, Weinstein describes the separate unions for Jewish tailors, cloak makers, raincoat makers, furriers, bakers, plumbers, bookbinders, mattress makers, seltzer workers, paper-box makers, jewelry makers, typographical workers, furniture movers, cab drivers, journalists, retail store workers, and even a Jewish actors union and union representing kosher slaughterhouse workers.[8]

In his 1903 book *History of Socialism in America*, Morris Hillquit describes the close bonds between the Socialist Party and the early Jewish trade unions:

> In the beginning of the eighties of the last century the immigration of Russian Jews to this country had assumed enormous dimensions. Thousands of these immigrants landed at the port of New York every week, and the majority of them settled on the Lower East Side of that city. Their principal industry was tailoring in all its branches, and within a few years they acquired a practical monopoly of the trade. Within the bounds of their settlement in the City of New York, which became the most congested spot on the face of the globe, hundreds of tailoring shops sprang up. These shops, popularly known as sweatshops, were conducted by middlemen or "contractors," within whose living rooms they were frequently connected. They were always dingy, uncleanly, and ill-ventilated, and in them scores of men, women, and children were indiscriminately crowded together, working at times 15 hours and more at a stretch for incredibly low wages.
>
> Several attempts had been made to organize them, but the attempts had met with but poor success, until the spring of 1888. By that time, however, the wages of the Jewish tailors had sunk so very low, and their conditions of work had become so very wretched, that even they, rebelled. A series of strikes was inaugurated by them. The knee-pants-makers were the first to open fire and they were soon followed by the pants-makers, the cloak-makers, the shirt-makers, and the jacket-makers, and within a very few weeks an army of no less than 15,000 Jewish tailors had laid down work, demanding better pay and shorter hours....
>
> It was on the initiative of the Jewish socialists that the United Hebrew Trades was organized. It is natural that there was at all times a strong bond of sympathy between the Jewish trade union movement and the socialist movement: most of the organizers, leaders, and speakers of the Jewish trade unions came from the ranks of the Socialist Labor Party, and in return the organized Jewish working men for a number of years heartily cooperated with the party in all it undertook, and promptly responded to all of its appeals.[9]

He was born Moshe Hillkowitz in 1869 in Riga. Unlike most Russian-Jews, he came from a well-to-do family and attended a Russian-language school. Young Moshe saw socialism "as a means to further the integration of Jews into a broader society [a view] shared by many other Eastern European Jews, especially students who attended secular gymnasia and universities" (p. 4). Following financial losses, the Hillkowitz family moved in 1886 to the United States to settle in the Lower East Side of New York. At age 17, Moshe found work as a cuff maker in a shirt factory and then worked as a picture frame maker. Along the way he changed his name to Morris Hillquit.

"Almost as soon as he settled in New York, Hillquit was drawn into East Side Jewish radical circles. ... He was immediately attracted to other young Jewish immigrants, mostly former students, now shop workers, who considered themselves intellectuals. ... For the most part their radicalism was rooted in their experiences in the European socialist and anarchist movements. But emigration and economic hardships in the United States also contributed to their further radicalization. ... The young intellectuals were interested in finding alternatives to their present circumstances" (pp. 6–7). With Abraham Cahan, he established the *Arbeter Zeitung* (Workers News), a Yiddish-language newspaper to spread socialist ideas. He helped form the United Hebrew Trades, a garment workers union. Seeing the Jewish struggle as part of a national workers' struggle, Hillquit joined the Socialist Labor Party. At age 24 years, he graduated from New York University law school and set up a law practice with his brother Jacob in Manhattan. In 1906, Hillquit, running on a socialist ticket, failed in his attempt to become the United States Representative from New York's 9th Congressional District.

In 1916, Meyer London and Morris Hillquit met President Woodrow Wilson in an attempt to keep America out of the war against Germany and its allies. The following year, Hillquit ran on an anti-war ticket for mayor of New York, collecting a respectable 22 percent of the citywide vote. His anti-war campaigning ended when America joined Britain and France against Germany. He served as legal counsel for the International Ladies Garment Workers Union (ILGWU). Many who achieved middle-class respectability turned away from radical ideas, but Hillquit remained a committed socialist to the end of his life. "To me, the Socialist movement with its enthusiasm and idealism, its comradeship and struggles, its hopes and disappointments, its victories and defeats, has been the best that life has to offer" (p. 243). Morris Hillquit died of tuberculosis in 1933, aged 64 years.[10]

Morris Hillquit, Socialist candidate, New York, c. 1915 (Library of Congress, LC-DIG-ggbain).

On June 3, 1900, 11 delegates representing seven small garment workers unions met at the Labor lyceum, 64 East 4th Street in New York City to form the International Ladies Garment Workers Union (ILGWU). Among them were Joseph Barondess, Philip Schwartz, I. Silberman, and A. Lebovitz—all of Russian Jewish heritage. The ILGWU began with 2210 members, with a budget of $185, too small to pay its officers.

Under the leadership of Herman Grossman, the union grew slowly. Membership, mostly female immigrants aged between 16 and 25 years old, grew with the labor unrest of 1909.

A meeting of ILGWU members was held in the Great Hall of Cooper Union in November 1909. Twenty-three-year-old Clara Lemlich, a member of Local 25 and a committed socialist, galvanized the crowd by declaring in Yiddish: "I am a working girl. I am tired of listening to speakers who talk in general terms. What we are here to decide is whether we shall or shall not strike. I offer a resolution that a general strike be declared—now." Seizing the excitement of the moment, the chairman of the meeting, Polish-born Benjamin Feigenbaum, an editor at the *Forward* and a founder of the American Socialist Party, took Clara's hand in his and declared: "If I turn traitor to the cause I now pledge, may my right-hand wither from the arm I raise."

Every arm in the hall went up in support of a strike. The next morning Clara and thousands of other garment workers took to the streets of New York. Dubbed the "Uprising of Twenty Thousand," they demanded better pay, work security and improved conditions. The strike pitted the Yiddish-speaking immigrants against the German-Jewish factory owners. Yielding to community pressure the owners settled the four months strike to the benefit of the workers.[11] Born in the Ukrainian shtetl of Gorodok, Clara Lemlich came to the United States at age 17 years. After the 1909 strike, she went on to become a leader in the women's suffrage movement, campaigning for the vote and better conditions for women in the home and in the workplace.

The Triangle Shirtwaist Factory was on the 8th to 11th floors of the Brown Building in the Greenwich Village neighborhood of New York City. Five hundred people, mostly young immigrant women, made women's blouses, known as shirtwaists. They worked nine hours a day, six days a week, earning between $7 and $12 a week. On Saturday, March 25, 1911, a fire engulfed the factory. The doors were locked to prevent theft and 146 garment workers, 123 women and 23 men, died by jumping out of the windows or being burnt to death. It was one of the deadliest industrial disasters in United States history. Most of the dead were recent Russian-Jewish and Italian immigrants, among them Anna Altman age 16, Ida Brodsky 16, Israel Rosen 17, Rosie Shapiro 17 and Sarah Weintraub 17. The ILGWU gained many members following the Triangle factory disaster.

During the 20th century, most of the presidents of the International Ladies Garment Workers Union (ILGWU) were Russian-born Jews who worked their way up the ranks of the union. Benjamin Schlesinger, union president in 1903, was born in Karkai, Lithuania. He came to the United States at age 15, to find work in a Chicago women's cloak and suit factory. Charles Jacobson, president in 1908, migrated at age 11, and began work in a Boston women's skirt sweatshop. Abraham Rosenberg, president, 1908–1914, came to New York at age 13. Morris Sigman, president 1923–1928, started as a presser in a cloak factory. David Dubinsky served as president from 1932 to 1966. Louis Stulberg, president 1966–1975, left Poland at age 14 to

Trade union procession for the victims of the Triangle Shirtwaist Company fire with Washington Square in the background, New York, 1911 (Library of Congress, LC-USZ62-83858).

find work in New York as a cloth cutter. They were followed as leaders of the ILGWU by American-born Sol Chaikin, president 1975–1986 and Jay Mazur, the last president of IWGWU, who served from 1986 to 1995.[12]

David Dubinsky was the most notable leader of ILGWU, serving over three decades as its president. When he took the position in 1932, during the Great Depression, the union, with fewer than 40,000 members, was on the brink of bankruptcy. "With extraordinary flair and boundless energy [he rebuilt it] into a dynamic organization that had $500 million in assets in 1966.... He pushed labor to greater social responsibility [and] demanded action against organized racketeering unions." Dubinsky built the ILGWU to 450,000 members. Short in stature, he "never lost his Yiddish accent, his tendency to wave his arms at the slightest provocation or his loud voice" and pointing his index figure as he spoke. After he was re-elected, he said: "I have accepted the presidency because I am foreign born, and I am proud of the great service we have performed for America." Under his watch, the union banished the sweatshops, increased wages, opened health centers, and introduced the 35-hour work week. "We eliminated worry, torture, hunger and starvation."

David Dobnievski was born in 1892 and raised in Lodz, in Russian Poland, where he attended an elementary school and learned to read and write Russian, Polish and Yiddish. He started working at age 13 and joined a union. At age 16 he was arrested by the Russian police and exiled to Siberia. In 1911, at age 19, he left Poland

Finger-pointing David Dubinsky, president of the International Ladies Garment Workers Union, with senator Jacob Kopel Javits, c. 1970 (Library of Congress LC-DIG-gtfy-01831).

to find work in New York as a cloth cutter. That year he joined ILGWU Local 10 and steadily worked to be president of the union. Dubinsky helped establish the Congress of Industrial Organizations (CIO), precursor of American Federation of Labor (AFL), in which he served as vice-president. He joined forces with Sidney Hillman of the Amalgamated Clothing Workers Union to form the Liberal Party. David Dubinsky retired from president of the ILGWU in 1966. He died in 1982, at age 90.[13]

Young Russian-Jewish women immigrants with socialist convictions, and fire in their bellies—like Clara Lemlich, Pauline Newman, Rose Schneiderman, Bas Sheva (Bessie) Rabinowitz, Channah Shapiro, Anna Rudinsky, Fannia Cohn and Rose Pesotta—played key roles in the labor movements. Pauline M. Newman was born in Kovno, Lithuania in 1887, the child of an Orthodox family. She was literate in Yiddish, Hebrew and Russian. After her father died in 1901 her mother took the family to America. Still in her teens, Pauline found work in the Triangle Shirtwaist Company. At age 16 she began writing commentaries for the *Jewish Daily Forward* about the terrible conditions for factory workers. Pauline joined the ILGWU and became its first full-time female organizer, rallying women in New York and around the country to join the union.

Rachel "Rose" Schneiderman hailed from a religious family in the shtetl of Sawin, near Chelm in Russian Poland. In 1890, at 8 years old, she came with her family to New York's Lower East Side. Two years later, her father died leaving the family in abject poverty. Rose and her siblings were placed in an orphanage. At age 13 she went out to work. In her twenties she was working in the garment industry as a cap maker, earning $8 a week, and was active in the ILGWU. Rose was a founding member, and then president, of the National Women's Trade Union League to improve the lives of working women through unionization, legislation and education. She campaigned for equal rights for women. In the 1930s Rose Schneiderman was a member of President Franklin D. Roosevelt's New Deal inner circle, working on the implementation of the National Industrial Recovery Act.[14]

Fannia Cohn, born in Belarus, was radicalized in her teens and joined the Russian Socialist Revolutionary Party. After her brother was brutally attacked in a pogrom, she emigrated at age 19 to the United States. She joined the Socialist Party of America and the ILGWU. She traveled around the country forming women's unions and organizing strikes. In 1918, she became the first female vice-president of the ILGWU, focusing on education to empower women to fight against race and gender inequities. Ukrainian-born Rose Pesotta worked in the education department of the ILGWU to welcome Black and Spanish women entering the needle trades.

Matilda Robbins was born in the Ukraine as Taube Gitel Rabinowitz. In her memoirs Matilda wrote:

> I became 14 in the new country on January 10, 1901. [She was shocked] by the ugliness and poverty of the Lower East Side of New York.... In thousands of tenements, cellars, dingy stores, decayed lofts, and firetrap buildings, men, women and children worked day and night; in bad light, foul air, they cut and sewed and dragged bundles and boxes and pushcarts and broken-down baby carriages through the New York Lower East Side streets. Competition was savage. Jobs were contracted at the lowest possible rates. Whole families worked to keep from starving.... I found a job clipping the threads off the finished shirtwaists at two-and-a-half dollars a week. I worked a 10-hour day and half-day on Saturday with a half-hour lunch break.

Matilda rose to become a senior member of the radical Industrial Workers of the World.[15]

In 1872, German-Jewish Max and Harry Hart, Joseph Schaffner and Levi Marx established Hart, Schaffner and Marx (HSM), to become one of Chicago's leading ready-to-wear men's clothing companies. The company gave employment to many recently arrived Russian-Jewish immigrants, but followed the prevailing pattern of poor working conditions, long hours and low pay. Born in 1889 in the shtetl of Linoveh, near Grodno in Russia, Bas Sheva Rabinowitz was one of 10 children of Emmanuel and Sarah Rabinowitz. Speaking only Yiddish, she arrived at Ellis Island in 1905 and was given the name Bessie. She found work in Chicago with HSM, Shop No. 5, sewing pockets to men's pants and jacket, earning four cents per piece.

In September 1910, the company announced a pay cut to three cents per piece. Acting spontaneously, 20-year-old Bessie led a walk-out of 16 co-workers, including

18-year-old Hannah Shapiro, born in Russian Ukraine, and 16-year-old Anna Rudnitsky. "I am not living," wrote Anna, "I am just working." Bessie, Hannah and Anna were soon joined by 8,000 other HSM workers, and by 30,000 more—mostly young immigrants—from other Chicago clothing companies. The bitter Chicago garment workers strike lasted from September 2, 1910, until February 18, 1911. The Chicago strike ended when Hart, Schaffner and Marx and other clothing manufacturers signed a collective bargaining agreement with their workers.

Sidney Hillman's life "reads like something out of Horatio Alger." He was born in 1887 in the Lithuanian shtetl of Zagare. His father wanted him to train for the rabbinate. Instead, young Sidney joined the Bund and was "an ardent idealist for the democratic revolution in Russia." He organized strikes in 1905, was arrested and held in prison facing exile in Siberia. He was released in a general amnesty, but soon rearrested. Following the dismissal of the Duma in 1906, Hillman saw no future for himself in Russia and decided to emigrate and join "the milling crowds of Russian exiles collecting in the great industrial cities of the West" (p. 20). Travelling on a false passport, he made his way to Manchester, England, and in August 1907 to New York.

Unable to find work in New York, Hillman moved to Chicago. He began as an apprentice cutter—one of the 10,000 workers at Hart, Schaffner & Marx (HSM)—receiving no pay for eight weeks, and then earning $6 a week. In September 1910, he met Bessie Rabinowitz and played a major role in organizing the strike against HSM. After the strike, Hillman entered union work full-time. At the start of the 20th century, most garment manufacturers in America, like HSM, were Jewish owned and "the great bulk of the production was centered in Jewish neighborhoods" (p. 36). In their early years as labor leaders, Sidney Hillman and Bessie Rabinowitz were organizing Russian-Jewish labor against German-Jewish management.[16]

In 1915, Sidney Hillman, Jacob Potofsky, Bessie Rabinowitz and 131 others broke from the United Garment Workers Union to form the more militant Amalgamated Clothing Workers of America (ACWA). Sidney and Bessie married in 1916. At home they spoke Yiddish together but remained decidedly secular. Hillman led Amalgamated for 25 years. In addition, he served as chairman of the Congress of Industrial Organizations (CIO) political action committee, and as chairman of the New York Labor Party. During World War II, he was a close advisor to President Franklin D. Roosevelt on national labor issues.

Hillman was an exponent of "harmonious industrial relations [believing that] the welfare of the workers was directly related to the welfare of industry itself." Using the skill of a diplomat, Hillman urged better pay and shorter hours for American workers. By the end of the war, the 44-hour work-week became standard. Hillman established nationwide agreements to pay textile workers the same wage for the same work, "thus reducing the inclination of employers to move their factories to centers where lower wages prevailed." Hillman suffered a series of heart attacks, but still "extended his activities in the national and international spheres." On occasion, when employers faced difficulties, Hillman loaned them union money to tide them over.

Hillman died in 1946 following his fourth heart attack. The funeral service was conducted by Rabbi Stephen Wise in the Riverside Memorial Chapel, after which the body lay in state at Carnegie Hall where many came to pay their respects. His death was "mourned by millions of Americans irrespective of political opinion or walk of life." President Harry Truman saluted Sidney Hillman as "a distinguished labor leader, and a great humanitarian." An immigrant from Russia, his achievements were "due to his own ability and character, and to the democratic ideals for which he fought." Eleonor Roosevelt, wife of President Franklin Roosevelt, called Hillman "a very beneficial citizen." Sidney Hillman's obituary was printed on the front page of *The New York Times*.[17]

Jacob Samuel Potofsky, an immigrant from Russian Ukraine, started working as a teenager for HSM, sewing pants pockets. Under the influence of Sidney Hillman, he joined the strike against the company. With the formation in New York City of the Amalgamated Clothing Workers of America (ACWA), Potofsky served as senior aide to Sidney Hillman. "I was a soldier in the ranks. Hillman was the chief, and I followed his orders." Frank Rosenblum and Hyman Blumberg—also Russian-Jewish immigrants—held senior positions in ACWA. After Sidney Hillman died, Jacob Potofsky, six-foot tall and sporting a Vandyke beard, was president of ACWA, from 1946 to 1972, and saw its membership rise to 400,000, with branches in most states as well as Puerto Rico and Canada. Bessie Rabinowitz Hillman served as vice-president of ACWA.[18] In its heyday, the ACWA owned banks, operated housing projects, ran employer-funded programs covering sickness, retirement and death. Amalgamated operated health and dental clinics for its members and their families.[19]

The immigrant Russian Jews were determined to leave the Lower East Side and the mind-numbing work in the cramped, foul-smelling sweatshops. Saving a little money, many moved uptown as clothing manufacturers in the Garment District, situated between W. 35th Street and W. 40th Street, and Broadway and Ninth Avenue, with Seventh Avenue as its center. By the 1910s, most "factories and workshops were owned by Russian Jews, and three-quarters of the workforce remained Jewish."[20] "Men who have risen from obscurity are in the foreground as the owners of the property in the new garment center. Some came to these shores without a cent, and from the humblest surrounding on the East Side, have risen to the front through hard work and sincere effort."[21] The man behind the building of New York's Garment District was Abraham E. Lefcourt, born Abraham Elias Lefkowitz to Russian Jewish immigrants. He started as a newsboy and bootblack on the Lower East Side to become an uptown real estate tycoon.[22]

7

Public Response to Russian-Jewish Immigrants

In 1880 the population of the United States was a little over 50 million. The great migration that took place between 1881 and 1914, helped double the nation's people. In 1880, there were 300,000 Jews in America; in 1914, there were three million. During those years, America saw the rapid growth of industries and cities, requiring a great expansion of public schools and universities, trade schools, orphanages, reform schools and hospitals for the physically and the mentally ill. Many immigrants sought opportunities outside New York, creating vibrant Jewish communities in Chicago, Boston, Philadelphia, Cleveland and other cities and towns across America. The migration to America of Eastern European Jews created a host of social problems too large for privately-funded Jewish social agencies alone to manage. Truancy, delinquency, abandoned mothers and children, illness, and the great need for job training among the Jewish immigrants required city and state services. The public response to the Jewish newcomers ranged from a warm welcome to outright rejection.

Public Schools

"The public school is the great savior of the immigrant district," said Jane Addams in 1908, "and is the one agency which imbibes immigrant children with American life."[1] Most Russian-Jewish immigrants who settled in the Lower East Side of New York or the ghettoes in Boston, Philadelphia and Chicago, sent their children—boys and girls—to the local free public elementary schools. Through the English language, these schools transmitted American values and customs, "promising students a share of American society and its opportunities." In New York, many went on to grammar school and then the tuition-free City College or Hunter College to find work as teachers in the New York City public school system, and were assigned to Jewish neighborhoods. These teachers greatly fostered the rapid Americanization of the children of Jewish immigrants.[2]

Mary Antin's family moved from the shtetl of Polotsk in the Russian Empire to "Chelsea, Massachusetts, speaking only Yiddish at home." She recalls:

> That wonderful September morning [in 1893] when I first went to school.... There were about half a dozen of us beginners in English, in age from six to 15. Miss Nixon made a special class of us, and aided us so skillfully and earnestly in our endeavors ... that we turned over page after page of the ravishing history, eager to find out how the common world looked, smelled, and tasted in the strange speech. The teacher knew just when to let us help each other out with a word in our own tongue—it happened that we were all Jews—and so, working all together, we actually covered more ground in a lesson than the native classes....
>
> Whenever the teachers did anything special to help me over my private difficulties, my gratitude went out to them, silently. It meant so much to me that they halted the lesson to give me a lift ... Dear Miss Carrol would be amazed to hear what small things I remember, all because I was so impressed at the time with her readiness and sweetness in taking notice of my difficulties.

Under the guidance of kind and capable public-school teachers, Mary Antin, who had never "been to school even in her own country and has heard English spoken only at school," within four months could read, speak and write the English language with the facility of a native-born child.... "Her experience showed what the Russian Jew can do with an adopted language."[3]

In her 1918 book *Out of the Shadow,* Rose Cohen tells how her starving family had to choose between education or going out to work.

> Winter was coming and none of us had even half warm enough clothing. Father decided that sister should leave school. She had just learned to read and write a little, and of course she could speak English. It was thought that she had made good progress in the short time, considering the drawback she had had, in not knowing the language. We all felt sad, mother particularly, that her education should end here. Her days in school had been happy ones. She had been known and loved by teacher and pupils throughout the little Henry Street school. And like the rest of us she did not look upon "free schooling in America" in a matter-of-fact way. She, a little Jewish girl from an out-of-the-way Russian village of which no one ever heard, was receiving an education! It seemed a wonderful privilege. But when she saw that this was not to be after all, she did not utter a single word of protest or complaint.[4]

Julia Richman epitomized the attitudes and actions of uptown German Jews towards the downtown Russian-Jewish immigrants. She was born in 1855 in the family home at 156 Seventh Avenue, Chelsea Village, New York City. Her father owned a paint and glazier business. When Julia graduated from Normal School, "her father, being in comfortable circumstances, objected to his daughter's going out into the world to work." Determined to be independent, Julia found work at age 17, as a teacher at Grammar School No. 59 on East 57th Street. Her talents for teaching and organization were soon recognized and she served 27 years as principal of Public School No. 77.

"In 1903, Julia Richman was made District Superintendent of Schools, choosing the Lower East Side as her field of work. The tremendous influx of immigrants in the previous 20 years had brought with it problems that no other section of the city faced." Julia Richman believed that "school is destined to become the greatest moral and social center of every community."[5] Running a school department with 600 teachers and 23,000 students, Richman was determined to integrate the children of immigrants into American life. "She established physical culture clubs, literary and debating clubs, for both girls and boys, and athletic leagues."[6]

Julia Richman's stress on rapid Americanization led to conflicts with religious Jews of the Lower East Side. In 1908, they submitted petitions "asking that Julia Richman be transferred to another district [because she was] entirely out of sympathy with the needs of this part of the community." The petitioners claimed that Richman "degraded and lowered parents in the eyes of their children, took advantage of every opportunity to suggest to the children that their parents were criminals, [and] delivered lectures reviling and maligning the inhabitants of the East Side and placed herself in an attitude of opposition to the residents of the East Side." Louis Marshall, a prominent Jewish leader of German background, supported Richman, saying she was "a loyal Jewess whose every act is inspired by good motives and a desire to be helpful to the community." Richman, Marshall and other uptown Jews of German origin gave their time and money to assist their co-religionists. Yet, many downtown Yiddish-speaking Jews viewed these efforts as a serious threat to their tradition-bound way of life.[7] Julia Richman successfully served nine years as superintendent of schools in the Lower East Side despite "influences that would have disheartened a woman of less strength of character, energy and enthusiasm."[8]

As early as 1905 the "prevailing impression was that pupils of poor Jewish immigrants from Russia are among the brightest in attendance at the public schools. Certainly, they rank high in all examinations for advancement to the secondary institutions of learning such as the high schools and city college. In spite of the bad industrial conditions prevailing among the Jews of the Lower East Side, the children themselves are quick to avail themselves of whatever privileges their new surroundings extend to them. Among these the privilege of most worth is the education offered them, and they are not slow to appreciate its advantages. The children begin attendance at the public school within a very short time after their arrival here. Very soon, the public-school teacher becomes a strong influence. They learn to look upon her as a model of good taste in clothes and manner of speech, as a pattern of deportment as well." In the elementary schools, many Russian Jewish children do well in English, history and mathematics, and are "exceedingly patriotic.... With the betterment of economic conditions, there has been a steady growth of attendance in the upper grades, the higher schools, and the professional institutions, in which a remarkably large number of Russian Jewish pupils show a high standard of scholarship."[9] For many bright Jewish children, the local elementary school led to the elite public high schools and on to Ivy League colleges to enter the golden pathway to the opportunities of America.[10]

Settlement Houses

Hull House at 800 S. Halsted Street, Chicago, founded in 1889 by Jane Addams and Ellen Gates Starr, was America's first settlement house. Two years later, Florence Kelley came to Hull House. The noble aim of these enlightened women was to welcome immigrants to America and lift them from poverty. Hull House offered English language lessons, health care, and recreation, and strove to improve work conditions in the sweatshops and factories. Hull House is close to Maxwell Street, once the teeming center of Russian-Jewish immigrant life. At first the Jews were suspicious of Hull House, believing it to be a missionizing institution. Hilda Satt's father died soon after the family arrived in Chicago. Her mother supported the family by scrubbing floors and taking in washing. The teenage Hilda was hesitant to accept an invitation to a Christmas party at Hull House. Once inside, she found

> children and parents at this party from Russia, Poland, Italy, Germany, Ireland, England, and many other lands, but no one seemed to care where they had come from, or what religion they professed, or what clothes they wore, or what they thought. As I sat there, I felt myself being freed from a variety of century-old superstitions and inhibitions. There seemed to be nothing to be afraid of. Then Jane Addams came into the room! It was the first time that I looked into those kind understanding eyes. There was a gleam of welcome in them that made me feel I was wanted. She told us that she was glad we had come. Her voice was warm and I knew she meant what she said. She made me glad that I had come to America.[11]

Missions were active in the ghettoes trying to convert the Russian-Jewish children to Christianity. Rose Cohen describes a mission school in the Lower East Side:

> The small school which the children attended was, I think, connected with a church or a missionary society. One day when the children came home, they told us that any child in the class who would say a prayer received a slice of bread and honey. Mother looked at them and asked them to tell her about it. Sister said, "There is nothing to tell. If you just bow your head as you sit at the desk, and repeat the prayer after the teacher you receive a slice of white bread and honey." We heard a great deal about the missionaries that winter. On Grand Street, at the corner of Attorney Street, there was a big store with green shades which were always drawn. In this store we knew the missionaries held a meeting every Saturday. We heard that the head of the missionaries was a baptized Jew. I heard my parents express their anger because the missionaries came and settled right in the heart of the Jewish neighborhood. We children used to run past the store with a feeling of fear and then stand at a little distance and look at it. I often went back to look inside through a worn part of the shade, and saw a man standing up and talking and a few people in the back of the room listening. Week after week the man preached almost to an empty room. Still, we hated to have them in the neighborhood to tempt our people.
>
> One Saturday afternoon father came home and said that he had just passed the missionaries' store on Grand Street. "They are doing good business these days," he said. "As I passed, the door opened and I saw the place crowded with people." We heard that anyone who went there and listened to the lectures received food and clothing.
>
> All our money was gone.... Mother walked about with slow shuffling steps from room to room. As the children were leaving for school, she asked them without looking at them, whether bread and honey was still given to the children at school. "Yes," sister said, "to those who bow their heads and pray." [Mother said:] "You can bow your heads and pray." Then she went into her dark bedroom.[12]

Lillian Wald was born in 1867 in Cincinnati into a well-to-do German-Jewish family. After graduating in nursing, she came to the Lower East Side to provide health services in the tenements of impoverished immigrants. The Lower East Side, wrote Wald, was "a vast crowded area, a foreign city within our own" (p. 12). In 1895, with funding from Jacob Schiff, Morris Loeb, John D. Rockefeller, and the Lewisohn and Warburg families, Lillian Wald established the Henry Street Settlement House. The settlement house was non-sectarian. "Protestants, Catholics, Jews, an occasional Buddhist ... served together in the Henry Street House, contented and happy, with no attempt to impose their theological convictions upon one another or upon the members of the clubs and classes who come in confidence to us" (p. 255).

"At Henry Street," wrote *The New York Times* in 1938, "all races, creeds and nationalities found a foretaste of utopia in which the barriers of prejudice were down, and men and women of goodwill could work and learn together."[13] Wald admired: "The passion of the Russian Jews for intellectual attainment [that] recalls the spirit of the early New England families and their willingness to forego every comfort that a son might be set apart for the ministry" (p. 99).[14]

Rose Cohen, newly arrived from Russia, had fallen ill. Lillian Ward came to the home to treat her.

> "How do you feel?" she asked me. Her lips smiled but her eyes remained almost sad. She spoke to mother in German, gave her a card and went away. I spelled out the printed name on the card, Lillian D. Wald, 265 Henry Street.... I wrote: "Miss Wald comes to our house, and a new world opens for us. We recommend to her all our neighbors who are in need. The children join clubs in the Nurses' Settlement and I spend a great deal of time there. Miss Wald and Miss Brewster treat me with affectionate kindness. I am being fed. I am to be sent to the country for health, for education.... In a week I felt well enough to go about again. But now the doctor and Miss Wald thought that I had better go to the hospital first and get quite strong. And so it was that I missed the opportunity of the education, for it never came again." Her parents feared sending Rose from their Lower East Side tenement to the hospital. "Miss Wald had a great deal of reasoning and persuading to do and my parents had a great deal to overcome to gain their consent."[15]

"Juvenile delinquency among Russian Jews has aroused the most discussion. The causes of this are again largely economic; housing conditions are bad; the parents are hard-working and too busy with earning the livelihood to pay sufficient attention to their children, who, left to themselves, learn idle or vicious habits on the streets and in the thousand ways of imitative childhood.... In the House of Refuge for boys at Glen Mills, Pennsylvania, out of a total of 766 inmates, 61—or 7.96 percent—were Jews, almost all of whom were Eastern European. Of these, 27 were charged with larceny, 24 with incorrigibility and the others with various delinquencies, such as running away from home, fighting, keeping bad company, malicious mischief, and the like. In the Girls' House of Refuge, out of a total of 127 inmates, eight were Jewish, all charged with being incorrigible" (pp. 358–9). The Jewish welfare agencies of Chicago were "in active co-operation with all the relief societies of the city; with the courts, with the loan organizations; with other societies engaged in preventive charity; and with all medical, housing, and correctional institutions or societies" (p. 93).[16]

Meyer Slein was born in 1898 in Odessa, oldest son of Rubin and Minnie Slein. The family immigrated in 1904 and settled in St. Louis. Rubin abandoned his wife

Lillian Wald (left) and Jane Addams, pioneers in the Settlement House movement, 1916 (Library of Congress, LCCN2016867092).

and five children and returned to Russia. In 1907, Minnie married Sam Bogdanow and had several more children. The broken home and poverty forced the children out in the streets, selling newspapers or stealing. Several of the Slein boys, including Meyer, were sent to reform school. Meyer Slein died in 1943 while serving his country during World War II, and was buried in the Fort Leavenworth National Military Cemetery, Kansas.

Twelve-year-old Meyer Slein was a newsboy who was on the streets until late at night with bad associates in St. Louis, Missouri. He is shown with three of his younger brothers, Abe, Louis and Max, 1910. Photographer Lewis Hine noted in May 1910, "He stole from large retail stores. Often stayed away from home all night." Meyer had recently returned from Missouri Industrial School for Boys, founded in 1889. The fifth Slein brother was in the reform school. The boys showed how a chaotic family and poverty led to "a street life and Juvenile Court" (Library of Congress, LC-DIG-nclc-03523).

Moses and Nechama Yoelson with their five children left their Lithuanian shtetl, near Kovno (Kaunas) and settled in Washington, D.C., where Moses found work as a rabbi and cantor. Asa Yoelson was eight years old when his mother died in 1895. He entered into a state of emotional withdrawal and was sent for four months to St. Mary's Industrial School for Boys, run by the Catholic Archdiocese of Baltimore. Determined to enter show business, he changed his name to Al Jolson to achieve national acclaim in the 1920s as a jazz singer.

Between 1909 and 1931, the Juvenile Courts of New York City assessed 171,119 cases of delinquency in boys and girls aged between 5 and 15 years. Of these 31,462—18.4 percent—were Jewish.[17] As the Russian Jews found their footing in America, delinquency fell. A review in 1945, found that Jews had the lowest rate of delinquency in New York.[18]

Opposition to Immigration

Many people in positions of power openly opposed the migration of Eastern European Jews to America. In 1891, the United States Senator from Massachusetts Henry Cabot Lodge claimed that "the races who have peopled the United States" were declining, while "the immigration of people removed from us in race and blood" was rapidly increasing.[19] In 1894, a group of Harvard men from old Boston families formed the Immigration Restriction Society to reduce the flow of "undesirable" immigrants from Eastern and Southern Europe and foster migration from northern and western Europe. Among its leading members were Robert Trent Paine, great-grandson of the signer of the American Constitution, Senator Henry Cabot Lodge, and A. Lawrence Lowell who, in 1909, was appointed president of Harvard College.

Jews were blamed for the rise of crime in American cities, especially bigamy, burning buildings, burglary, prostitution and pickpocketing. In 1897, president of the New York Board of Police Commissioners Frank Moss, in a book chapter entitled "New Israel: A Modern Source of Crime," accuses Jews of "prejudice, stubborn refusal to yield to American habits, and clannishness." The Lower East Side, which

"Uncle Sam: Why should I let these freaks cast whole votes when they are only half American?" (J.S. Pughe, *Puck* magazine August 9, 1899).

Moss calls New Israel, is "a distinct center of crime. It is infested with petty thieves and housebreakers, many of them desperate. Criminal instincts are so often found naturally in the Russian and Polish Jews ... to warrant the opinion that these people are the worst elements in the entire rank of New York life.... A large proportion of the people of New Israel are addicted to crime." The Lower East Side, writes Moss, is an over-crowded area with "degenerate Jews, filled with old-clothes shops, sweat-shops and second-hand shoe-shops" (p. 51).[20]

In 1908, the New York Police Commissioner Theodore Brigham published an article on "Foreign Criminals in New York" in the *North American Review.*

> The crimes committed by the Russian Hebrews are generally those against property. They are burglars, firebugs, pickpockets and highway robbers—when they have the courage; but though all crime is their province, pocket-picking is the one to which they seem to take most naturally. Indeed, pickpockets of other nationalities are beginning to recognize the superiority of the Russian Hebrew in that gentle art.... Among the most expert of all the street thieves are Hebrew boys under 16, who are being brought up to lives of crime. Many of them are old offenders at the age of 10. The juvenile Hebrew emulates the adult in the matter of crime percentages; 40 percent of the boys at the House of Refuge and 27 percent of those arraigned in the Children's Court, being of that race. The percentage of Hebrew children in the truant schools is also higher than that of any others.[21]

The Jewish community countered these figures to show that Jews accounted for only 16.4 percent of delinquency and crime in New York.[22]

William Zebina Ripley, born 1867 in Medford, Massachusetts, received his doctorate from Columbia University and went on to an acclaimed academic career as professor of political economy at Harvard University. He believed that races differed from each other in appearance and intellect—a view popular at that time. He classified the peoples of Europe as Teutonic in the north (long-skulled, fair eyes and blond hair); Nordic in the center (round-skulled, stocky, and intermediate in eye and hair color); and Mediterranean in the south (short stature, dark eyes and dark hair). The Jews "were without a country" of their own, and were concentrated in western Russia (actually Poland, Latvia, Lithuania, Belarus, Ukraine). Jews were "undersized and often absolutely stunted, had narrow chests, dark hair, hooked noses, thick eyebrows and even a particular separation of the teeth."[23] Ripley's book came out in 1899, when the immigration to America of Russian Jews was high.

The United States Immigration Commission (known as the Dillingham Commission after its chairman, Senator William P. Dillingham of Vermont), was formed in 1907. In 1911, the Commission issued a 41-volume report, stating that the continued arrival of Eastern and Southern European immigrants was a serious threat to American culture and values. The Commission recommended the use of a literary test to turn away persons deemed intellectually inferior. Jewish immigrants from the Russian Empire were deemed clannish and non-assimilable.[24] The Commission regarded Jews as a separate race. The Dillingham Commission wrote: "The primary causes have been a desire for better economic conditions, and the persecutions directed against the Jewish population."[25] Jews arrived in families rather than as unattached young adults. It recommended limiting the number of each race arriving each year to a percentage of that race arriving over several years. The Dillingham Commission also advocated the continuation of immigration restrictions against Chinese, Japanese and Koreans.

The Dillingham Report emboldened anti-Semites like New York lawyer Madison Grant. Using William Z. Ripley's pseudo-scientific racial theories, Grant called a halt to Jewish migration to America. In his 1916 book *The Passing of the Great Race*, Grant claimed that the Nordic race, stemming from northern Europe, was biologically and culturally superior to others. Grant stated that with mass immigration to the United States "the man of the Old School is being crowded out … of the streets of New York by the swarms of Polish Jews [who] adopt the language of the native American, they wear his clothes; they steal his name; and they begin to take his women: but they seldom accept his religion or understand his ideals; and he is being elbowed out of his own home." If Jewish immigration continues, writes Grant, "the true American will entirely disappear."[26] Hitler's most valued book on America was Madison Grant's *The Passing of the Great Race.* In a letter, Hitler told Grant "The book is my bible." Hitler often quoted from it in his vitriolic speeches.[27] Madison Grant was a senior member of the Immigration Restriction League. He played a key role in the 1924 passage of the Johnson-Reed Act that reduced Eastern European Jewish migration to a trickle.

About 250,000 Jews—many of them Russian immigrants—joined the United States Army during World War I. America emerged from the war an isolationist county with many in Congress determined to cut immigration, especially from Russia, now under Bolshevik rule. The automobile mogul Henry Ford stoked anti-Semitism through his newspaper *The Dearborn Independent* alleging that there was a Jewish conspiracy to control the world's economy. In 1920, these articles were assembled into a vituperative book entitled *The International Jew: The World's Foremost Problem.* "The Jew does not assimilate," alleged Ford's newspaper.

> From the sale of old clothes to the control of international trade and finance, the Jew is supremely gifted for business … the Jewish boy prefers to begin as messenger, salesman or clerk—anything—so long as it is connected with the commercial side of the business.… His emergence in the financial, political and social spheres has been so complete and spectacular since the war [World War I].… In America alone most of the big business, the trusts and the banks, the natural resources and the chief agricultural products, especially tobacco, cotton and sugar, are in the control of Jewish financiers or their agents; Jewish journalists are a large and powerful group here. … The theatrical business, of course, as everyone knows, is exclusively Jewish. Play-producing, booking, theater operation, are all in the hands of Jews.… The motion picture industry. The sugar industry. The tobacco industry. Fifty percent or more of the meat packing industry. Upward of 60 percent of the shoemaking industry. Men's and women's ready-made clothing. Most of the musical purveying done in the country. Jewelry. Grain. More recently, cotton. The Colorado smelting industry. Magazine authorship. News distribution. The liquor business. The loan business. These, only to name the industries with national and international sweep, are in control of the Jews of the United States, either alone or in association with Jews overseas.… Bolshevism everywhere, in Russia or the United States, is Jewish.[28]

Responding to pressures to significantly reduce immigration of Jews and Italians, on May 19, 1921, President Warren G. Harding signed the Quota Act, while allowing greater immigration from Western and Northern European countries. The Peace Conference at Versailles in 1919 gave Poland and Lithuania independence from Russia. In 1921, 74,700 Jews from Poland entered the United States but their numbers fell sharply with the implementation of the Quota Act.

In the Immigration Restriction Act of 1924, United States Senator David Reed and Representative Albert Johnson proposed even lower immigration quotas from Eastern and southern Europe. "Genetic theories played such a role in the enactment of the Immigration Restriction Act of 1924. Passage of that law required popular sentiment in its behalf; the genetic arguments advanced by members of the eugenics movement helped organize and direct that sentiment."[29] Senator David Reed, co-sponsor of the Johnson-Reed Act, said Eastern Europeans "arrive sick and starving and therefore less capable of contributing to the American economy, and unable to adapt to American culture."

In an April 1924 article in (*sic*) *New York Times*, Senator Reed announced: "America of the Melting Pot Comes to an End." He claimed that "Americans are beginning to smart under the irritation of her foreign colonies—these groups of aliens, whether in the city slums or country districts, who speak a foreign language, and live a foreign life, and want neither to learn our common language or to share our common life." Reed wanted to keep "American stock up to the highest standard—that is, the people who were born here."[30]

Following the passage of the 1924 immigration act, Senator Reed proudly proclaimed: "The racial composition of America at the present time thus is made permanent." The 1924 Act greatly favored immigration from Great Britain, Germany and Sweden but offered low quotas for immigrants from Eastern and Southern Europe, capping total immigration to 164,667 a year. Poland, with 3.5 million Jews, was allotted a quota of 5,982, and Romania, with a million Jews, was allowed only 295. Soviet Russia was allocated a quota of 2,784 but "emigration from the USSR had not been permitted, except for a tiny handful, since the early 1920s."[31]

With doors closing on further large-scale Jewish immigration, "by 1927 Jewish communities existed in every American state with the largest concentrations in New York (1,900,000 people), Illinois (405,000), Pennsylvania (405,000), Massachusetts (220,000), Ohio (174,000), New Jersey (225,000), California (123,000) and Michigan and Maryland (each about 90,000). By the close of 1927 about 4,250,000 Jews lived in the country, comprising 3.58 percent of the entire population."[32]

8

Response of the Jewish Community to Immigrants

> "Our chief aim is and always should be to make of the children of the recent immigrants, good American citizens. The older generation is often beyond reform; the younger should never be allowed to grow up into the state of dependence on public relief."[1]

> "Russian Jews are filled with a genuine desire of becoming part and parcel of this great republic yet wish, at the same time, to remain loyal to their heritage."[2]

In the 1870s, the Jewish population of New York numbered barely 60,000, mostly German Jews who had deep roots into American life. United Hebrew Charities (UHC) of New York was founded in 1874 to help the Jewish poor, the ill and the aged. Henry Rice, served 34 years as president of UHC. Born in Bamberg, Bavaria, he came to the United States in 1850, at age 15. Rice served in the United States Army during the Civil War. After the war, he established a wholesaling company.[3] Beginning in 1881, impoverished Yiddish-speaking immigrants, fleeing the Russian Empire, greatly swelled the Jewish population of the city. "Immigration was adding its hundreds of Jewish lads to the streets of New York City. Other boys were placed at sewing machines in tailors' shops, or at some branch of cigar-making." Henry Rice observed Jewish boys "selling papers, matches and sundry articles, blacking shoes or working for a pittance in crowded manufactories. [He took on the task] to teach these boys above 13 years of age some useful trade or occupation."[4]

The Jewish Sheltering House Association was formed in 1892. A decade later, the Hebrew Immigrant Aid Society (HIAS) was established at 229 East Broadway, New York City, with funds supplied by Baron and Baroness Maurice de Hirsch, Mortimer Schiff, Oscar Straus, Julian William Mack and other Jews of German origin. These organizations joined together in 1909 at the height of Russian-Jewish immigration to form the Hebrew Sheltering and Immigration Society. The aims of the society were: "To facilitate the landing of Jewish immigrants at Ellis Island; to provide them temporary shelter, food, clothing … to guide them to their destination; to prevent them becoming public charges and help them to obtain employment; to discourage their settling in congested cities … and to foster American ideals among the newcomers and to instill patriotism and love for their adopted country."[5] Staff members of the Society met new immigrants at Ellis Island and railroad stations, helped them find relatives, and assisted migrants deemed unfit and sent back to Europe. The Society set up the Industrial Removal Office at 174 2nd Street, New York City, to disperse immigrants from New York to other parts of the country.

At the close of the 19th century, the German Jewish elite established several educational institutions to help the children of Russian-Jewish immigrants rapidly embrace American life. The Hebrew Technical Institute, founded by UHC, began in 1884 at 209 East Broadway, New York. Three years later it moved to a larger building at 9th and Stuyvesant Streets. All students, between 14 and 17 years, "pursue the same course for two years. In the third year the student specializes in woodworking, pattern making, metal working, tool making, instrument-making, mechanical drawing, architectural drawing, free-hand drawing, applied electricity, radio physics, automotive engineering or auto electricity." Joseph Bloomingdale, founder of Bloomingdale's department store on 59th Street, served as president of the institute from 1900 to 1904.

The school housed up to 380 students a year, with 3,300 graduating over a 50-year period. Albert Einstein, himself a recent immigrant, visited the school on March 30, 1934, and complimented the school for providing "theoretical and practical education so as to render the students useful as self-reliant workers in different branches of industry.... The focusing of both theory and craftsmanship in a single technical subject I have nowhere else seen realized in so perfect a manner."

Max "Marty" Friedman was born in the Lower East Side. After graduating from the Institute, he played professional basketball and was admitted to the Basketball Hall of Fame. Another graduate, Arthur Aaron Hamerschlag, of Austro-Hungarian parentage and a member of the Class of 1889, specialized in the new field of electricity. His skill became known to Andrew Carnegie who invited him to Pittsburgh to became the first president of Carnegie Mellon University. The Hebrew Technical Institute closed in 1939.[6]

Chicago's German-Jewish elite reckoned that little could be done to improve the lot of the Russian-Jewish parents, but their children should be helped to become "clean, honest, useful, educated Americans" and become skillful manual workers. Leon and Emanuel Mandel, owners of Mandel Brothers, a leading Chicago department store, at the corner of State and Madison, led the fund drive to lift the children of poor Russian Jews out of poverty. In 1887, "Leon Mandel donated the magnificent sum of $20,000 towards the establishment of a school to equip the sons and daughters with the power of making a healthy, honest and honorable livelihood, with the desire of living a respectable and self-respecting manner."

The founders commissioned Dankmar Adler and Louis Sullivan, architects of the Transportation Building at the 1893 World's Columbian Exposition, to design the four-story Jewish Training School on Judd Street, in the middle of Chicago's Jewish ghetto.[7] The school aimed "to acquaint the children of Russian Jews with the

Chicago's Jewish Training School, designed in 1890 by Dankmar Adler and Louis Sullivan, pictured c. 1910.

English language, our American methods and American institutions and to help them advance themselves." In the machine- and joinery shops and the chemistry laboratory, the boys learned carpentry, printing and other trades, while the girls were connected "with domestic and commercial worlds."[8]

In 1878, Jacob H. Hecht was appointed president of the United Hebrew Benevolent Association to help the poor and the aged of Boston's small German-Jewish community. Only 6,000 Jews lived in Boston in 1880. Within 15 years, the Russian-Jewish migration swelled the Jewish population of the city to 60,000 with many settling in the historic but run-down North End. "I cannot believe I am in America," observed Zvi Hirsh Masliansky, "The streets of Boston remind me of Vilna; Synagogues, Talmud Torah study groups, Hebrew schools in the old style; almost all the shops closed on Saturdays."[9] As it happened in New York and Chicago, the arrival of Russian-Jewish immigrants changed the focus of Jewish charity. Despite "some doubt that these Russians could become worthy Americans," Hecht and his wife Lina in 1891, financed the Hebrew Industrial School in the North

End to help the immigrants find their way in America. "At the end of five years, the Industrial School had taught 1,200 children to be wage earners, breadwinners, and self-respecting intelligent citizens."[10]

His father was banker to the king of Bavaria. Born in 1831 in Munich, Maurice de Hirsch was educated in Brussels and joined a banking house where he made his first fortune. He added to his great wealth by running railroads in Europe. He was a major supporter of the Alliance Israelite Universelle. He funded the Jewish Colonial Society to help Russian Jews establish farming communities in the Argentine and Brazil. In 1891, he established the Baron de Hirsch Fund in New York to assist Russian Jews settle in America. Providing $2.5 million (worth $90 million in 2024), de Hirsch recruited fellow German Jews Jacob Schiff, Oscar S. Strauss and Mayer Sulzberger to run his fund.

The de Hirsch fund supported the Woodbine Agricultural School in southern New Jersey, to train young Jews in farming. In 1895, the fund opened the Baron de Hirsch Trade School to train boys in carpentry, plumbing, machinery, house painting, sign painting, fresco painting and in the new trades related to electricity and automobiles. The de Hirsch trade school had fully equipped plumbing, carpentry and machine shops. The training would prepare the students to be intelligent apprentices, as a major step towards becoming skilled trades people. Tuition was free.[11]

German financier and philanthropist Baron Maurice de Hirsch, c. 1894. He established a fund to assist Russian Jews settle in America (Library of Congress, LC-USZ62-112175).

The 97 students who graduated in June 1903, were advised to be "zealous, efficient and hard-working. When you get a job, do your work well.... You must strive to make yourself the very best kind of American. Be loyal and patriotic citizens. Many of you come from Russia. Remember that such a crime [*sic*] could not be committed in the land of the Stars and Stripes." Prizes were awarded to David Glickman, machinery department, Joseph Weinberg, plumbing, Max Greenwald, electricity, Joseph Shapiro, sign painting and Samuel Herman, house and fresco painting.[12] The Baron de Hirsch Trade School closed in 1927.

The Baron de Hirsch Agricultural School on 300 acres near the town of Woodbine, southern New Jersey, was launched in 1894 with the purpose of training Jewish immigrant boys between the ages of 14 and 18 years to become successful farmers. The residential school taught classes in English and business, as well as how to grow fruits and vegetables, landscape gardening, animal care, and agricultural chemistry. "During the spring and summer term the school work is devoted exclusively to practical out-of-door work." In 1905, the 53 graduates of the agricultural school were told of the "advantages of the farm over work in the large cities because there was a demand for farmers."[13]

The de Hirsch school imposed strict disciple and was determined to instill the boys with "American manners and ways of living." A culture clash ensued between the demonstrative Russian-Jewish boys and the strict rules of the German-Jewish sponsors. "On many occasions the pupils rebelled, organized strikes, and caused considerable confusion."[14] Farming in rural New Jersey did not appeal to many inner-city Jewish boys. Instead, they were entering universities in large numbers. Difficulties in recruiting new students forced de Hirsch Agricultural School to shut down in 1917.[15]

Nathaniel Myers "often said that there were hundreds interested in helping Jewish boys but few to help girls." Born in 1848 into a German-Jewish family that settled in St. Louis, Myers left school at age 15 to start work as a telegraph messenger boy. He found the energy to study the law, passed the bar examination and set up practice in New York in corporate law. In 1897, he took part in the establishment of the Hebrew Technical School for Girls, sited at 267 Henry Street. The school aimed to elevate "working-class Jewish immigrant girls." From 1900 and until his death in 1921, he served as president of the school.[16]

The girls, age 15 to 18, who attended the Hebrew Technical School, were graduates of New York's public grammar schools. They were largely American-born girls of Russian-Jewish parentage. Early in the 20th century, the school moved to a new building at 15th Street and Second Avenue. The commercial department taught bookkeeping, stenography, typewriting, penmanship and rhetoric. The domestic department taught embroidery, dressmaking, knitting, sewing and drawing. With many applicants, the enrollment of the school rose from 100 in 1900 to 650 in 1921.[17] When the New York public schools began offering similar training, the enrollment of the Hebrew Technical School for Girls declined and the school closed in 1932.

In 1897, Clara de Hirsch, widow of Baron Maurice de Hirsch, donated $200,000 to establish the Clara de Hirsch Home for Working Jewish Girls at 225 East 63rd Street, New York. Charging $5 to $6 dollars a week for board and lodging, and accepting girls between 14 and 18 years, the home aimed to improve their mental, moral and physical conditions. Focused on the needle trades, the home gave classes in machine operation, dressmaking and millinery.[18] Mrs. Oscar S. Strauss served as president of the home. She was the wife of German-born Oscar Solomon Strauss who rose to become United States secretary of commerce and labor, 1906–09, in the Theodore Roosevelt administration. Oscar Strauss was America's first Jewish cabinet secretary. The Clara de Hirsch Home closed in 1960.

Adolphus Solomon and other sponsors of the Columbia Religious and Industrial School for Jewish Girls saw the risks to Jewish identity of rapid Americanization. Founded on Columbia Street in New York's Lower East Side in 1888, this girl's school stressed equally Jewish religion, Jewish identity and work. In addition to learning how to operate garment-making machinery, knitting, embroidery and dress-making, the girls were offered classes in religion, Jewish history and Hebrew. Solomon, a founder of New York's Mount Sinai Hospital, was a descendant of Haym Salomon, who helped finance the American War of Independence. His daughter Rosalie served as president of the Columbia Religious and Industrial school. She was a "leader in political and civic organizations and helped a number of important Jewish philanthropic organizations" including Hadassah, the Union of Orthodox Jewish Congregations, as well as serving as president of the Columbia Religious and Industrial School.[19] At its peak, the school had 300 students. The Columbia Religious and Industrial School for Jewish Girls shut down in the 1940s.

The Educational Alliance has served the City of New York since 1889. Prominent Jewish philanthropists Isidor Straus, owner of Macy's department store, banker Jacob H. Schiff, Myer Isaacs and Edwin R.A. Seligman raised the funds to build a grand five-story building at 197 East Broadway. The underlying purpose of the Institute was to render the children of Russian-Jewish immigrants "physically, mentally and morally, better men and women; better American citizens, and better Jews." The principal aim of the Institute, reported *The New York Times* on November 9, 1891, was "the Americanization of the large mass of foreign-born Jews in the city." The Institute offered classes in the English language, civics, American history, cooking and stenography. Over time the Institute opened a library and a children's theater, offered concerts, clubs, lectures in Yiddish and English, and sponsored evening college-level classes. By the 1910s, 10,000 children and adults a day were passing through its doors.

Speaking in 1915, in Yiddish at the 25th-anniversary of the founding of the Educational Alliance Joseph Friedlander noted: "During the last 25 years a complete change has taken place in the makeup of the American Jewish community due to the influx of Jews from Eastern Europe."[20] With its stress on Americanization at the expense of the Russian-Jewish heritage, the Educational Alliance was "regarded by a very large number of East Siders with absolute antipathy and mistrust."[21] By the 1940s most Jews had left the Lower East Side and the Institutional Alliance was repurposed to serve newer immigrants.

The National Council of Jewish Women established settlement houses in several cities to Americanize Jewish immigrants and their children. "Tensions based in

The Education Alliance at 175 East Broadway, New York, c. 1906. German Jews financed centers for Russian Jewish immigrants to teach them the English language and how to adjust to American ways (*Brockhaus-Efron Jewish Encyclopedia*, published 1908–1913, St. Petersburg, Russia).

differences in social class, political orientations, and religious practice often proved particularly poignant in these institutions, especially in debates between workers and clients on the use of Yiddish and support for Zionism."[22]

In 1903, under German-Jewish leadership, the Chicago Hebrew Institute opened on the Near West Side to hasten the Americanization of Russian-Jewish immigrants. Modeled on New York's Educational Institute, it offered classes in English, citizenship, Jewish culture and sports activities. During Lincoln Week, February 1909, it held a program for "Yiddish speaking people, especially for newly arrived Jewish immigrants." The institute had a library, offered lectures on Abraham Lincoln and George Washington, had a glee club and held religious services on Saturdays.[23] The institute was "frankly Jewish and staunchly American." In 1926, the institute moved from the Jewish ghetto to the new center of Jewish life in Lawndale. Its work in Americanizing immigrants done, the Chicago Hebrew Institute evolved into a Jewish Community Center.[24]

The Hebrew Technical Institute, the Baron de Hirsch trade school and the Clara de Hirsch Home for Working Girls, all of New York, the Jewish Training School of Chicago, the Baron de Hirsch Agricultural School, the Chicago Hebrew Institute and the Hebrew Industrial School of Boston were all funded by prominent secular German-Jewish philanthropists who had made their money in business, department stores, banking and manufacturing. Trade schools for Jewish children also opened in Philadelphia, Cleveland and Cincinnati. The curricula closely followed those of trade high schools all over America to prepare boys to enter the workforce as apprentice carpenters, plumbers, bricklayers, automobile mechanics, electricians and telegraph engineers, and girls to work in the needle trades, in offices, schools and hospitals. Their aim was to Americanize the Russian-Jewish child: to keep the Jewish religion, but minimize the differences between Jew and Gentile in accent, dress, language, habits, and occupation.

The German-Jewish elite who funded the Jewish trade schools expected boys and girls to leave public schools after completing the 8th-grade and spend the years from age 15 to 18 learning a trade, like plumbing and carpentry, and office work and millinery for the girls. By the 1920s it was clear that they had misread the capabilities and ambitions of the children of Russian Jewish immigrants. Despite their impoverished background, many of these children aspired to complete public high school and go on to four-year-colleges, to enter the professions. Others chose careers in business, sports or entertainment. Others channeled their ambitions into sports. Still others showed little interest in discipline and learning. Instead, they joined street gangs, getting into fights, making mischief and stealing.

Jewish Education

"The most far-reaching opposition is between those whose aim is to preserve Jewish group life, and those who wish to amalgamate with non–Jews in this country. [The German-Jewish elite was] anxious to put the [Russian] Jews in this country on a level at least equal to that of other Americans." Many immigrants wanted an educational system to preserve in America the Jewish religion, culture, values and way of life, including the dietary laws, and keeping the Sabbath and observing the holy-days. With limited financing, religious members of the Russian-Jewish immigrants establish a network of Talmud Torah schools to teach Hebrew, religion, the Bible, and Jewish customs. Among the largest was Machzikim Talmud Torah, 227 East Broadway, with 800 students, and Downtown Talmud Torah at 394 E. Houston Street, New York City. "But the Talmud Torah was not sufficient for the demands of some of the Eastern European Jews, because it failed to make proper provision for the study of the Talmud" (p. 72).

Intensive-study Yeshivot, based on the European model, were established by the zealously Orthodox, beginning in 1886, Etz Chayim Talmudic Academy located at 85 Henry Street. Etz Chayim was followed by the Beth Seder Tifereth Jerusalem

Yeshivah, and by the Rabbi Jacob Joseph Yeshivah at 165 Henry Street. Under the leadership of Dr. Solomon Schechter, the Jewish Theological Seminary became one of America's leading Jewish schools. Alexander Dushkin estimated that in 1915, in New York City, only one in four Jewish children of elementary school age were receiving any form of Jewish education (p. 115). After bar-mitzvah at age 13, very few children continued a Jewish education.[25] The Rabbi Jacob Joseph School, the last yeshivah in the Lower East Side, left in 1972.[26]

As in New York City, but on a far smaller scale, the Russian Jews who settled in Chicago, Boston, Philadelphia and other cites, tried to keep alive the flame of Jewish education, especially with children of elementary school age. Everywhere, the magnetic pull of Americanism won out.

Social Disruption

"The Jewish boy criminal is a new phenomenon," wrote Boris D. Bogen in 1905. "One-third of the complaints drawn in the Children's Court of the City of New York are against Jewish children.... Poverty drives thousands of children into the streets in search of a trifling earning. Selling newspapers, bootblacking, running errands, working around theaters and other places of amusement, serve as preparatory schools for the juvenile delinquent."[27] The migration of hundreds of thousands of impoverished Russian Jews created a host of problems including broken homes, abandoned wives and children, drunkenness, truancy and delinquency. Fathers came to America alone, planning to earn the money to pay the passage of wives and children. Many of these lonely men "contracted new ties and are unwilling to maintain responsibilities originally contracted before they left their native places.... The United Hebrew Charities of New York has in its records for the year 1909, 1,046 deserted women and 1,655 widows.... Jewish delinquency spread on the East Side with great rapidity.... It was a problem of how to breach over the gulf between the parents and their children. Reverence for parents used to be the foundation for Jewish social life, the children of immigrants are losing it through getting hold of American ideas in the wrong way."[28]

In 1905, United Hebrew Charities set up the National Desertion Bureau to trace fathers who had abandoned their wives and children. Pictures and descriptions of many of these men were published in the "Gallery of Missing Husbands" column of the New York Yiddish-language *The Daily Forward*. In 1908, a despondent young woman wrote the following letter to the "Bintel Brief" section of *The Daily Forward*:

> Max: The children and I now say farewell to you. You left us in such a terrible state. You had no compassion for us. ... Have you ever asked yourself why you left us? Max, where is your conscience; you used to have sympathy for the forsaken women and used to say their terrible plight was due to the men who left them in dire need. And how did you act? I was a young, educated decent girl when you took me. You lived with me for six years, during which time I bore you four children. And then you left me. Of the four children, only two remain, but you have made them living orphans. Who will bring them up? Who will support us? Have you no

> pity for your own flesh and blood. Consider what you are doing. My tears choke me and I cannot write anymore.

Such letters appeared quite frequently in *The Forward* and other Yiddish newspapers in the early years of the 20th century. The desertion by the bread-winner had become a fact of life for numerous immigrant Jewish families during this period. In 1905, 14.6 percent of the cash relief funds administered by the United Hebrew Charities were granted to deserted women, second only to that provided to widows and their children."[29]

"The proverbial Jewish family, known for its traditional strength, was rapidly showing signs of weakness as a result of its transplantation from Eastern Europe to America.... The Jewish family structure, replanted in America, was greatly affected by the stresses of immigrant life. It was not long before the issues of crime, prostitution, and particularly family desertion were to confront many Eastern Europe Jewish immigrant families in America.[30]

Molly Picon's father abandoned his family. When Walter Matthau was age three, his father walked out leaving his wife and two young sons in a desperate situation. Walter "never had a father [and] saw him just a couple of times." Walter and brother Henry "really hustled to take care of their mother."[31] Despite their early privations, Molly Picon and Walter Matthau became stars of the Yiddish and then of the English-language stage and film.

The National Conference of Jewish Charities learned in 1906 that

> Delinquency is on the increase among our boys; no longer is the Jewish girl a synonym for virtue. Between 28 and 30 percent of all children brought to the Children's Court of New York are Jewish children. There are three and a half times as many children among this number who are the children of recently arrived immigrants as there are of native-born parents.... In the Ghetto, families are huddled together in a few dingy rooms; large families live and frequently several boarders besides, ... the home life is unbearable for the children, disease must thrive and immorality has a breeding place amid such wretched surroundings.... The New York Truant School contains a large number of Jewish children; a general average would be about 35 percent of the total number.... The parents send the children out to sell papers, shine shoes and peddle, when the father or the bread winner of the family is out of work, and such children are compelled to fall in line and thus help to support the family.... The children are on the streets nearly all day long, finding nothing to attract them in their dingy homes, and in the streets many bad habits are formed. [Due to a lack of Jewish resources a] large number of Jewish children are being committed to Catholic institutions and those of other denominations.[32]

The family and social problems of many Russian-Jewish immigrants severely taxed the resources of Jewish social organizations across America. In 1916, in Manhattan 1,558 Jewish children were arraigned in the Juvenile Court. At that time Jewish charities debated whether there was a "need of specific Jewish institutions for Jewish juvenile delinquents." Some advocated "the establishment of an intermunicipal institution for Jewish delinquent children" while others "insisted that the state institutions ought to handle this problem."[33]

In 1906, the Jewish Board of Guardians established the Hawthorne School for boys and, six years later, Cedar Knoll School for girls, in Westchester County, to care for Jewish children declared delinquent by the Children's Courts of New York. Until the 1920s, most of the girls and boys sent to these reform schools were Russian-born.[34] "The problems of the delinquent Jewish girl," explained the principal of Cedar Knoll, stem from the conflict between "their strong religious principles and high ideals ... thrown into new surroundings, where the customs of the country are strange and incomprehensible to them, amid different economic conditions, where the struggle for mere existence is so keen."[35]

In 1922, some 23 percent of the 2,094 children arraigned before the Juvenile Courts of New York City were Jewish. The Jewish Education Association devised a plan "to take 10,000 children off the streets and place them in Jewish religious schools [in the hope this would] inculcate reverence in the child [and] establish habits of regularity."[36] By 1933, only 14.6 percent of the arraigned delinquents were Jewish.[37] As Jewish immigrants settled into American life fewer of their children were arraigned for delinquency.

Quite a number of Jewish delinquents went on to careers in crime, too extensive for the Jewish institutions alone to handle. Benjamin "Bugsy" Siegel was a Lower East Side Jewish juvenile delinquent. He was born in 1906 on Cannon Street, the son of Orthodox Eastern European-born Max and Jennie Siegel. Max worked as a presser in a men's pants factory, earning $50 a month. At age 12 Bugsy dropped out of school to launch his criminal career as a petty thief. He joined the Lafayette Street gang demanding protection money from struggling pushcart peddlers under the threat of poisoning their horses and burning their pushcarts. Bugsy and his Lower East Side pals Meyer Lansky, Arthur Flugenheimer, Jacob "Gurrah" Shapiro and Louis "Lepke" Buchalter—members of the Jewish Mob—embarked on lives of crime, with gambling, drugs, high-jacking liquor cargoes, bootlegging, corrupting trade unions, robbery and murder. The "Bugs and Meyer" gang built an extensive crime syndicate that stretched from the Lower East Side to the American West. Siegel moved to Los Vegas where he built the lavish Flamingo Hotel, that became a gambling mecca for Hollywood celebrities. Along the way he made enemies. In June 1946, the 40-year-old Siegel was in a lavish house on North Linden Drive, Hollywood. Concealed in the bushes, a sniper fired shots through the window, killing Siegel.[38]

Meyer Lansky was born in 1902 in Grodno, in the Russian Empire. His name at birth was Maier Suchowljansky. At age 8 he came with his family to America to endure an impoverished childhood in the Lower East Side. He attended Public School No. 34, but dropped out after the 8th grade to find work as a tool and die maker. To add to his meager wages, Lansky set up a floating dice game, where he met Charles "Lucky" Luciano and Bugsy Siegel. Lansky "maneuvered his way up through the ranks of organized crime and parlayed Prohibition profit into hundreds of illicit and legitimate businesses." He developed gambling operations in New Orleans, Florida, the Bahamas and Cuba, and was a major investor in Siegel's Las Vegas gambling empire.

Lansky's Havana operation ceased with the Castro revolution. Standing 5 foot 4 inches and weighing 135 pounds, the smart, well-organized and dapper Meyer Lansky employed high-priced lawyers to evade prosecution. Crime syndicates expanded greatly after World War II, with the financial wizard Lansky setting up casinos, skimming money from trade unions and businesses and evading taxes. He was arrested only once—in 1953—to spend a mere two months in prison. At his death in 1983, at age 81, Meyer Lansky left a fortune of $200 million.[39]

Described as "the worst industrial racketeer in America," Louis Buchalter was arrested by the FBI in 1939 and charged with leading a gang that collected millions of dollars from major industries, and with trafficking in narcotics. He was born on the Lower East Side in 1897 to a respectable Jewish immigrant family. His mother called him "Lepke" and the name stuck. He quit school at age 14 years, after his father had died, and embarked on thievery, leading to reform school and jail. In his 20s, Lepke formed a partnership with the Russian-born, slow-thinking, rough and tough Jacob Shapiro, nicknamed "Gurrah" for his repeated snarling "Get out of here."[40] Gaining control of the bank accounts of textile, trucking and baking unions, they skimmed money for high living. In the 1930s, Buchalter and Shapiro established Murder Inc. to commit contract killings for pay. They arranged the murders of fellow Jewish gangsters "Dutch Schultz" (Arthur Simon Flegenheimer) and Harry Greenberg. In 1941, Lepke was found guilty of murder. On March 4, 1944, he was taken to the electric chair at Sing Sing Prison. Rabbi Jacob Katz recited prayers in Hebrew. Minutes before his execution, Lepke Buchalter claimed it was "a framed-up case.... I want to thank judge [Irving] Lehman. He knows me because I am a Jew."[41]

Mugshot of mobster Benjamin "Bugsy" Siegel, 1928, New York Police Department.

Bugsy Siegel, Meyer Lansky and Lepke Buchalter were but three of a sizeable number of Russian-born, or the children of Russian-born immigrants, active in crime during the first half of the 20th century. Morris Sidwirtz (better known as Moe Sedway, born in 1894 in the Russian Empire) was a faithful lieutenant of the "Bugs and Meyer Gang." After Siegel was murdered, Sedway and

Gustav "Gus" Greenbaum successfully took over the running of Flamingo Hotel and helped establish Los Vegas as a gambling mecca. Jack Zelig (born in 1888 as Selig Henry Lefkowitz, on the Lower East Side) was a skillful pickpocket by age 6. Later, he took over as head of the Eastman gang after Max "Kid Twist" Zuckerbach was murdered. In 1912 Zelig, "the notorious gun-fighter," at age 24, was gunned down.[42] The brothers Hymie, Joseph and Louis Amberg engaged in labor racketeering and threatening small shopkeepers. Using a smuggled weapon, Hymie in 1926 attempted to break out of the Tombs prison. When the attempt failed, he used the weapon to commit suicide. On September 30, 1935, Joseph was gunned down by members of Murder Inc.[43]

Meyer Lansky, known as the Mob's Accountant and a member of the Jewish Mob, 1958 (Library of Congress, LC-USZ62-12071).

Maxwell Street, Chicago, had its peddlers and pushcarts, but also gangs and gambling. Davey, Hirschie, Al and Max, "the notorious Miller brothers [were] famous in vice, gambling, booze, politics and gang warfare in the Ghetto."[44] Davey Miller "was Jewish Chicago's highest-profile figure in the citywide gangster confederation that emerged in the early years of Prohibition."[45] Isaac Gittelson Bloom, known as Ike Bloom, ran prostitution rings and bootlegged booze during Prohibition to serve his many Chicago nightclubs as well as selling to the general public. Al Capone invested in Bloom's nightclubs.

Benjamin "Zuckie the Bookie" Zuckerman skillfully negotiated the amalgamation of a number of Jewish-run illegal gaming establishments to become the gambling kingpin of the 24th Ward on Chicago's West Side. On January 14, 1944, he was about to enter his house on Roosevelt Avenue, when he saw "a slightly built man slowly walking in front of him ... that man turned suddenly, drew a gun and fired a bullet that hit Zuckerman in the chest. [The man fired] two more times hitting Zuckerman in the eye and in the throat, and then he stepped into a car, where two other men had been waiting to help him get away." The murder was never solved but appeared to be the work of the Chicago Syndicate.

Other American cities had their Russian-Jewish mobsters. Charles Solomon and Hyman Abromowitz ran illegal gambling and prostitution in New England. Abe Bernstein, his brothers Joseph, Raymond and Isadore and their Purple Gang were the chief suppliers to Al Capone of smuggled Canadian whiskey. Alex Birns (born Alexander Birnstein) moved from a Cleveland street-fighter to theft, organized crime and bootlegging. In 1975, then aged 68 years, Birns was killed by rivals who planted a bomb in his car. Hyman "Pittsburgh Hymie" Martin was a Pittsburgh mobster and bootlegger. Harry Rosen was a leading Philadelphia mobster and bootlegger.

Exclusion and Acceptance

"The Grand Union Hotel, a late 19th-century playground for the rich, attracted American elites—among them Joseph Seligman, a Bavarian-born Jewish banker. For nearly a decade he and his family decamped from their Manhattan home to vacation at the hotel. On May 31, 1877, however, the hotel's manager, Henry Hilton, denied the Seligmans accommodations. Hilton said they were unwelcome because they were Jews."[46] Joseph Seligman was among the wealthiest, best known and most Americanized of American Jews. During the late 19th century and well into the 20th century, Jews—both established German Jews and more recently arrived Russian Jews—faced restriction in hotels, golf clubs, universities, businesses, law schools and medical schools. (Chapter 9: From Public School to Ivy League College discusses the quota system to lower Jewish admission to leading universities.) In response they formed their own institutions, especially in the Jewish neighborhoods of large cities. The Belmont Country Club (of Belmont, Massachusetts), Fenway Gold Club (of Scarsdale, New York), the Lake Shore Country Club (of Glencoe, Illinois), and many other private clubs across the nation served well-to-do Jews.

"American Jewish hospitals were founded, starting in 1854, to serve indigent Jews, to respond to anti-Semitism, by creating opportunities for graduate medical education and medical practice, to provide culturally sensitive care to observant Jews, and to fulfill a religious commitment to healing. Jewish hospitals were governed, administered, staffed, and philanthropically supported predominantly by Jewish communities.... Approximately 113 Jewish hospitals were founded in the history of the United States."[47] Among them were the Barnes Jewish Hospital of St. Louis, Missouri, the Jewish Hospital of Cincinnati, Ohio, the National Jewish Hospital of Denver, Colorado, and the Mount Sinai Hospital of New York. The Beth Israel Hospital of New York's Lower East Side, and the Beth Israel Hospital of Boston provided a familiar environment and kosher food to Jewish immigrants and Jewish physicians and nurses. After World War II, discrimination lessened and Jewish clubs and hospitals began to wither.

The Zionist Movement in America

Between 1881 and 1914, more than two million Russian Jews came to the United States. During that period 60,000 Jews left Russia for Ottoman-ruled Palestine. Among them were David Ben Gurion, Levi Eshkol and Yitchak Ben-Zvi (founding fathers and future prime ministers and president of the State of Israel). Golda Meir chose a different route to become one of the great leaders of Jewish nationhood.

"Golda Meir is unique among Israeli leaders: no other prominent Israeli of the pioneer generation came from America; only Golda was brought up in the United States and left its security for a precarious vision. Goldie Mabovitch was born in Kiev in southwestern Russia on May 3, 1898. Most of Russian Jewry lived within the Pale of Settlement—the Russian districts in which Jews were permitted to reside under the Czarist regime. Within or outside the Pale, the Jew was a second-class citizen.... Moshe Mabovitch, the head of the family, was a skilled carpenter and cabinetmaker who had won the right to live there because special dispensations were given to superior craftsmen." In 1905, Moshe left alone for the United States. Three years later he sent money for his wife and three daughters to join him in Milwaukee, Wisconsin. Golda was 8 years old when she came to America. The family of five settled into "a little store with two rooms in the back located on 10th Street, then a poor Jewish section of Milwaukee.... Life at first proved little better than in Pinsk."

Golda attended public school in Milwaukee's Sixth District. "Golda learned English quickly and within two years was at the head of her class, a record which she was to maintain until graduation." Golda attended the North Side high school. On Saturdays she worked in Schuster's department store wrapping parcels and running errands, earning $1 for a 12-hour shift. Golda gave English lessons to newly arrived immigrants at 10 cents a lesson, carefully saving his money to buy a railroad ticket to Denver, Colorado, and at age 15, she ran away from home, to join her older married sister, Sheyna Korngold.

"In Denver, there was a colony of Jewish intellectuals who had been patients at the Jewish Hospital for Consumptives.... Isolated in the mountain city, they often congregated in Shana's house for glasses of tea with lemon and much talk. Mainly East European in origin, they reflected the ideological currents of the countries they had left. Socialists, anarchists, Marxists, Zionists, they sat in Sheyna's house quarreling feverishly about their various social creeds.... Golda was enchanted by the political debates and charged atmosphere." In Denver, Golda "obtained a job in a department store where she sold linings and took measurements for skirts."

At age 16 she met Morris Myerson, a young Russian-Jewish immigrant four years older than herself "and a romance soon blossomed. Morris, as penniless as she, self-educated and with no prospect of acquiring professional training and earning a precarious living as a sign painter.... No one in her circle had as yet made the ascent, characteristic of her immigrant generation, from working class to petty bourgeois." With Eugene Debs as her girlhood hero, Golda was drawn into socialist circles. Rising anti-Semitism during World War I evoked her nationalistic interests. Golda joined Yiddish-speaking Poale Zion to combine socialism and Zionism. Her Zionism was strengthened on meeting David Ben Gurion and Yitzhak Ben Zvi, then on a tour of America urging American Jews to settle in Palestine. Golda told Morris that she would marry him on the condition that they would migrate to Palestine. He reluctantly agreed and they married in 1917. Golda became a full-time worker in the American labor Zionist movement. In 1921, the 23-year-old Golda and Morris boarded S.S. *Pocahontas* to begin their journey to British-ruled Palestine. Golda and Morris were accompanied to Palestine by her sister Sheyne Korngold, and Sheyne's children.[48]

During the years between the world wars, there was a substantial migration of German and Polish Jews but only "a barely perceptible trickle of American Jewish immigration to Palestine."[49] Golda and her family settled on kibbutz Merchavia in the Valley of Jezreel. Golda became a senior member of the Histadrut labor union. In 1948, she placed her signature to Israel's Declaration of Independence. She served as minister of labor (1949–1956), foreign minister (1956–1966), and from 1969 to 1974,

Golda Meir, raised in Milwaukee, Wisconsin, became prime minister of Israel. She is shown with President Richard Nixon and Secretary of State Henry Kissinger at the White House, November 1, 1973 (Library of Congress, LC-U9-28671-30A).

as the fourth prime minister of the State of Israel. Golda Meir died in 1978, aged 80 years.

David Ben Gurion was in the United States from 1914 to 1917 recruiting American Jews to settle the land in Palestine. Born in Minsk, Paula Munweis immigrated with her family to the United States in 1910, at age 18. She trained in nursing at the Beth Israel Hospital in Newark. In 1915 David met Paula at a Poale Zion meeting Newark, New Jersey. David Ben Gurion and Paula Munweis married in New York two years later. "She was not a Zionist," Ben Gurion told a reporter in 1968. "She had very little Jewish feeling, she was an American, she was an anarchist." At that time, all the progressive youths were anarchists. And her hero was an anarchist woman, Emma Goldman. She had no interest in Israel. "America is better, why do we need the land of Israel?" But I told her: "You will have to go to Israel and she agreed."[50] Paula joined her husband in Palestine in 1919, two years before Golda Meir, arrived. Paula Ben Gurion died in 1968 at age 76.

Fellow American Zionists Judah Leon Magnes and Henrietta Szold played key roles in establishing the framework of the Jewish state. Born in 1877 in San Francisco, Judah Magnes was a founder in 1906 of the American Jewish Committee. In New York he established the Kehillah "to wipe out invidious distinctions between East European and West European, foreigner and native, Uptown and Downtown Jew, rich and poor, and make us all realize that the Jews are one people with a common history and with common hopes." In 1919, Magness helped establish the Hebrew University of Jerusalem. Henrietta Szold was born in 1860 in Baltimore, Maryland, the oldest of eight daughters of rabbi Benjamin Szold. Henrietta set up a school in Baltimore offering lessons in English and vocational guidance to recently arrived Russian immigrants. In 1912, she established Hadassah to provide health care in Palestine. She migrated to Palestine in 1933 and was active in Youth Aliyah, rescuing Jewish children from Nazi Europe.

9

From Public School to Ivy League College

The children of Russian Jewish immigrants, like others, attended public elementary schools in their neighborhoods. In his book *The Immigrant Jew in America,* published in 1908, Edmund J. James, president of the University of Illinois, described the rapid adaptation of these children to American life and values. In the East Side of New York "the schools below Hester Street ... had a preponderance of Jewish children." The student body of the elementary schools on East Houston, Remington, Suffolk, Delancey, and Henry Streets were 70 to 95 percent Jewish. The teachers reported that these children of poor Russian Jewish immigrants were "among the brightest at the public schools.... They rank high in all examinations for advancement to secondary institutions of education such as high schools and city colleges. They are quick to avail themselves of whatever privileges extended to them.... They are bright, attentive and studious." Already by the start of the 20th century, there was "a great increase in the number of Jews in attendance upon the classes at Columbia and the University of New York."

Early in the 20th-century Philadelphia, Russian Jewish immigrants clustered in the section bound by Lombard Street in the north, Moore Street in the south, the Delaware River in the east, and 19th Street in the west. The kindergartens, elementary schools—such as the Fletcher School—and high schools in this section were largely filled with Jewish children. Yiddish was their mother tongue but very soon they were proficient in English and adapted "to the prevailing customs and habits." In Chicago, Russian Jews settled in the West Side around Maxwell Street. The Washburn and Garfield public schools in the West Side were more than 90 percent Jewish. Jewish students also predominated at the Smythe, Foster and Goodman schools. In Chicago, as in New York, Philadelphia, Boston and other cities, the children of Russian Jewish immigrants yearned for education.[1]

In 1902, the *Daily Forward* commented on the high value Russian Jewish immigrants placed on education. "It shows our capacity to make sacrifices for our children ... as well as our love for education, for intellectual effort." They saw education as the way forward, to escape the grime and gloom of ghetto life and to enter the American mainstream. From elementary school, most of these Jewish children went on to the neighborhood high schools. A large number, who showed intellectual promise, took the examinations to gain entrance into the elite examination public high schools, such as New York's Bronx High School of Science (founded 1938), Stuyvesant High School (founded 1904), and DeWitt Clinton High School (founded 1897), Central High School of Philadelphia and the Boston Latin School. This required leaving the neighborhood early each morning and travelling by streetcar to school, returning home late in the afternoon, and handling a heavy study load that included Latin and Greek.

For much of the 20th century, the student body of these elite public schools was heavily Jewish. (In the 1930s, Boston Latin was 50 percent Jewish, in 1973, Stuyvesant High School was 90 percent Jewish.) Bronx School of Science educated eight future Nobel Prize winners, including Sheldon Glashow, Stephen Weinberg, Melvin Schwartz, Roy J. Glauber, Leslie Lamport, and Robert J. Lefkowitz. Bronx School of Science also educated seven Pulitzer Prize winners, among them Joseph Lelyveld, Buddy Stein, William Safire, Gene Weingarten, and Spencer Ackerman. Abraham Lincoln High School, founded 1928 in Brooklyn, produced Nobel Prizewinners Arthur Kornberg, Jerome Karle and Paul Berg.

Established in 1836, the all-boys Central High School was the first high school in Philadelphia. Known for its academic excellence, the school attracted many bright Jewish boys. In 1919, Judah Medoff and Harold Lipshutz , and in 1920, Herbert Lowenstein, led the honor rolls. The class valedictorian in 1916 was Herbert Mandel, in 1917 Howard Steinberg and Hirsch Allman, in 1919 Alfred Meyer Klein and in 1924 Morris Aarons.[2]

Founded in 1635, the Boston Latin was the first school established in America. Four governors of Massachusetts, and five signers of the Declaration of Independence—Samuel Adams, Benjamin Franklin, John Hancock, William Hooper, and Thomas Paine—were educated at Boston Latin. Many other distinguished Americans, including four Harvard presidents, received their education at Boston Latin. Until the early 20th century, most students admitted to Harvard came from Massachusetts. For generations Boston Latin contributed more Harvard freshman than any other school—public or private—in the nation.[3] The admission standards for acceptance to Boston Latin were high with many competing each year for the 100 places. During the first three decades of the 20th century, Jewish students, sons of recent immigrants from Russia, comprised one in five of Boston Latin School students.[4]

Boston Latin School taught Latin, Greek, English and the classics. The English High School of Boston opened in 1821 with a strong emphasis on mathematics, and prepared schoolboys for business, engineering and mechanics. Many Jewish students—the sons of poor Russian Jewish immigrants—entered Boston English as well as the high schools in Cambridge, Chelsea and Malden. The most academically gifted applied for admission to prestigious colleges. Jewish college freshmen coming from other states were also graduates of public high schools. They stood out in high school and were determined to shine at Harvard, Yale and Columbia.

At the start of the 20th century, the nation's most prestigious colleges, Harvard, Yale and Princeton—The Big Three—were virtually the exclusive homes of the Protestant establishment. These colleges had "a broad influence on the national culture."[5] Pupils coming out of Phillips Andover, Choate, Groton, and St. Paul moved smoothly to Cambridge, New Haven and Princeton to join the sports clubs, enter the secret societies, and edit the college magazines. In 1909, 79 percent of the Princeton students, 65 percent of Yale students and 47 percent of the Harvard students came from these private preparatory schools.[6] Combining their high Protestant lineage, with a "Gentleman's C" was sufficient to achieve leading positions in politics, business, banking or industry.

Before 1900, few Jews graduated from Harvard, Yale, Princeton or Columbia. The highly intelligent Boris Sidis was one of the first Russian Jews to gain admission to Harvard in the 19th century. He was born in 1867 in the Ukrainian town Berdychiv. At age 17 he was imprisoned by Tsarist police and spent two years in solitary confinement. In 1887 he escaped from Russia and settled in the grime and poverty of the Lower East Side, earning a pittance in the sweatshops. Hoping for a better life, he made his way to Boston and earned his keep teaching English to recent Russian immigrants. One of his pupils was Sarah Mandelbaum. The two fell in love, married and motivated each other to rise higher. In 1892, a few years after coming to the United States, Boris was admitted to Harvard College and Sarah to the Boston University School of Medicine. At Harvard, Boris was greatly influenced by the psychologist William James, who started America's first academic department of psychology. Graduating magna cum laude Boris went on to complete doctorates in philosophy and medicine to begin a distinguished career as a psychiatrist.

Their son was born in 1898. Boris and Sarah named him William James Sidis, in honor of his godfather and Boris's mentor at Harvard. The boy displayed exceptional mathematical and language skills. He was able to read newspapers at 18 months old and soon taught himself to write and speak 20 or more languages including English, French, Latin, Russian and Hebrew. His IQ tested above 250. His ambitious parents were determined to hasten the career of their child prodigy and applied for his admission to Harvard when he was nine years old. He was admitted to the college two years later and graduated in 1914, cum laude. He failed as a college lecturer, dropped out of law school and in 1919, was arrested under the Sedition Act for opposing the entry of the United States into World War I. William's emotions began to unravel and he spent several years in mental institutions. Once called the world's greatest child prodigy, William cut himself off from his parents and from the intellectual life to become reclusive, living alone in Boston's South End and earning a living running adding machines. William James Sidis died in Boston at age 46 in 1944.[7]

The Harvard historian Samuel Eliot Morison observed that the few "German Jews who came were easily absorbed into the social pattern. At the start of the [twentieth] century the bright Russian Jewish lads from the Boston public schools began to arrive."[8] Reaching college age in the early 1900s, the youngsters flocked to the universities. With New York the epicenter of Jewish life, by the 1910s, City College was 90 percent Jewish and Columbia College 40 percent Jewish. In 1905, the *New York Post* wrote: "The thirst for knowledge fills our city colleges and Columbia's halls with the sons of Hebrews who came over on steerage." Fearing students "of Anglo-Saxon, Dutch, German and Huguenot descent" would go elsewhere, these colleges devised ways to greatly reduce Jewish admissions. Princeton limited Jews to fewer than the proportion of Jews in the population of the United States.

Louis Mayer Cahn graduated from Harvard in 1895. After law school he set up practice in Chicago. He was "interested in social and charitable work ... and am [he said] at present a member of the board of directors of a social settlement, and secretary of the Jewish Aid Society of Chicago, which has charge of the general relief and aid among the Jewish poor of Chicago." Later, Cahn served as executive director of the Association of Jewish Charities of Chicago.[9] Born in Minsk in 1880, Morris Raphael Cohen migrated with his family to New York's Lower East Side when he was 12 years old. Displaying exceptional intelligence, he went from City College of New York (CCNY) to complete a Ph.D. at Harvard in 1906. He returned to CCNY as a professor of philosophy and helped the school gain the reputation as the "proletarian Harvard." Morris Cohen became "almost a legendary figure in American philosophy, education and liberal education and the liberal tradition, [displaying] a wide range of learning and intellectual rigor."[10]

In 1902, Isadore Hyam Lazarus graduated from the Latin School to enter Harvard College. In 1906, 20 Jewish students, led by Henry Hurwitz, Horace Kallen and Abraham Simon, formed the Harvard Menorah Society for the Study and Advancement of Jewish Culture and Ideals. Henry Hurwitz was born in 1886 in a Lithuanian shtetl. At age five, he came with his family to the United States and settled in the fishing town of Gloucester, Massachusetts. Henry was class valedictorian at Gloucester High School. After graduating from Harvard College in 1908, he attended the law and business schools. Hurwitz established the Intercollegiate Menorah Society and served as editor of the *Menorah Journal* to advance Jewish culture and ideals in America.

In December 1907, Henry Hurwitz invited Harvard president Charles William Eliot to address a meeting of the Harvard Menorah Society in Peabody Hall, Phillips Brooks House. "Representatives of Brown University, Dartmouth, Massachusetts Institute of Technology, Tufts, Boston University and Radcliffe will be present. The purpose of the meeting is to urge the formation of similar societies in other colleges, and members of the University interested in the objects of the society, the study and promotion of Hebraic culture and ideals."[11] At the meeting of the Harvard Menorah Society, Eliot "advised the Jewish students at Harvard to take more care of their physical development ... asserting that the Jewish race physically was inferior to other races and that it was the duty of the coming Jewish generations to remedy this deficiency.... Here at Harvard, you young men of the Jewish race, neglect the out-of-door life and do not get out for the fresh air and develop physically as you should, although you are taking every advantage of the intellectual opportunities offered you."[12] Eliot's focus on race and physical inferiority suggests he was influenced by his Harvard colleague professor William Zebina Ripley who claimed that Jews were narrow-chested, undersized and lacked the vigor of the Teutonic races.[13]

Charles William Eliot served 40 years, from 1869 to 1909, as president of Harvard College. As early as 1907, admission to Harvard was measured less by "one's mastery of a traditional curriculum, including Latin and Greek [than by] the ideal of the well 'all-round man' of sturdy character, sound in body, and proper social background."[14] In 1909, A. Lawrence Lowell succeeded Eliot as president of Harvard. In the 1920s, Lowell advocated a drastic reduction in immigrants from Eastern Europe. By changing the definition of merit from objective academic achievement to the subjective assessment of character and manliness, he sought also to limit the admission of Jews to Harvard.

An analysis of the 1030 members of Harvard Class of 1920 shows that one in 10 were of Jewish origin. Four out of five of them were born in the United States of Russian Jewish parents. One-fifth were born in Tsarist Russia, but came to the United States as young children and were educated in American schools. Most grew up in the Jewish sections of Boston (Dorchester, Mattapan, Roxbury and the North End) and surrounding towns (Cambridge, Malden and Chelsea). Nearly all of them had attended the local public school from first to twelfth grades. Many of those residing in the city of Boston had passed the grueling entrance examination to attend the elite Boston Latin or Boston English high schools. Several of these Jewish students entered Harvard from high schools in Chelsea, Cambridge, Malden, Salem, New Bedford or Gloucester. Most of them served in the United States military during World War I.

The 25-year follow-up of the Class of 1920 shows that many went on to graduate school to qualify as physicians, lawyers, accountants, engineers or academics. They experienced the Great Depression and had come through World War II. By 1945, they were well-established in their various fields and living in comfort, with their own children entering university life. Many had left Boston and the Jewish enclaves of Chelsea, Lynn and Malden with their Orthodox synagogues, and moved to the affluent suburbs of Newton, Brookline, Swampscott or Marblehead, to open Conservative and reform temples. A number of them had achieved fame and fortune. The Jewish members of the Harvard Class of 1920 reached levels of success in their careers and economic well-being that were equal to that of their non–Jewish classmates.[15] Here are some examples:

Harold Henry Berman was born in 1899 in Boston, the son of Julius and Rebecca Berman. His academic journey took him to Boston Latin School, Harvard College, Tufts medical school and training in psychiatry. He enlisted at age 42, in World War II, and served as chief neuro-psychiatrist at the U.S. Submarine Base, New London, Connecticut. After the war he was director of St. Lawrence State Hospital, Ogdensburg, New York. After graduating from Boston Latin School Arthur William Marget served with the U.S. Army. In 1920 he graduated from Harvard summa cum laude, and went on to complete his doctorate. He was appointed professor of economics at the University of Minnesota. His major work *The Theory of Prices* was published in 1938. In World War II he again joined the armed forces, served in Europe, and rose to the rank of lieutenant colonel. After the war, Marget served as chief of the finance and economic division of the United States section of the Allied Commission for Austria and then, as chief of the United States finance division in Paris. Returning to the United States, he joined the Board of Governors of the Federal Reserve System Federal Reserve System in Washington as director of its international finance division.

Joseph Shalom Shubow was born in 1899 in Olita, Lithuania. He came to Boston with his parents Morris and Hayve, where he attended Boston Latin School. In 1920 he graduated cum laude from Harvard to go on to train as a rabbi. Able to speak seven languages, Shubow was committed to Jewish life. He was a leader in the American Jewish Congress and the Zionist movement. In 1936, he was a delegate to the World Jewish Conference held at Geneva. In his 40s, during World War II, he served in Europe as chaplain of the 4th battalion. In 1945, he crossed the Rhine with the troops into Germany and held a Passover seder in Joseph Goebbel's castle. He was awarded the Bronze Star for helping Holocaust survivors locate surviving family members.

"For a long time," rabbi Shubow wrote in 1945, "it was felt that Hitler's persecution and degradation of the Jews of Germany was essentially an internal problem and, therefore, was no affair of the rest of mankind. The lesson of being one's brother's keeper was forgotten … and the world demonstrated for an entire decade a most amazing demoralization. From 1933 to the time of our entry into the war, many people of America … still spoke in terms of isolation and indifference, indicating a complete moral carelessness to the great burning issues of the world." Shubow served until his death in 1969 as rabbi of the Conservative Temple B'nai Moshe in Boston. His younger brother Leo, Harvard Class of 1924, also became a rabbi.

Born in Russia, Charles James Isber went from Boston English to Harvard College and then law school. He moved to Washington, D.C., to work as a tax attorney, Bureau of Internal Revenue. His brother William, Class of 1926, followed his path to Harvard, and law school.

Leo Max Davidoff was born in 1898 in Latvia to Liebe and Israel Davidoff. At age 8 he came with his family to the United States. He entered the Harvard Class of 1920 from Salem Classical High School. While attending Harvard Medical School he took part in the Students' Army Training School. He completed his medical internship at Boston University Medical Center, followed by training in neurosurgery at Peter Bent Brigham Hospital. In 1925 he served as surgeon to the MacMillan Arctic Expedition. In the 1930s he was chief of surgery at the Jewish Hospital in the Bronx. In the 1940s he was an attending neurosurgeon at Montefiore Hospital and then director of the department of neurosurgery at the Beth Israel Hospital, and professor of neurological surgery, College of Physicians and Surgeons, Columbia University. Professor Davidoff was a pioneer in the field of neurosurgery. He authored 200 scientific papers and wrote 12 books. He died in 1975.[16]

After graduating from Harvard, Frank Samuel Freeman completed his doctorate. In 1925, he joined the faculty at Cornell, rising to professor of psychology and education. His research interests focused on individual differences. Freeman served as chair of the New York State Board of Examiners of Psychologists, and was active in the New York State Psychological Association. Freeman died in 1966. His classmate Joseph Albert Freiberg left Cambridge to attend the College of Medicine of the University of Cincinnati. He trained in orthopedic surgery at the Massachusetts General Hospital and Boston Children's Hospital, followed by training in European clinics including Edinburgh, London, Berlin, Munich, Heidelberg and Bologna. Freiberg served from 1939 to 1962 as professor of surgery at the University of Cincinnati, director of the orthopedic service at Cincinnati General Hospital, consultant to the Veterans Administration hospital, Cincinnati Children's Hospital, and the Jewish Hospital. Samuel Richard Goodstone also trained in medicine. During World War II, Goodstone served in the medical corps of the United States Army.

The town of Chelsea lies directly across the Mystic River from Boston. It was founded in 1624 and its 2.5 square miles render it the smallest town in Massachusetts. During the first three decades of the 20th century, Chelsea was second only to New York's Lower East Side in holding the highest concentration of Jews in America. It was known as the Jerusalem of America. By 1930, its 20,000 Jews (40 percent of the total population) supported 18 synagogues (mostly Orthodox), several kosher food stores and butcher shops, and a network of Hebrew afternoon schools. The children of these Russian Jewish immigrants attended the Shurtleff, Carter and Williams schools before entering Chelsea high school.

Chelsea was one of the first high schools in America to offer classes in classical and modern Hebrew. Mary Antin's Russian Jewish family settled in Chelsea when she was 10. Within a year she spoke and wrote fluently in English. Her 1912 biography *The Promised Land* lovingly describes her education at the Williams school. Samuel Bertram Horovitz, Hyman Bernard Horovitz, Jacob Joseph Tutun, and Joseph Israelite graduated from Chelsea High School to enter the Harvard Class of 1920.

Samuel B. Horovitz graduated magna cum laude and went on to gain his law degree at Harvard law school. Born in Odessa, Hyman Bernard Horovitz served in the Massachusetts Coast Artillery, then was called to federal service at Fort Andrews, Massachusetts. Later, he sailed for France to serve in the Marne-Aisne, Aisne-Oise and Meuse-Argonne offensives. After his discharge from the Army in February 1919, Horovitz returned to his studies, graduated in 1920 and went on to Harvard law school. In 1945, he was employed as a lawyer by the Commonwealth of Massachusetts, Division of Employment Security.

Born in Russia, Jacob Joseph Tutun was a member of the Chelsea high school debating team. At Harvard he received the Coolidge Debating Prize, awarded annually to the best speaker on the University team. In 1919, the Princeton debating team beat Harvard. "The best speech for Harvard was made by Jacob Tutun '20, while Hendrickson and Stevens of Princeton were judged superior in rebuttal."[17] Jacob Tutun graduated from Harvard cum laude, went on to law school; and established a law practice in Chelsea. He was much involved in Jewish affairs including the Judaean Credit Union, B'nai B'rith, Chelsea Zionist organization; he became chairman of the Chelsea Hebrew School. Tutun had "faith in the influence of Harvard in making the world a decent place in which to live.... I have tried to take part in the communal life and have been active in several organizations. My views are liberal, and I am ready to recognize an able man regardless of his party affiliations."

Joseph Israelite was born in Chelsea. Like Tutun, he graduated from Harvard cum laude, attended law school and then returned to his home town. Israelite served on the Chelsea board of aldermen, and as city solicitor. Born in Chelsea in 1906, David Littmann was a cardiologist and Harvard Medical School professor. He invented the Littmann stethoscope, with much improved sound performance.

Moses Koppel was born in 1898 and attended Malden high school. After graduating from Harvard, he trained in medicine to become a pathologist. In World War II, he served as chief of laboratory service, Camp Wallace, Texas. In 1944 he was promoted to major and served as chief of laboratory service, 49th General Hospital, New Guinea. "My religious convictions are Jewish," Koppel reported in 1945. "My hobbies are the usual ones—books, music, theatre, lodges, medical meetings, and the like—common to medical men living in New York. My life has been rather quiet, peaceful, and pleasant. I have no complaints, and manage to enjoy life and keep busy."

Born in 1898, Abraham Lincoln Green graduated from Boys' High School, Brooklyn, New York. During World War I, he joined the U.S. Army Medical Corps to serve in France. Discharged in May 1919 he returned to his studies at Harvard. After taking his law degree, he entered government service in the Foreign Economic Administration. In 1941, at age 43, he re-enlisted in the U.S. Army to serve abroad for two years until disabled in the line of duty.

Another New Yorker, Aron Seth Walter Steuer enlisted in the U.S. Army and was assigned to Company B, 304th Battalion, Tank Corps. In July 1918 he sailed for France. Upon discharge in 1919 he returned to his studies at Harvard and then Columbia law school. For eight years he was in a private law practice. In 1930, Steuer became a City Court Justice and two years later, was elected to serve on the State of New York Supreme Court. He urged an investigation of Nazi Germany before the United States took part in the 1936 Berlin Olympic Games. He was a director of the Young Men's Hebrew Association and supported Jewish philanthropic organizations. Judge Aron S. Steuer died in 1985 at age 87.

Arnold Horween was born was born in 1898. His parents Isadore and Rose (Rabinoff) Horwitz left Russia six years earlier and settled in Chicago. In 1905, Isadore established a leather tanning factory. Arnold played football for the Francis

W. Parker School before entering the Harvard Class of 1920. At 5 foot 11 inches and weighing 205 lbs., he was recruited for the Harvard football team as a fullback, experiencing its undefeated 1919 and 1920 seasons and serving as team captain in 1920. Arnold was a pitcher with the Harvard baseball team and, as a member of the Harvard track team, excelled at shotput. During the years of World War I, he served as a U.S. Navy lieutenant on a destroyer in the Atlantic. With his older brother Ralph, he joined the National Football League (NFL), playing for the Chicago Cardinals.

From 1926 to 1930, Horween served as coach of the Harvard football team. Arnold Horween's prestigious appointment faced considerable opposition. "I am really doubtful if we could expediently invite any member of the Hebrew race to become head coach no matter how skillful he might be," wrote Henry Pennypacker, dean of Harvard admissions and tasked with cutting Jewish admissions. "There is a settled feeling, apparently very widespread, that we must do something at once to check certain growing influences and that Horween's appointment in the present ticklish situation would be perilous."[18]

In 1928, Arnold married Marion Eisendrath, daughter of the leather tycoon, William Nathan Eisendrath. In 1930, he returned to Chicago to run the Horween Leather Company located at 2015 North Elston Avenue. For many years the Horween company supplied the leather for the footballs used by NFL. "I left college with the firm conviction that rugged individualism ... was the most progressive type of thinking, and I haven't changed since. The tanning business requires so much time and attention that my activities have been largely confined to this job. Any free time for recreation is spent mostly in cruising the waters of Lake Michigan and Lake Huron, particularly the North Channel of Georgian."[19] Arnold Horween served as trustee of the Chicago Symphony Orchestra. He died in 1985.

Arnold's older brother Ralph was a member of the Harvard Class of 1918. Ralph proudly listed his military service during World War I: "Seaman 1st class U.S. Naval Force when United States entered the war; called to active duty April 13, 1917, and assigned to patrol boat *Talofa*; promoted quartermaster 2nd class in May; entered Cadet School, Massachusetts Institute of Technology, June 1; appointed ensign Sept. 26; assigned to U.S.S. *Connecticut,* Atlantic Fleet, Oct. 15; commissioned ensign U.S. Navy March 1, 1918; assigned to destroyer *Maury* July 1; promoted lieutenant September 1; transferred to destroyer *Gregory,* Mediterranean Squadron, April 2, 1919; resignation accepted July 1, 1919."

Like his brother Arnold, Ralph played on the Harvard football team and then, the Chicago Cardinals. A yen "for the law led me back to the Harvard Law School in 1926, although I was married and had a daughter at the time. My wife and I spent three delightful years in Cambridge, and added a son to the family by the time I got the LLB, in 1929. Starting to practice law immediately in Chicago, I was soon admitted to partnership in the firm of Cassels, Potter & Bentley." During 1934–1935 he was special assistant to the United States Attorney General, executive assistant to the Secretary of the Interior, for oil, and a member of the First Federal Tender Board in the East Texas field.

Brothers Ralph (left) and Arnold Horween from Chicago were members of the Harvard College football team in 1918.

"I started my own firm, Topliff & Horween, in Chicago. I soon found myself engaged more and more in the highly exciting field of anti-trust law litigation and trade association law. In 1940 I rejoined the Horween Leather Company, where I am at this writing, in charge of research, technical processes, production and personnel. My hobbies are sailboat cruising, chamber music, naval history, and chemical research and experimentation. I sailed as navigator in the New London–Annapolis race in 1939. I keep my ketch in Green Bay, at Ephraim, Wisconsin. Every summer my wife and children cruise with me from there, across Lake Michigan, through the Straits of Mackinac to Georgian Bay. I play the violin or viola in a string quartet, in which my wife plays the cello." He endowed the Horween Professorship at the University of Virginia. Ralph Horween's remarkably full life ended at age 100 years.

By 1945, the Jewish members of the Harvard Class of 1920 had long since shed their immigrant roots. The lawyer George Sidney Levenson was worried about his son Jim "who has been in the Naval Air Corps for 16 months and hopes to get those 'gold wings' soon." Paul Palais reported that his children "have given me much happiness and fill me with pride." His son Donald was a pupil at the prestigious Governor Dummer Academy, founded in 1743, and "will be entering Harvard in June. Richard has been entered there for next year. Nancy is the best athlete. I shall expect her to get letters in every sport. Even the youngest, Stephen, is a chip off the old block." Solomon Rotenberg moved from Boston to the affluent town of Newton, where in 1934, "there was no modern house of Jewish worship. We were quite active in the founding and development of Temple Emanuel there. I was on the original building committee and chairman of the committee, which rebuilt and enlarged the structure to its present size."

In 1908, Jews comprised 8 percent of the 1,000 Harvard freshmen. Abraham M. Sonnebend was born in Boston in 1898 to Esther and Joseph Sonnebend. He graduated from Boston Latin School and entered the Harvard Class of 1918. After graduation he started in the real estate business and rose to head the Hotel Corporation of America, director of Columbia Pictures and many other organizations. Sonnebend served as president of the American Jewish Committee.[20]

The Castleman disease of the lymph nodes is named after Benjamin Castleman, who first described the condition in 1956. He was born in 1906 in Everett, Massachusetts, the eldest of three sons, to religious Russian-Jewish parents, Samuel and Rose. The family moved to Dorchester, Massachusetts, where Benjamin attended Dorchester Hugh School, while working to support the education of his younger brothers. Despite the Jewish quota, Benjamin was accepted into the Harvard Class of 1927. Upon graduation from Harvard, he entered Yale Medical School. In the 1930s he joined the pathology department of the Massachusetts General Hospital (MGH), to conduct pioneering research into diseases of the parathyroid and the lymph glands. He married Wellesley College graduate Anna Siegel, like him, the child of Russian-Jewish immigrants. Benjamin Castleman was an editor of the prestigious *New England Journal of Medicine* and served as director of pathology at MGH.

In 1922, Jews were 22 percent and in 1925, 28 percent of the Harvard class. In that year Harvard president A. Lawrence Lowell called for a quota on Jewish admissions. Too many Jews, he said, were frightening away White Protestant admissions. Limiting Jewish admissions to Harvard was "good for the Jews" by reducing antisemitism.

Abbott Lawrence Lowell (1856–1933) was a member of the Brahmin Lowell family. His ancestors immigrated to the New World in 1637. In 1814 Francis Cabot Lowell built his water-powered textile mill, bringing the industrial revolution to America. The textile city of Lowell, Massachusetts, was named in his honor. Lawrence, the second textile city of Massachusetts, was named for Abbott's maternal grandfather. A. Lawrence Lowell was a member of the sixth generation of Lowell sons to enter Harvard.

In 1896, Lowell published the two-volume *Government and Parties of Continental Europe* to gain the position of professor of economics at his alma mater. The central theme of his work was: "Democracy cannot be strong until the people are sufficiently homogeneous to form a real public opinion and this cannot happen while the classes in society are out of harmony with one another." The need for harmony "justifies democracies in resisting the influx in great numbers of widely different races.... Americans feel that Asiatics cannot be assimilated so as to become an integral and indistinguishable part of the population. The essential point is that all elements of the population should be capable of common aims and aspirations, should have a common stock of political traditions. Without homogeneity a nation may be great, but it can hardly be a successful democracy." Lowell was vice-president of the Immigration Restriction League, formed in 1894 by three Harvard alumni, determined to preserve the hegemony of the Anglo-Saxons by severely restricting admission of Eastern and Southern Europeans, viewed as inferior and unassimilable.

A. Lawrence Lowell served as president of Harvard from 1909 to 1933. His early reforms stressed academic merit and led to an increase in admission of public-school students. In 1909, the Jewish student body at Harvard was 6 percent. By 1922, the influx of Jewish students who had attended public schools like Boston Latin, Boston English, and Philadelphia's Central High School increased the Jewish students to 22 percent, when Jews constituted 3 percent of the U.S. population. Lowell applied to Harvard his conviction that democracy required homogeneity. To this end he refused to consider the admission of women, accepted few Asians and wanted to significantly reduce the number of Jews, no matter how academically qualified they were.

In 1922, Lowell wrote that anti–Semitism was rising in America and that Jews were being excluded from Gentile clubs, private schools and even hotels. Anti-Jewish attitudes were increasing among Harvard students. To restore homogeneity and reduce anti–Semitism, it was necessary, said Lowell, to significantly dilute the Jewish pool at Harvard. Jews were "not easily assimilated.... It is the duty of Harvard," he said, "to receive just as many boys who have come, or whose parents have come, to this country without our background as it can effectively educate.... If every college in the country would take a limited proportion of Jews, I suspect we should go a long way toward eliminating race feeling among the students." Anti-Semitism has increased, wrote Lowell "with the immigration from the Old World." Lowell called on Jews "to help us" by agreeing to lower Jewish college applications, especially to Harvard.[21]

Lowell was not alone in calling for fewer Jews at Harvard. After attending the Harvard-Yale football game in 1925, a Harvard alumnus W.F. Williams wrote to him: "Naturally, after 25 years, one expects to find many changes, but to find that one's University had become so Hebrew-ized was a fearful shock. There were Jews to the right of me, Jews to the left of me, in fact they were so obviously everywhere that instead of leaving the Yard with pleasant memories of the past I left with a feeling of utter disgust of the present and grave doubts about the future of my alma mater.... Are the Overseers so lacking in genius that they can't devise a way to bring Harvard back to the position it always held as a 'white man's' college."[22]

To prevent what he considered "a dangerous increase in the proportion of Jews," A. Lawrence Lowell decided to change the criteria for Harvard admission from examinations to "the estimate of character ... based upon the probable value to the candidate, to the college and to the community." Lowell wanted to exclude candidates "of defective character." After the fall of 1926, Harvard applicants were required to complete a form listing race, color, religion, maiden name of mother, birthplace of father, and whether the applicant had changed his birth name. Headmasters and school principals were required to list the applicant's religion: Protestant, Catholic, Hebrew or Unknown. Lowell set into motion a process in which the subjective assessments of physical and mental fitness, assimilability and character, rather than academic merit, became the criteria for acceptance. To lower Jewish admissions, students were classified as J1—conclusively Jewish, J2—evidence strongly suggests candidate is Jewish, and J3—possibility candidate is Jewish. In November 1926, President Lowell attended the final practice session of the Harvard football team before its match against Princeton, reported *The New York Times* on November 4, 1926. It is not known whether Lowell knew that Arnold Horween—a Harvard alumnus, former captain of the Harvard football team and now its head coach—was Jewish.

By the end of Lowell's tenure in 1933, Jews were restricted to 10 percent of the student body.[23] Other elite colleges such as Yale, Princeton and Columbia also imposed quotas on Jewish admissions. In his book *Joining the Club,* Daniel Oren tells that in order to limit "the alien and unwashed element," Yale University, from the 1920s to the 1960s, kept Jewish enrollment to about 10 percent. Students of German-Jewish background, such as the J. Robert Oppenheimer, Harvard Class of 1925, gained admission but many well-qualified students of Russian-Jewish heritage were excluded from Harvard, Yale, Princeton and Columbia.

Despite the restrictions on their admission, many sons of Russian Jewish immigrants brought great distinction to themselves and to their alma maters. Leonard Bernstein, born in Lawrence, Massachusetts, in 1918, composed the music for the Broadway hit shows *West Side Story, Candide, On the Town* and *Wonderful Town* as well as many enduring orchestral pieces. He attended Boston Latin School before entering Harvard, Class of 1939. Harvard alumni Sheldon Glashow, Ronald Hoffman, Eric Kandel, Martin Karpas, David Lee, Merton Miller, Paul Samuelson, Robert Morton Solow, William Howard Stein, and Ralph M. Steinman each won the Nobel Prize. Israel Isaac Rabi, Roald Hoffman, Leon Max Lederman, and Arthur Ashkin—graduates of Columbia University—were Nobel Prizewinners.

The achievements of children of Russian Jewish immigrants were by no means limited to East Coast Ivy League university graduates. Denied admission to Harvard, Yale or Princeton, many Jewish students found a welcome home at other colleges. The 1961 Nobel Prize winner in Chemistry was Melvin Calvin, son of Elias and Rose Hurwitz, a graduate of the University of Minnesota. Herbert Charles Brown (born Herbert Brovoarnik), Nobel Prize for Chemistry in 1979, attended the University of Chicago. Paul Berg, Nobel Prize for Chemistry in 1983, attended Pennsylvania State University. Jerome Karle (born Jerome Karfunkle) and Herbert Aaron Hauptman jointly won the Nobel Chemistry Prize in 1985; both attended City College of New York. Julius Axelrod was born in 1912 in the Lower East Side of New York. His father supported the family as a basket weaver. After graduating from City College of New York (CUNY), Julius hoped to become a physician but was rejected by every medical school to which he applied. Instead, he found work as a laboratory technician. His research in catecholamine metabolism led to the Nobel Prize in Medicine 1970.

Arthur Kornberg, Nobel Prize in Medicine 1959, Julian Schwinger, Nobel Prize in Physics 1965, Leon Max Lederman, Nobel Prize in Physics 1986, Kenneth Joseph Arrow, Nobel Prize in Economics 1972, and Ralph Hofstadter, Nobel Prize in Physics

***Left:* Portrait of Milton Friedman taken in 1986 by Bachrach Studios. *Right:* Biochemist Julius Axelrod. His father was an immigrant basket weaver. Born 1912 in New York, Axelrod won the 1970 Nobel Prize in Medicine (National Institute of Health).**

1961, were other graduates of City College of New York. (At its prime, CUNY was known as "the poor man's Harvard.") Alan Jay Heeger, born in Sioux City, Iowa, and educated at the University of Nebraska, won the 2000 Nobel Prize in Chemistry. Rosalyn Sussman Yalow. Nobel Prize in Medicine 1977, attended Hunter College. Daniel Nathans, Nobel Prize in Medicine 1978, attended the University of Delaware. Stanley Cohen, Nobel Prize in Medicine 1986, attended Brooklyn College. Martin Rodbell, Nobel Prize in Medicine 1994, graduated from Johns Hopkins University. Donald Arthur Glaser, Nobel Prize in Physics 1960, graduated from Case Western Reserve. Burton Richter, Nobel Prize in Physics 1976, attended the Massachusetts Institute of Technology. Steven Weinberg, Nobel Prize in Physics 1979, attended Cornell University. Martin Lewis Perl, attended the Brooklyn Polytechnic Institute, and Frederick Reines, who attended the Stevens Institute of Technology, were co-winners of the Nobel Physics Prize in 1995.

Milton Friedman was born in 1912 in New York City of a working-class Jewish immigrant family. He received a scholarship to attend Rutgers University, and completed his doctorate at Columbia University. As a professor at the University of Chicago, he was one of America's leading economists and in 1976 he was awarded the Nobel Prize in Economics. Robert Fogel attended Cornell University and in 1993 was awarded the Nobel Prize in Economics.

"The passion for education of Eastern European Jews," wrote noted sociologists Nathan Glazer and Patrick Moynihan in 1963, "showed almost from the beginning of their arrival in this country: a passion ... that was unique in American history."[24]

10

Sports

Russian Jews came largely from the shtetl "with no familiarity with sports. [They] were stereotyped as weak, unhealthy, and physically unfit." Coming to America, the parents were against sports as a distraction from learning. Yet, "the second generation avidly participated in sports ... as a means to become Americanized [and] to display manliness ... Jews were among the very first professional baseball players and among the most outstanding early American track stars. They dominated inner city sports such as basketball and boxing during the 1920s and 1930s."[1]

The German-Jewish-sponsored Educational Alliance in New York advocated "education of the body as well as the mind. The importance of physical training, for our downtown brethren cannot be over-estimated. Our co-religionists are often charged with a lack of physical courage and repugnance of physical work. Nothing will more effectively remove this than athletic training. Let a young man develop his body and he will neither shrink from danger or from manly work."[2] The Educational Alliance actively sponsored sports camps, believing that "fraternal feelings" are best developed on the athletic field.[3]

Boxing

Boxing was once America's favorite sport. It offered tough young men, Italian, Irish and Jewish, the chance to leave the ghetto. Many ghetto boys learned early to use their fists to defend themselves and to protect their territory to sell newspapers. During the years 1900 to 1940, there were 30,000 Jewish professional fighters, comprising 7 to 10 percent of the boxing talent of the period. Few of them made real money at it. Most, like Johnny "The Ghetto Hercules" Mendelsohn of Milwaukee, have long since been forgotten. Among those who succeeded were 29 Jewish world boxing champions, about 16 percent of the total number of world champions. They were mostly short, wiry fellows fighting in the six lighter weight class: flyweight (up to 112 pounds), bantamweight (up to 118 pounds), featherweight (up to 126 pounds), junior lightweight (up to 130 pounds), lightweight (up to 135 pounds) and junior welterweight (up to 140 pounds).[4]

Like others, the Jewish boxer fought for the money and the glory. But he also fought to express ethnic pride and to refute the stereotype of Jewish physical weakness. In their fights, several proudly wore the Star of David on their boxing trunks. "The Jewish boxers did not just box for themselves," wrote Teddy Atlas. "They were representing a race of people and the reputation of that race. Jewish immigrants and their children lived in a rough and tumble environment. Within this environment it was very important for some Jews to be able to go into the ring and be as tough as the next guy.... The Jew had to prove he could be as tough as anyone and could be as proud as anybody."

Reuven Goldstein, "The Jewell of the Ghetto," was a 1920s contender for the world's lightweight boxing championship. Vincent Morris Sheer, who boxed under the name Mushy Callahan, was the world's light heavyweight champion from 1926 to 1930. Harry Besterman, who went by Harry Lewis, was the world's welterweight champion from 1909 to 1911. Isadore Schwartz, "The Ghetto Midget," standing 5 feet 1 inch, was the world's flyweight champion from 1927 to 1929. Samuel Mosberg was the lightweight champion at the 1920 Olympic Games, held in Antwerp, Belgium. Joe Bernstein, "The Pride of the Ghetto," turned professional in 1894 at age 17. He fought three times between 1899 and 1901 for the world's featherweight championship but lost all three bouts.

Dov-Ber David Rosofsky, better known as Barney Ross, was world champion in three divisions; lightweight, light welterweight and welterweight. Jack Bernstein held the world championship in 1923 as a junior lightweight. Charley Phil Rosenberg was world bantamweight champion from 1925 to 1927. Solly Krieger was the NBA world middleweight champion from 1938 to 1939. Al Singer, "The Bronx Beauty," was the world lightweight champion in 1930. Abraham Attell Goldstein, fought under the name Al Goldstein and was the 1924 world bantamweight champion. All were from Russian-Jewish immigrant families that settled in New York, mainly the Lower East Side. Several grew up in orphanages. Their success in the ring brought delight and pride to the Russian-Jewish residents of the Lower East Side.

From the South Philadelphia ghetto came Barney Lebrowitz, Lew Tendler and Benjamin "Benny" Baruch Bass. Born in 1904 in the Ukraine, Benjamin came with his family to the United States when he was two years old. At age 10 he was selling newspapers on Philadelphia streets. Standing five feet 1½ inches, he fought 243 bouts. During 1927, before a crowd of 30,000, he defeated fellow Jewish boxer Morris Kaplan, to become the world featherweight champion. Two years later he won the world junior lightweight championship. From Chicago's Maxwell Street ghetto came Harry Harris, Samuel Berger and Jackie Fields; and from Connecticut came Max Rosenbloom. Abraham Washington Attell, known as "The Little Hebrew," came from San Francisco, California. He was the world featherweight champion from 1906 to 1912.

Born in 1899 in the Lower East Side, John Dodick, the second of seven children, dropped out early from school to help his father, a fruit peddler. He fought under the name Jack Bernstein, winning the world junior lightweight championship in 1923. Barney Lebowitz was born in 1891 in the Philadelphia ghetto, the son of Russian immigrants. To help the family, he shined shoes and sold newspapers. Fighting under the name Battling Levinsky, he was the world's light heavyweight champion from 1916 to 1920. Isadore "Izzy" Schwartz, born in 1900, grew up in a New York Jewish orphanage. Standing 5 feet 1 inch, and known as the Ghetto Midget, he was the world's flyweight champion. Reuven "Ruby" Goldstein was born in 1907 on Cherry Street, Lower East Side. After his father died, Ruby was sent to an orphanage. He was a serious contender for the world lightweight championship. Later he was a prominent boxing referee. David Mondrus, born in 1905 in Russia, settled with his family in Sioux City, Idaho. Despite the sub-zero winter temperatures, young David walked the streets selling newspapers, defending his turf by fighting. He boxed professionally under the name Davis Montrose. Nicknamed Newsboy Brown, he was the world flyweight champion in 1928.

Morris Scheer was born in 1905 in the Lower East Side, and grew up in Los Angeles. Under the name Mushy Callahan, he was the world light welterweight champion from 1926 to 1930. After he retired from boxing, he served many years as a boxing referee as well as establishing a career in Hollywood as a stuntman and actor. After his father died, Charley Phil Rosenberg was placed in a Hebrew orphanage. He was trained in boxing by Ray Ancel and Whitey Bimstein. His manager was Harry Segal. Charley was world bantamweight champion from 1925 to 1926. Born in the Williamsburg section of Brooklyn, Solly Krieger took up boxing despite the opposition of his observant immigrant parents, and had a 13-year professional boxing career, holding the world middleweight championship between 1938 and 1939. Born in 1909 in a Lower East Side tenement, Abraham "Al" Singer, known as The Bronx Beauty, won the world lightweight championship in 1930. Isadore Schwartz was orphaned at age 2 and he spent his youth in an orphanage. During World War I, he served with the United States Expeditionary Force and, in his boxing career, was known as Corporal Izzy. He was in 115 fights, leading to world flyweight champion in 1927–1929. Jacob Finkelstein was born in 1908 on Maxwell Street, the heart of Chicago's Jewish ghetto. His Russian-Jewish father worked as a butcher. At the start of his boxing career Jacob was told that his name gave the wrong image. He changed Jacob to Jackie and Finkelstein to Fields. Boxing under the name Jackie Fields he won the gold medal in the featherweight division at the 1924 Summer Olympics in Paris, and was twice, in 1927 and 1932, the world's welterweight champion.

"Benny Leonard was perhaps the greatest lightweight of all time."[5] On July 27, 1922, two Jewish boxers, Benny Leonard and Lew Tendler, "two of the greatest lightweights in the ring today," fought for 12 rounds in Jersey City for the world's lightweight championship. "It was a battle that will be long remembered by the 60,000 who witnessed Tendler's futile effort to snatch the crown from Leonard who has held it since 1917."[6] The two fought again on July 23, 1923. "Leonard's victory was glorious—a perfectly harmonious piece of fighting humanity working in coordination and admirably concentrated. … Tendler though beaten, earned the plaudits of the crowd by a truly great stand. At the end of the fight, and before the result was announced, Tendler said to Leonard: 'It's all right Benny. I don't need a decision. You beat me tonight. It comes from the heart when I say: You're a better man than I am.'" *The New York Times* commented: "Benny Leonard still is world's lightweight champion. The wonderful Harlem lad retained his title last night at the Yankee Stadium when he battered his way to a clear victory on points over Lew Tendler, Philadelphia southpaw, a most dangerous challenger for the title."[7]

When the legendary boxing coach Ray Arcel was asked who was the best boxer ever, he replied: "Who was better than [Jack] Dempsey the day he knocked out Willard to win the title? Who would've beaten him? Joe Louis might've had a chance. Maybe Ali would've had a chance. And pound for pound, who was better, [Sugar Ray] Robinson or Benny Leonard? I hesitate to say either one, but Leonard's mental energy surpassed anybody else's.... Benny would tell the kids, 'Think, think. Learn how to think. You've got to talk to yourself. I'm going to jab this guy. I'm going to hook this guy.' We learned all those tricks by listening to what was Leonard's main stock in trade: to teach."[8]

Benny Leonard, "the Ghetto Wizard" (left), and southpaw Lew Tendler, July 27, 1922, world's lightweight championship.

Benjamin Leiner was born in 1896 in the heart of the Jewish ghetto of the Lower East Side. His parents were religious Jews from the Russian Empire. Father Gershon worked long hours in a sweatshop to support his wife Minnie and their eight children. Benny turned professional at age 15, changing his name to Benny Leonard so his parents would not know he was earning money from boxing. He had 219 fights and held the world's lightweight championship for eight years from 1917 to 1925. Leonard's star opponent was Lew Tendler. They shared a similar deprived childhood. Born in 1898 in the South Philadelphia ghetto. Lew was age two years when his father died. At age six, Lew Tendler earned money selling newspapers. A southpaw—known as Lefty Lew—he turned professional at age 15 and had 159 fights during his professional career. Tendler was regarded as one of the greatest fighters who never won a world title.

Benny Leonard, Lew Tendler and Barney Ross were three of the greatest fighters of the Golden Age of Jewish American boxing. Dov-Ber "Beryl" David Rosofsky was born in 1909 in a dingy apartment on Rivington Street, Lower East Side, to Isidore "Itchik" and Sarah Rosofsky. Hoping for a better life, the Rosofsky family took the train to Chicago in 1911, where Itchik ran a small grocery store on Maxwell Street, the teeming center of immigrant Jewish life. In 1922, Itchik was shot dead in his store, resisting a robbery. Sarah suffered a nervous breakdown. Age 14 at the time, Dov was left to his own devices. He dropped out of school, ran with the local gang, and served briefly as a messenger boy for the Al Capone gang. He found his true vocation in the boxing ring. Under the name Barney Ross, he turned professional at age 19. He was world champion in three divisions—lightweight, light welterweight and welterweight—and was known as "The Pride of the Ghetto." He fought Jimmy McLarnin three times for the world welterweight championship. Their November 28, 1934, bout, at the Garden Bowl, was watched "with enthusiasm by a typical fight crowd drawn from all circles of life—from the ghetto and from Park Avenue."[9] Barney Ross retired from the ring in 1938.

"Barney Ross, former world lightweight boxing champion, was sworn into the United States Marines," announced *The New York Times* on April 22, 1942. "He will serve as a boxing instructor." Instead, Ross insisted on going abroad to fight for his country. During the epic battle at Guadalcanal, he was part of a patrol that ran into Japanese machine gun fire, wounding all except Ross. He gathered all the rifles and grenades and single-handedly fought 22 Japanese soldiers over 13 hours, killing them all. "I never expected to get out. I was crying and praying and shooting and throwing grenades." He calmed himself by repeating Sh'ma Israel—Hear O Israel, The Lord is One. "The night I spent in that shell-hole was by all odds the toughest round I ever slugged through. I thought the bell would never sound.... I got a leg and arm full of shrapnel. I was just too busy to notice. I had malaria at that time, too." Weighing 140 pounds, Ross carried fellow marine Freeman Atkins to safety. For his bravery and saving American lives, Ross was awarded the Silver Star. On his

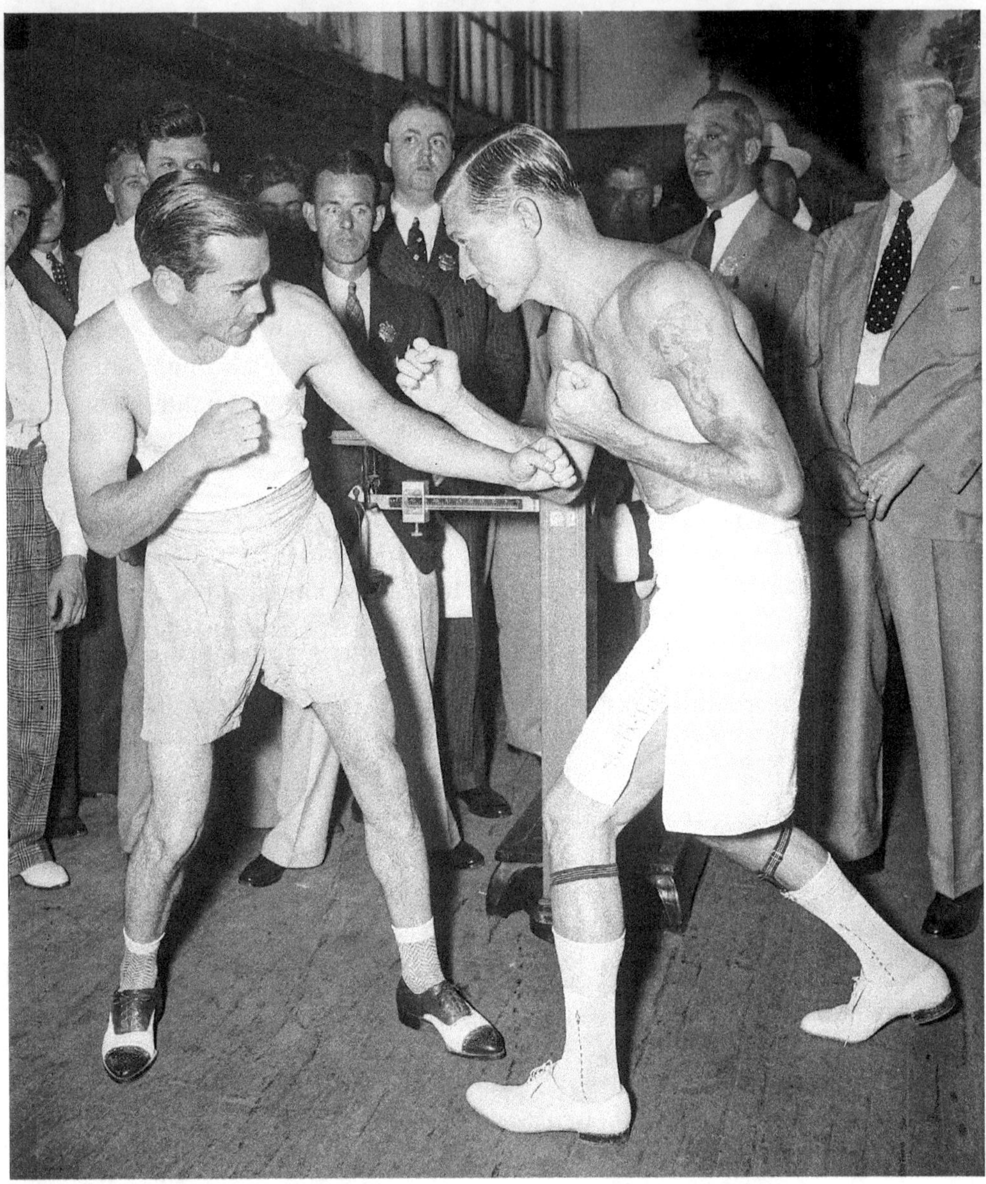

Barney Ross (left) vs. Phil Furr, 1936. Ross was a world champion boxer in three weight divisions. He was a decorated veteran of World War II (Library of Congress, LC-DIG-hec-33437).

return home, Ross "kneeled humbly on American soil and kissed the ground." "This I vowed to do if ever I saw American soil again."[10]

In addition to the contenders, Jews of Russian descent took part in every aspect of boxing as promoters, managers, trainers, gym owners, cornermen, publicists, equipment makers, and fans. Ray Arcel was born in Terre Haute, Indiana, on August 30, 1899, but grew up in New York's East Harlem—he liked to say his was the only Jewish family living there. "Because of that, as a kid I was in a fight every day," said Arcel. Over half a century, starting in the 1920s, Arcel trained thousands of fighters at Stillman's Gym on Eighth Avenue. Twenty-two of them became world champions, including the Jewish boxers Benny Leonard, Barney Ross, Abe Goldstein and Charley Phil Rosenberg. "If you take a piece of gold out of the ground," said Arcel, "you know it's gold but you have to polish it. You have to give it a form. But there aren't many guys capable of polishing a fighter."[11] Ray Arcel "had a genius for devising the right battle plan for his fighters."[12] Morris "Whitey" Bimstein moved from the Lower East Side to partner with Ray Arcel as boxing trainers, working with Jack Dempsey, Gene Tunney, Benny Leonard, and Max Behr. Hymie Cantor was the boxing coach at the Educational Alliance and trained Ruby Goldstein. Slapsie Maxie Rosenbloom learned the craft of boxing at the 92nd Street YMHA.

Several of the Jewish kids switched from using their fists to wielding the pen. Nathaniel "Nat" Stanley Fleischer grew up on the Lower East Side. "At age 12 he was bitten by the boxing bug and never recovered."[13] Only 5 feet 2 inches in height, he was knocked out in his first fight and turned instead to journalism. In 1922, he founded *The Ring* magazine that became the authoritative voice of the sport. He wrote many books on boxing, including the annual *Ring Record Book*. Known as "Mr. Boxing," Nat Fleischer was the referee or judge in more than a thousand boxing matches. He died in 1972. Herbert "Bert" Sugar "descended from a long line of Hungarian pots-and-pans peddlers."[14] He was the editor of *Boxing Illustrated* and then *The Ring* magazine. Known for a fedora on his head and a cigar clenched between his teeth, he was "boxing's human encyclopedia."[15]

Jacob Golomb, born in Riga, Latvia, in 1893, arrived as a young boy in the United States. His father was a tailor in the Bronx. "Starting in his 20th year with $5 and a sewing machine, donated by his father, he built up an enterprise that became one of the largest of its kind in the world." He was an avid swimmer but was dissatisfied with the available swimsuits that lasted only one season. Golomb established the Everlast company to produce longer lasting swimwear. In 1917, Golomb met the rising heavyweight boxer Jack Dempsey who asked him to make longer-lasting boxing headgear and boxing gloves. Golomb manufactured the boxing gloves worn by Dempsey on July 2, 1921, in his defense of his world's heavyweight title against Frenchman Georges Carpentier. The fight drew a crowd of 91,000, with millions more listening in on the RCA broadcast of the nation's first nationwide radio broadcast. Everlast became the world's leader in boxing equipment including trucks, shirts, mouthguards, boxing gloves, punching bags, boxing rings, ropes, corner stools and footwear.[16]

Basketball

Isadore Gottlieb was born in 1898 in Kiev, Ukraine. As a little boy he moved with his family to Philadelphia. Besotted with sports, in 1917 he organized a basketball team out of the South Philadelphia Hebrew Association, using the acronym SPHAS. "Gottlieb was around basketball since the days when the sport was trying to survive, as the prelude to dances. He remembered the days in Philadelphia in the grand ballroom of the Broadwood Hotel, when the admission was 65 cents for men and 35 cents for women and you could get into the Saturday night habit of watching the SPHAS play. Mr. Gottlieb was on the bench wearing a loud, flowered tie, managing the team and counting the house.... In those days many of the Jewish people wouldn't let their daughters go to an ordinary dance except when the SPHAS were in action before the dance."[17] The SPHAS, with mainly Jewish players, was a leading Eastern professional team winning 12 league championships between 1919 and 1959. Gottlieb promoted the Negro League and the Harlem Globetrotters. Gottlieb was one of the founders of the National Basketball Association and earned the moniker Mr. Baseball. He was the owner and coach of the Philadelphia Warriors that won the league championship in 1947. Eddie Gottlieb died in 1979, aged 81.

Howard "Red" Rosan, born in 1911 in South Philadelphia, played 10 seasons for the SPHAS before moving to the Baltimore Bullets as head coach. He coached the 1945 Bullets to ABL champions. Ralph Kaplowitz, born 1919, in New York, was a basketball star while a student at New York University. After serving with the U.S. Army during World War II, he signed with the SPHAS for a year, joined the New York Knicks and then the Philadelphia Warriors.

Arnold Jacob "Red" Auerbach (1917–2006) was one of America's greatest and most respected basketball coaches. As head coach of the Boston Celtics, Auerbach won nine National Basketball Association titles, including eight in a row between 1959 and 1966. A pioneer in opening basketball to Black players, he hired Bill Russell to play on the team, and in 1966, appointed Russell head coach of the Celtics. After he retired from coaching, Auerbach continued with the Celtics as general manager from 1966 to 1997 and as president from 1997 until his death at age 89, in 2006. Red Auerbach was an icon in Boston, indeed in all of New England.

Red's father Hyman "Hymie" Auerbach, was born in Russia in 1883. He "was only 13 years old when he said goodbye to his mother and father and made his way to the ship, which would carry him to a better life in what everyone said was a land of opportunity on the other side of the ocean.... He and his brothers Louis and Sam, eventually settled in Brooklyn. The new arrivals were eager to learn the ways of their adopted homeland and they worked hard at becoming Americans." Hymie married "a young office worker named Marie Thompson" and the couples settled into a third-floor apartment on Lynch Street in Williamsburg, close to "the elevated trains rumbling over Broadway that provide access to the rest of New York." Arnold, the second of four children, was born there in 1917. He was called Red for his flaming red hair. Hymie owned "a small restaurant in Manhattan, just across from Radio City," moved to a delicatessen in Brooklyn and then operated a dry-cleaning store earning "15 cents for pressing a suit." Still a boy, Red helped out, pressing up to a hundred pairs of pants a day.

Like many other New York boys from Russian-Jewish families, Red Auerbach had a passion for basketball. "I grew up in Williamsburg section of Brooklyn and basketball was the sport because there was no way out there. You couldn't play football. They had no fields for baseball. Everything was basketball." His father "thought basketball was a waste of time. He was opposed to me spending so much time playing it.... I'd just tell him, 'Look. I'll help you after school and during the summer, but I still want to play basketball. Basketball is important to me.'"[18] At 5 feet 10 inches, he was an outstanding player at Eastern High School in Brooklyn, and won an athletic scholarship to George Washington University. He served three years with the Navy during World War II. In 1946 he was appointed coach of the Washington Capitals. In 1950, Red Auerbach took over the struggling Boston Celtics. During his 57 years with the Boston Celtics the cigar-chomping Red Auerbach transformed the franchise into a basketball powerhouse. "Auerbach had a relentless will to win and he was a supreme judge of talent."[19]

Like "Red" Auerbach, William "Red" Holzman was a red-headed New Yorker of Russian-Jewish parentage who gained fame as a basketball coach. "William Holzman was born on Aug. 10, 1920, on the Lower East Side of Manhattan and moved with his family to a tenement in the Ocean Hill–Brownsville section of Brooklyn when he was 4 years old. His parents were Jewish immigrants, his mother from Romania, his father from Russia. His father, Abraham, was a tailor who discouraged his son from playing sports. But 'Roita,' Yiddish for Red, as the youngster was called—Yiddish was the language Holzman grew up with—became a standout athlete at Franklin K. Lane High School."[20] He attended City College of New York and joined the United States Navy during World War II. After the Navy, he played professional basketball until 1954 when he began coaching. For 15 years. Holzman was head coach of the New York Knicks, leading his team to NBA championships in 1970 and 1973, and gaining more wins than any other coach, but Red Auerbach.

The third red-headed Jewish basketball player-turned-coach was Louis "Red" Herman Klotz, born in 1920 in South Philadelphia. Standing 5 foot 7 inches, Klotz attended Villanova University on an athletic scholarship. He left college to serve with the United States Army. Klotz was a point guard with the Baltimore Bullets and later with the Philadelphia SPHAS, before joining a team that played worldwide as a foil, losing almost every game, against the famed Harlem Globetrotters.[21] Abraham "Abe" Michael Saperstein, of Polish-Jewish heritage, founded the Harlem Globetrotters to highlight the skills of Black basketball players. Their games were a combination of talent and showmanship to entertain the crowds. The Globetrotters were capable of beating the leading all–White teams of the NBA. Saperstein's Harlem Globetrotters helped integrate basketball.

New York produced many Jewish basketball players who excelled at high school and college, served in the United States Army, and went on to play and coach in the National Basketball Association. Jack "Dutch'" Garfinkel, born in 1910 in Brooklyn, played for the Boston Celtics, 1946–1947. Harry Boykoff, born on the Lower East Side in 1922, at six foot 10 inches was among the first of the Big Men to enter the game. Known as "Big Hesh" he played for the Boston Celtics 1950–51. During a game at

DeWitt Clinton High School, Lou Bender connected on a long two-handed shot, prompting a response, "Now that was a lulu of a basket." The nickname Lulu stuck and followed Bender to Columbia University and into a career in the American Basketball League.[22] Sidney "Sonny" Hertzberg, born 1922 in Brooklyn, began his professional career in 1946, playing for the New York Knicks, and then the Boston Celtics. Later he served as a scout and commentator for the Knicks. Harry Rosenstein, born 1920 in Brooklyn, was a member of the New York Knicks in 1946. Max "Slats" Zaslofsky, born 1925 in Brooklyn, played for the New York Knicks from 1950 to 1953, and later was coach of the New York Mets. Ralph Kaplowitz, born 1919 in the Bronx, played for the New York Knicks, 1944–1947. Oscar "Ossie" Benjamin Schectman, Howard "Howie" Rader and Sidney Harold Tannenbaum—all Brooklyn born—had professional basketball careers. "During the 1940s these Jewish players were often showered with anti-Semitic catcalls."[23]

Baseball

Many boys of Russian-Jewish heritage took to baseball with the same enthusiasm that others took to boxing and basketball. Success at baseball lifted them from the ghetto to regional and even national fame. Starting in the early days of professional baseball there were Jewish players, writers, statisticians, manufacturers, managers, and more recently, Jewish owners of major league teams. Lipman Emanuel Pike (born in 1845 of Dutch-Jewish heritage) was the first Jewish ballplayer. Barney Pelty "The Yiddish Curver" and Erskine Mayer were leading pitchers early in the 20th century. During the years between the Great Wars, many Jews, including Hank Greenberg, played for major league teams. Jacob Albert Pitler played for the Pittsburgh Tigers, and later was coach of the Brooklyn Dodgers. Jonah Goldman played for the Cleveland Indians. Isadore "Izzy" Goldstein was born in Odessa, moved to the Bronx, picked up the game and briefly joined the Detroit Tigers, as a teammate of Hank Greenberg. Leo Fishel was the game's first Jewish pitcher, playing for the New York Giants. Goodman "Goodie" Rosen and Max Rosenfeld played for the Brooklyn Dodgers. Phil Weintraub was first baseman with the New York Giants.

Andrew "Andy" Howard Cohen was born in 1904 in New York of Russian-Jewish immigrants. When he was four, the family moved to El Paso, Texas, where Andy developed a passion for baseball. Early in his baseball career he was advised to change his name, but Andy "had pride in his race.... He said Cohen was a good enough name for him. To take any other would be an attempt to hide the fact that he was a Jew. Besides, it would hurt his mother if he played under an assumed name." His skill and his name paid off for him. John McGraw, manager of the New York Giants, "had long nursed the idea of having a Jewish ballplayer on the Giants. He wanted one as an attraction to New York fans."[24] Andy Cohen was second baseman for the Giants from 1934 to 1937.

Henry "Hank" Benjamin Greenberg was born 1911 in "a second-floor apartment of a tenement house at 16 Barrow Street, Greenwich Village, New York. When I was about a year old, we moved a few blocks to a sixth-floor walk-up on Perry Street. A small group of Jewish families lived in the same building. We all spoke the same language. This was common among the immigrants who came from Europe." Greenberg recalled: "I grew up into a typical Jewish family whose objective was to send their children to college to become doctors or dentists or lawyers or schoolteachers.... But I loved baseball and stuck with it." His father owned a company that shrunk cloth before it was made into suits, giving the Greenberg family a middle-class life. The neighbors would say: "Mrs. Greenberg has such nice children. Too bad

Andrew "Andy" Howard Cohen in his New York Giants uniform in 1993.

All-Star Game, Washington, D.C., July 7, 1937. From left: Lou Gehrig, Joe Cronin, Bill Dickey, Joe DiMaggio, Charley Gehringer, Jimmie Foxx, and Hank Greenberg (Library of Congress, LC-DIG-hec-22989).

one of them has to be a bum. ... Mother said: 'Why are you wasting your time playing baseball? It's a bum's game.' ... My father used to holler at me that I would never make anything of myself." Ira Berkow wrote: "Greenberg did not change his name, and although he didn't flaunt his Jewishness, he didn't hide it either."[25]

Known as The Hebrew Hammer, Hank Greenberg played for the Detroit Tigers as first baseman, to become one of the greatest sluggers in baseball history. He famously declined to play on Yom Kippur in 1934. He played in the 1937 All-Star game held at Griffith Stadium, Washington, D.C. On October 16, 1940, at the height of his baseball career, Greenberg registered for the military draft, to take a pay cut from $55,000 a year with the Tigers to $252 a year with the Army. "I never asked for a deferment. I made up my mind to go when I was called. My country came first."[26] Greenberg served 47 months and saw action in China and Japan. After the war, he returned for a couple of seasons with the Detroit Tigers.

Olympic Games

Laurence "Lon" Eugene Myers, born in 1859 in Richmond, Virginia, was an early, and pre-modern Olympic Games, Jewish track star. "The second annual winter meeting of the New York Athletic Club attracted a crowd of 5,000 'despite the bitter weather.' ... L.E. Myers of the Knickerbocker Yacht Club handily won the 440-yard race in 57 seconds."[27] Myers set national records in every distance between 50 yards to one mile, and held world records in 100 yards, 440 yards and 880 yards. He died at age 41 of pneumonia.

The track star Myer Prinstein represented the United States in the 1900 and 1904 Olympic Games. Daniel Frank was also on the 1904 track team; Charles Jacobs (track, 1908), Harry Simon (shooting, 1908), Alvin T. Meyer and Abel Kiviat (track, 1912), Fred Meyer won a bronze medal and Samuel Gerson a silver medal in wrestling at the 1920 Antwerp games; Sydney Jelinek (crew, 1924), Louis A. Clark (track, 1924), Lillian Copeland (track, 1928), Albert Schwartz (swimming, 1932), Philip Ehrenberg and George Gulak (gymnastics, 1932), Irving Jaffee (won two gold medals in skating, 1932), and Samuel Balter (basketball, 1936). Several Jewish boxers of Russian descent represented the United States in the Olympics Games. The heavyweight Samuel Berger won gold at the 1904 Olympics, lightweight Sam Mosberg won gold at the 1920 Olympics, featherweight Jacob Fields won a gold medal at the 1924 Olympics, featherweight Harold Devine won a bronze medal in 1928, and lightweight Nathan Bor won a bronze medal at the 1932 Olympic Games.

Myer Prinstein was born in Russian-ruled Poland. He came as a boy to the United States and settled in Syracuse, New York, where his family operated a grocery store at the corner of Orange and Harrison Street. Standing 5 feet 8 inches and weighing 145 pounds, he excelled on the track team at Syracuse High School. Prinstein won the triple jump at the Paris Olympics in 1900. At the 1904 games in St. Louis, he was the gold medalist in the long jump and the triple jump.[28] Fellow Jew

Myer Prinstein was the gold medalist in the long jump competition at the 1904 Olympic Games, held in St. Louis, Missouri.

Daniel Gordon Frank was the silver medalist at the 1904 games with a long jump of 6.89 meters, well behind Prinstein's jump of 7.34 meters.

Abel Richard Kiviat, born in 1892 on the Lower East Side to immigrant parents, was a high school track star. He served as captain of the Irish American Athletic Club track team. In 1908 he set an American record for the 1,500 meters race. He won the silver medal for 1,500-meters at the Stockholm Olympic Games in 1912. At Stockholm, Kiviat was a member of the American relay team that won the gold medal for 3,000-meters.[29]

Lillian Copeland of Russian-Jewish heritage, was the national women's shotput and discus champion. She won a gold medal in discus at the 1932 Olympic Games with a throw of 136 feet 8 inches. Because of Nazi anti–Semitism, she boycotted the 1936 Berlin games, retired from sports and joined the Los Angeles Sheriff's Department to serve as a juvenile officer. She died in 1964, aged 59 years.[30] Frederick Julius Meyer began wrestling as a boy while attending the Chicago Hebrew Institute. After the 1920 Olympic Games he became a professional wrestler. Abe Cohen represented the United States in fencing at the 1956 Olympics and his brother Herbert competed for the United States in the 1964, and in the 1968 Olympics.

Samuel Balter, born in Detroit in 1909, was a member of the basketball squad that won the gold medal at the 1936 Summer Olympic Games in Berlin. Marty Glickman, 18, and 21-year-old Sam Stoller were members of the United States 4 × 100

Left: Abel Kiviat, silver medalist in the 1,500 meters at the 1912 Stockholm Olympic Games. _Right:_ Lillian Copeland (shown here in 1928), was born in New York of immigrant Jewish parents. She was an Olympic champion who excelled in javelin, discus and shot put.

meters relay team. Hours before the final race, they were dropped from the team and replaced by Jesse Owens and Ralph Metcalfe. The revised American team easily won the gold medal. There were accusations that the two Jewish athletes were excluded so as not to embarrass the German chancellor, Adolf Hitler. Sam Stoller described it as: "the most humiliating episode of my life." Years later, "Glickman was relentless in his claim that Avery Brundage, the head of the United States Olympic Committee, and Dean Cromwell were members of the America First Committee and sympathetic to the Nazis." Glickman believed: "Sam and I became the unfortunate objects of bigotry." Like Sam Stoller, Marty Glickman went on to a long and distinguished career in sports broadcasting.[31]

Football

In 1893, Isadore and Rose Horwitz left their shtetl near Kiev, Ukraine, to settle in Chicago. A decade later they owned a thriving leather tanning company, and changed their name to Horween. They sent their sons Ralph and Arnold to a private school where they excelled in their studies and in sport. Both boys were accepted to Harvard College, Ralph in the Class of 1918 and Arnold in the Class of 1920. Big and strong, both boys donned the crimson uniform of the Harvard football squad. Arnold was team captain and led his team to victory over other Ivy League colleges. Later, Arnold served as head coach of Harvard football. (A fuller description of the Horween brothers can be found in Chapter 9.)

By 1918 the sons of Russian-Jewish immigrates were entering colleges "in sufficient numbers to give them adequate representation in football and to make the public conscious of the Jew.... In 1926 an All-Jewish team that year could have included Benny Friedman of Michigan, Dave Mishel of Brown, Izzy Zarakov and Al Miller of Harvard, Harry Kaplan of Columbia, Ed Baruch of Princeton and Jonah Goldman of Syracuse in a star-studded backfield, while the line could have been recruited from such stout fellows as "Buss" Friedman, Harvey Levy and Walter Winick, the center trio of a very good Syracuse team, Tack Ruben of Dartmouth, Dave Skudin of New York University, Saul Mielziner of Carnegie Tech and Shon Klein of Ohio State" (p. 116).

Benjamin "Benny" Friedman (shown here in 1926), was born in Cleveland, Ohio. He played football for the University of Michigan and was All-American. 1926.

Among the early Jewish All-Stars were: "Joe Alexander of Syracuse, 1918 and 1919; Benny Friedman of Michigan, 1925; Fred Sington of Alabama, 1930; Marchmont Schwartz of Notre Dame, 1931; Harry Newman of Michigan, and, Aaron Rosenberg of Southern California" (p. 120).[32] Benjamin "Benny" Friedman was born 1905 in Cleveland, the son of a Russian-Jewish tailor. He played for the University of Michigan Wolverines, elected All-American, 1925–1926, and voted most valuable player in 1926. Michigan had "a new and dazzling gridiron meteor."[33] Benny Friedman played eight seasons in the National Football League. From 1949 through 1963, he served as athletic director at Brandeis University.

Harry Lawrence Newton was born in 1909 in Detroit. During his teen years he attended a baseball camp where Benny Friedman taught him how to throw the football. Like Benny, Harry was on the University of Michigan Wolverines football team.

In 1932 he was elected to the first team of the All-Stars and was voted football's most valuable player. He played professionally for the New York Giants.

Tennis

Julius "Julie" Seligman was born in 1909 in New York City. From 1925 to 1926, he was the national boys' 18-and-under tennis champion. In 1928 he was the national intercollegiate men's singles tennis champion. Richard "Dick" Savitt won the Australian and Wimbledon tennis championships in 1951. After the Wimbledon victory, *The New York Times* announced: "Dick Savitt of Orange, New Jersey, who never took a tennis lesson, established himself as the World's No. 1." Savitt "has been called the greatest Jewish tennis player of all time ... but, in the 50s, there was no escaping the fact that Savitt's Jewishness worked against him."[34] Savitt was ranked among the top 10 American players six times in the 1950s and among the world's top 10 four times. Richard Savitt was born in 1927, in Bayonne, New Jersey, of Russian-Jewish descent. "He taught himself to play tennis in his early teens when he was a ball boy at the Berkeley Tennis Club in Orange, New Jersey."[35]

11

Composers and Authors

Throughout the 20th century, many Americans of Eastern European Jewish background gained prominence as composers of classical and popular music, and as authors.

Composers

Irving Berlin, George Gershwin, Aaron Copland, Leonard Bernstein, Philip Glass, Stephen Sondheim, and Bob Dylan were the sons or grandsons of Russian-Jewish immigrants. They helped define American popular and classical music. (The other great songwriters, Jerome Kern and Marvin Hamlisch, were of German-Jewish heritage.)

Thirty-year-old songwriter Irving Berlin was drafted into the 77th Division. Rather than train for war, he was given the task of entertaining the troops. He wrote the musical *Yip Yip Yaphank* with the hit songs *Oh! How I Hate to Get Up in the Morning, The Girl I Left Behind*, and *Dream On, Little Soldier Boy.* The tryout was held at Camp Upton and it went on to a smash Broadway opening. Berlin wrote *God Bless America*, but decided it did not fit the tempo of the show. Twenty years later, at the start of World War II, Kate Smith made it America's second anthem.

The immigrant boy from the shtetl of Tolochin in Tsarist Russia and growing up in the mean streets of the Lower East Side was America's beloved songwriter with such hits as *Alexander's Ragtime Band, Annie Get Your Gun, Top Hat, This Is the Army, White Christmas* and *Follow the Fleet.* In addition to his many hit songs, Irving Berlin wrote the musical scores for the films *Top Hat, Blue Skies, Easter Parade, There's No Business Like Show Business,* and *Holiday Inn.*

Neither parent provided George Gershwin with support for his musical ambitions. In 1929 he said, "There is no such thing as tradition for me. Whatever I know about music, I've wrenched out for myself. I had no parents to stand over me and encourage me in the little tunes that I used to make up. No one ever urged me on by telling me that Mozart was a great composer when he was 11."[1]

Moishe Gershovitz was born in 1872, Rosa Brushkin in 1875; both from privileged Jewish families permitted to live in St. Petersburg, Russia. Now "Morris" and "Rose," they met and married in New York, changing their surname first to Gershvin and then to Gershwin. They moved frequently, with Morris pursuing various occupations including leather worker, shoemaker, bookmaker, working in a stationery store, a cigar shop, running a Turkish bathhouse, operating a bakery, working in eateries and running a summer resort. There was always enough money to eat and live well, enjoy Yiddish theater and pay for the children's music lessons. Their first child, Israel (better known as Ira) was born in 1896, then George in 1898, followed by Arthur in 1900 and Frances in 1906. George showed little interest in music until age 10 years when he heard his friend Maxie Rosenzweig play the violin.

His parents bought a piano for Ira, but it was George who loved to play it. At age 15 he dropped out of school to plug music for the Jerome H. Remick Company, earning $15 a week. At age 17, he published his first song. Two years later his *Swanee* was taken by the Broadway star Al Jolson, and became a national hit. In 1924 Gershwin displayed his classical music skills with *Rhapsody in Blue*, followed in the 1920s by a string of Broadway hits including *Lady Be Good, Oh Kay, Funny Girl* and *Strike Up the Band*, mostly in collaboration with songwriter brother Ira. George traveled to Paris to study with Nadia Boulanger and Maurice Ravel. In 1928, he completed *An American in Paris*. The next year he wrote the music for *Show Girl*; in 1930, *Girl Crazy* with such enchanting songs as *Embraceable You* and *I Got Rhythm*. In 1935 he completed the opera *Porgy and Bess*.

George Gershwin, composer of Broadway hits and the opera *Porgy and Bess* (Library of Congress, LC-USZ62-60866).

Moving to Hollywood in 1936, George wrote the music for the movie *Shall We Dance*, featuring Fred Astaire and Ginger Rogers. In 1937 he began having violent headaches with hallucinations and difficulty with coordination. He was diagnosed with an inoperable brain tumor and died on July 11, at age 38, the same age that Felix Mendelsohn died, three years more than Wolfgang Mozart and seven years longer than Franz Schubert. George Gershwin's music remains a vital and delightful part of the American musical repertoire to our day, and likely well beyond. "What he wanted to do most, he said, was to interpret the soul of the American people. Thus, in the tempo of jazz he jabbed at the dignities of American life, while he won the plaudits of the musical élite with the classic qualities of *Rhapsody in Blue*."[2]

Aaron Copland's decision to devote his life to music was "a blow" to his father. "Where did you get such a strange idea. Can you make a living out of it?" His father "had no particular interest in music, but, doubtful or not, he supported his son's musical education, and over the years, took increasing pride in his career." Aaron's mother was "more sensitive [and] had some musical ability." The proudest moment of her life was in 1927 while "watching her son perform his Piano Concerto with the Boston Symphony."[3]

Aaron Copland was born in Brooklyn in 1900, the son of Harris and Sarah Copland, both Russian-Jewish immigrants. The family name was originally Kaplan. Harris and Sarah were "loyal Americans, staunch Democrats, and loving but busy parents," who owned a small department store on Washington Street in Brooklyn. They spoke Yiddish at home and observed the major Jewish holidays, but were eager to integrate into American life. Aaron was the youngest of five children. "Copland grew up with a large extended family of uncles, aunts and cousins." In the summers he attended Jewish camps. He was a sensitive boy who "felt very different" and was "rather delicate by comparison with the other kids."[4] Aaron had his bar-mitzvah at Congregation Baith Israel Anshei Emes in Brooklyn. Copland had "the great luck [to be] born with a musical gift." At age eight he started "to compose, or at least to improvise and make up tunes at the piano."[5]

Aaron Copland was born in Brooklyn, New York, in 1900. His works included *Appalachian Spring, Billy the Kid, Rodeo* and *Fanfare for the Common Man*.

At age 15 years he decided to become a composer. With financial support from his family, he traveled to Paris to study under the famed pedagogue Nadia Boulanger. Returning to the United States he was supported by two Guggenheim Fellowships, in 1925 and 1926. He found a sponsor in Serge Koussevitzky, who premiered Copland's work with the Boston Symphony Orchestra. During a creative period in the 1940s, Copland composed such quintessential American works as *Appalachian Spring* (for which he received the Pulitzer Prize), *Billy the Kid*, *Rodeo*, *Fanfare for a Common Man*, and his Clarinet Concerto. Aaron Copland's music functioned as "a mirror of America [and] played a central role in the shaping of the national consciousness."[6]

Leonard Bernstein came from a Russian-Jewish immigrant home with little appreciation of classical music. At age eight Leonard began his Hebrew studies at the Conservative Temple Mishkan Tefila, then located in the Boston suburb of Roxbury. Two years later, at a religious service, he was so emotionally moved by the rich, baritone singing of the cantor accompanied by the organ and choir "that he began to cry." When Leonard was 10 years old, Aunt Clara gifted him with a piano. "From the moment he touched the piano, Leonard couldn't tear himself away from it." He displayed an "exceptional ear and instinctive grasp of theory." Leonard's father reluctantly agreed to pay for Leonard to have piano lessons with a neighbor Freda Karp who charged $1 an hour for each lesson. Leonard soon surpassed her skills and she suggested he continue his studies at Boston's New England School of Music. When his father refused to pay the added expense, Leonard began earning money by teaching piano to children and playing at weddings. His father was "a shrewd businessman and ardent religionist. He was also an implacable opponent of Bernstein's pursuit of a career in music, and relations between father and son were often strained. His mother, by contrast, provided a warm, supportive household in which her son's ambitions flourished."[7]

Leonard Bernstein was born August 1918, the first child of Samuel and Jennie Bernstein who had immigrated from Russia to the textile city of Lawrence, on the Merrimack River, 25 miles north of Boston. The family moved to Pleasanton Street, Roxbury, then the center of Jewish life in Boston. He attended the elite Boston Latin school, the first public school in America. "It was here that Bernstein's interest in languages and literature began to flourish, but what already obsessed him as a teenager was music." His love and knowledge of music developed further during his years at Harvard College, where, as a sophomore, he met the famed conductor Dimitri Mitropoulos. From Harvard he attended the Curtis Institute in Philadelphia.[8] Bernstein wrote the music for the film *On the Waterfront*, as well as Broadway hits *On the Town*, *Candide*, and in 1957, *West Side Story*. He wrote symphonies and masses in a career that gained him seven Emmy awards, two Oscars and many other prizes. In 1947, he was appointed principal conductor of the New York Philharmonic, the first American-born conductor to lead a major American symphony orchestra. Leonard Bernstein was "one of the most prodigiously talented and successful musicians in American history."[9] Leonard Bernstein died in 1990 at age 72.

Philip Glass was born in 1937 in Baltimore, the son of American-born parents of Russian-Jewish heritage. His mother was a librarian and his father owned a record store on Howard Street. "My father was self-taught, but he ended up having a very refined and rich knowledge of classical, chamber, and contemporary music. Typically, he would come home and have dinner, and then sit in his armchair and listen

Leonard Bernstein, composer of *West Side Story* and *Candide,* pictured in 1965 (Library of Congress, LC-USZ62-127784).

to music until almost midnight. I caught on to this very early, and I would go and listen with him." His parents did not encourage Philip to devote his life to music. "The general view in my family was that musicians were somehow living on the fringes of respectability and that the life of music was not the life an educated person would pursue."[10] Despite these obstacles, Glass became a leading American composer, writing many symphonies and concertos, chamber music, operas and film scores.

Robert Allen Zimmerman, better known as Bob Dylan, was born in 1941 in Duluth, Minnesota, the son of Abram and Beatrice Zimmerman of Russian-Jewish descent. The Zimmerman family was part of a small, closely-connected Jewish community. His father "was stricken with polio and it kept him out of the war [World War II], but my uncles all had gone and came back alive. Uncle Paul, Uncle Morris, Jack, Max, Louis, Vernon and others had gone off to the Philippines, Sicily, North Africa, France and Belgium."[11] Dylan wrote and performed many songs, including *Blowin' in the Wind* (1963) and *The Times They Are a' Changin'* (1964). In 2008, the Pulitzer Prize committee awarded him a special citation for his "profound impact on popular music and American culture, marked by lyrical compositions of extraordinary poetic power." In 2016, he was awarded the Nobel Prize in Literature "for having created new poetic expressions within the great American song tradition."

Stephen Joshua Sondheim began life in 1930 in the luxury 27th floor San Remo apartment at 145 Central Park West, New York City. His father Herbert was of German-Jewish heritage. His mother Janet Fox came from a family of Orthodox, Yiddish-speaking Lithuanian Jews who settled first in Fall River, Massachusetts, and moved to Harlem, then a Jewish area of New York City. Janet found work as a dress designer for Sondheim-Levy, a successful Seventh Avenue high-end women's clothing manufacturer, and married the owner, Herbert Sondheim. The snobbish Janet chose to raise her son in the established German-Jewish manner. With his upwardly mobile parents busy in New York and attending fashion shows in Paris, Stephen, an only child, was raised mostly by servants. He attended Felix Adler's Ethical Culture School.

"As for religious instruction, Stephen Joshua Sondheim received none at all. He never had a bar mitzvah ceremony, he knew nothing about the observances of the Jewish calendar, and he did not enter a synagogue until he was 19 years old." In the summers he attended Camp Androscoggin in Maine, "patronized by prominent German-Jewish families from New York and emphasized athletics from dawn to dusk."[12] Stephen's love of theater began as a boy of nine, attending live Broadway shows. When he was 10, his parents divorced.

At a preparatory school he started writing lyrics for musicals, and focused on theater arts as a student at Williams College in Massachusetts. His mentor was the famed composer and lyricist Oscar Hammerstein II. Sondheim wrote the lyrics for *West Side Story* (1957) and *Gypsy* (1959); and wrote the music and lyrics for such musical gems as *A Funny Thing Happened on the Way to the Forum* (1962), *Company* (1970), *Follies* (1971), *A Little Night Music* (1973), *Sweeney Todd: The Demon Barber of Fleet Street* (1979), *Sunday in the Park with George* (1984), and *Into the Woods* (1987). Sondheim won 8 Tony awards, 8 Grammy awards, the Presidential Medal of Freedom, the 1985 Pulitzer prize for *Sunday in the Park with George*, among many other accolades. He was one of the leading figures in 20th-century musical theater. Stephen Joshua Sondheim died in 2021 at age 91.

"The *Great American Songbook* is the canon of the most important and influential American popular songs and jazz standards from the early 20th century that have stood the test of time in their life and legacy. Often referred to as 'American Standards,' the songs published during the Golden Age of this genre include those popular and enduring tunes from the 1920s to the 1950s that were created for Broadway theater, musical theater and Hollywood musical film." Many of these songs were the work of Jews of Eastern European lineage.

Irving Berlin gave us *Alexander's Ragtime Band* (1911), *All by Myself* (1921), *Always* (1928), *Cheek by Cheek* (1935), *Easter Parade* (1933), *Blue Skies* (1926), *Change Partners* (1938), *God Bless America* (1938), *Heat Wave* (1933), *How Deep Is the Ocean* (1932), *I've Got My Love to Keep Me Warm* (1937), *Let's Face the Music and Dance* (1936), *Oh! How I Hate to Get Up in the Morning* (1943), *Say It Isn't So* (1932), *There's No Business Like Show Business* (1946), *A Pretty Girl Is Like a Melody* (1919), *Top Hat, White Tie and Tails* (1935), and *White Christmas* (1942).

George and Ira Gershwin gave us *Bidin' My Time* (1930), *But Not for Me* (1930), *Embraceable You* (1928), *Fascinating Rhythm* (1924), *A Foggy Day* (1937), *I Got Plenty of Nuttin'* (1934), *I Got Rhythm* (1930), *It Ain't Necessarily So* (1935), *I've Got a Crush on You* (1930), *Of Thee I Sing* (1931), *'S Wonderful* (1927), *Somebody Loves You* (1924), *Someone to Watch Over You* (1926), *Summertime* (1934), *That Certain Feeling* (1925) and *They Can't Take That Away from Me* (1937).

Harold Arlen (born Hyman Arluck, the son of a Jewish cantor) wrote the music for *Over the Rainbow* (1939), *It's Only a Paper Moon* (1933), *I've Got the World On a String* (1932), *Let's Fall in Love* (1933), *That Old Black Magic* (1942), *The Man Who Got Away* (1953), *One for My Baby* (1943), *Stormy Weather* (1933), and wrote the music for the hit 1939 movie *The Wizard of Oz*.

Arthur Schwartz wrote the music for *That's Entertainment* (1952), *The Band Wagon* (1931), *A Tree Grows in Brooklyn* (1937), *Cover Girl* (1944), *Alone Together* (1932), *Dancing in the Dark* (1931).

Frank Loesser wrote *Baby, It's Cold Outside* (1941), *Luck Be a Lady Tonight* (1950) and *Slow Boat to China* (1948).

Cy Coleman wrote *The Best Is Yet to Come* (1959), *Big Spender* (1962), *I've Got Your Number* (1962) and *Witchcraft* (1957).

Al Jolson wrote *Me and My Shadow* (1927) and Leonard Bernstein wrote *New York, New York* (1944).

Authors

In her 1912 autobiography *The Promised Land,* Mary Antin tells why Russian Jews, including her family, chose to leave the Old World in the hope that life in the New World would be better. Antin's book allows us "to see our own country as a Russian refugee sees it," commented *The New York Times* review on April 12, 1912, "and we may understand why the journey from Russia to America was like the Exodus of old; and why this country of ours, with all its poverty, with its slums, with its industrial problems, and its armies of unemployed, is still a land of promise."

Mary Antin (born Maryasne Antin) was the second of six children of Israel and Esther Antin from the shtetl in Polotzk in the Pale of Settlements. Jewish life revolved around religion and tradition, fear of their Russian neighbors and loathing of the Tsarist state. When she was 13 years old, the family came to the United States and settled in the town of Chelsea, Massachusetts. None could speak any English. The eight of them lived in a three-room tenement without a bathroom. Mary and her siblings entered the public schools, soon mastered the English language and identified with American ways and values, and embraced citizenship with a passion. Mary's book, completed when she was 33 years old, tells of her "flight from the scourge of despotism to take shelter under the American flag. I brought nothing with me but my memories of the old order of things and a great hunger for the bread of freedom." Her work appeared first in *The Atlantic* and in 1912 in book form: *The*

Promised Land, wrote the reviewer, "stands out among the books of the years; stirring, human, poignantly alive [and] a unique contribution to our literature." Mary Antin died in 1949 at age 67.[13]

In the 1930s Henry Roth launched his literary career with *Call It Sleep*, Delmore Schwartz published *In Dreams Begin Responsibility*, and Nathanael West (born Nathan Weinstein) published *Miss Lonelyhearts* and *The Day of the Locust*. Sidney Joseph Perelman (better known as S.J. Perelman) began his career as a Broadway playwright and short story writer. Albert Hirschfeld (better known as Al Hirschfeld) began a brilliant 50-year career with his black-and-white portraits of Broadway and Hollywood stars, politicians and celebrities. After the birth of his daughter Nina in 1945, Hirschfeld imbedded her name in his drawings.

"Harold Bloom, the prodigious literary critic who championed and defended the Western canon in an outpouring of influential books that appeared not only on college syllabuses but also—unusual for an academic—on best-seller lists.... Professor Bloom was frequently called the most notorious literary critic in America." From a vaunted perch at Yale, he flew in the face of almost every trend in the literary criticism of his day. Chiefly he argued for the literary superiority of the Western giants like Shakespeare, Chaucer and Kafka ... over writers favored by what he called "the School of Resentment," by which he meant multiculturalists, feminists, Marxists, neoconservatives and others whom he saw as betraying literature's essential purpose. "Harold Bloom was born on July 11, 1930, in the East Bronx. He was the youngest of five children of William and Paula (Lev) Bloom, struggling immigrants from Eastern Europe. His father was a garment worker." The family was Orthodox and Yiddish-speaking. Harold was six years old before he learned English.

"The first book Harold read was an anthology of Yiddish poetry. He soon discovered the New York Public Library's branch in the Melrose section of the Bronx and worked his way through Hart Crane, W.H. Auden and T.S. Eliot. He graduated from the Bronx High School of Science ... and went to Cornell on a scholarship, where he dazzled his professors. 'And I am very Jewish,' he told a reporter, 'and lower-class Jewish at that.... I really am a product of Yiddish culture.'" He wrote 40 books including *The Western Canon* (1994). Harold Bloom, Sterling Professor of Humanities at Yale University, died in 2019, age 89.[14]

Norman Mailer, Joseph Heller, Herman Wouk and Leon Uris wrote World War II epics. They were close in age. Joseph Heller and Herman Wouk, like Mailer, were from New York. Uris was born in Baltimore, Maryland.

Norman Mailer was born in Brooklyn in 1923 as Nachum Malach. He was the son of Itzchak Isaac Benjamin Mailer, born of Lithuanian-Jewish parents in 1892 in Cape Town, South Africa, and Feigne Schneider Mailer, born in the Russian Empire and raised in Brooklyn. Itzchak used the name Bennett and Feigne went by Fanny. Norman studied Hebrew and had his bar-mitzvah at Congregation Shaarei Zedek in Brooklyn. Despite his clear Jewish lineage, Norman Mailer claimed that his "knowledge of Jewish culture is exceptionally spotty.... I am not a typical Jew." Like most

Jewish intellectuals his age he spent his childhood "rejecting Jewishness at a great rate."[15]

"As a child," wrote David Denby in the *New Yorker,* "Norman was quiet and obedient [and] preoccupied with his studies.... On the way to school (Boys High, in Bedford-Stuyvesant), he kept his head down, avoiding fights with the local Italian and Irish street gangs, and with the local Jewish toughs as well." He built model airplanes ... and in a spare room, he would write fiction. "In September, 1939, Mailer showed up at Harvard in an outfit of orange-striped trousers, a gold jacket, and saddle shoes. He was 16, and found himself as ignorant about ruling-class undergraduates and the social rituals of the college.... In his first year on campus, he ate dinner with other Jewish boys at the Harvard Union and began to feel his way around. Until the end of his sophomore year, he lived almost entirely within the protected boundaries of the American Jewish middle class."

After graduating from Harvard, he married Beatrice (Bea) Silverman and was soon drafted into the U.S. Army. "He was sent for basic training to Fort Bragg, North Carolina, where many of the men were from Pennsylvania, the South, and the Upper Midwest. Mailer was from middle-class Jewish Brooklyn; he had landed in the great working-class Gentile world, and was eager to observe."

Stationed in the Pacific during World War II, Mailer sent 400 letters to his wife. After the war he transformed these letters into *The Naked and the Dead*, "a book that only a nice Jewish boy could write. A nice Jewish boy, that is, in flight from his background.... He wrote *The Naked and the Dead* at a rate of 5,000 words a week.... The book received rave reviews and was an overnight best-seller, remaining on *The New York Times* list for more than a year." The two Jewish characters in *The Naked and the Dead*, "Roth and Goldstein, struggle especially hard for dignity—an obvious point of concern for Mailer, who had his own anxieties to resolve. [Roth is] an irritable guy, he's snobby, morose, and too weak to survive—clearly Mailer's disapproving version of himself. Mailer endowed Goldstein with greater physical and moral strength. Like some earlier Jewish writers, Mailer saw virtue in a life of physical activity and advanced moral adventure.... Goldstein's consciousness as a Jew keeps him from letting go, for, if he fails, the men will think badly not just of him but of all Jews. In the character of Goldstein, Mailer's fear that he was not tough enough for the Army ends in a portrait of formidable endurance."

"The Brooklyn Jewish boy was no longer abashed, no longer inadequate, and certainly no longer quiet. Beginning in the nineteen-fifties ... Mailer transformed himself into a barrel-chested macho—a man six times married, the father of eight children and an adopted son, and the author of more than 40 books, some of them American classics.... He believed that physical courage was necessary equipment for a great writer (Hemingway was the model), and that Jewish men in particular had to overcome all sorts of weaknesses."[16]

"Herman Wouk was born 1915, in the Bronx, to Abraham and Esther (Levine) Wouk. His father, an immigrant from Minsk, had started out sorting and marking laundry for $3 a week but rose to become president of an industrial steam-laundry business. Herman, the middle child of three, excelled at school and earned a place at Townsend Harris High School, an accelerated three-year public institution for gifted students in Manhattan. At Columbia University he majored in comparative literature and philosophy ... [and] he temporarily moved away from the Orthodox Judaism in which he was raised and that later became a mainstay of his personal life and the subject of a best-selling nonfiction book, *This Is My God* (1959), and a follow-up, *The Language God Talks* (2010). With *The Caine Mutiny*, Mr. Wouk struck gold. A crackling drama on the high seas leading up to a riveting courtroom scene, it introduced readers to the unforgettable Capt. Philip F. Queeg, a seething blend of paranoia and incompetence, constantly fiddling anxiously with two steel ball bearings in his left hand. When he steers the ship toward certain disaster in a typhoon, his junior officers remove him from command, an act for which they later face court-martial. The book, which sold more than three million copies in the United States alone, won the Pulitzer Prize for fiction in 1952 and was made into a movie in 1954 with Humphrey Bogart as Queeg."[17]

One of the major influences of Wouk's life was his father, "the stern busy boss of a steam laundry all week, at dinner on Friday night was Papa, convulsing us kids with his drolleries in Yiddish and Shalom Aleichem."[18] In 1955, Wouk was featured on the cover of *Time Magazine*. The accompanying story said: "He is a devout Orthodox Jew who had achieved worldly success in worldly-wise Manhattan while adhering to dietary prohibitions and traditional rituals which many of his fellow Jews find embarrassing.... Wouk made Jewish religious observance appear mainstream in his books. Scenes of a Passover seder and a bar mitzvah service became scenes of middle-class American life in 'Marjorie Morningstar.'"[19]

Like Herman Wouk, Leon Uris wrote about Jews and Jewish history. His books sold very well. His "best-known works are *Exodus*, a popular novel about Jews trying to establish modern Israel (selling five million copies), and the screenplay for *Gunfight at the O.K. Corral*, perhaps the archetypal Hollywood Western." His 1961 book *Mila 18* deals with the Warsaw Ghetto Uprising. "Leon Marcus Uris was born in 1924, in Baltimore, the second child and only son of Wolf William Uris, a shopkeeper, and Anna Blumberg Uris, Jews of Russian-Polish origin. His mother was a first-generation American and his father an immigrant from Poland, who on his way to America had spent a year in Palestine after World War I and had derived his surname from Yerushalmi, meaning man of Jerusalem.... Mr. Uris quit high school shortly after the Japanese attack on Pearl Harbor (he was halfway through his senior year) and joined the United States Marines. He served as a radio operator in the campaigns at Guadalcanal and Tarawa."[20]

"Joseph Heller was the author of *Catch-22*, the darkly comic 1961 novel became a universal metaphor not only for the insanity of war, but also for the madness of life itself.... *Catch-22* was based on Heller's experiences as a bombardier with the 12th Air Force in the Mediterranean in World War II.... *Catch 22* would become an

American classic, selling more than 10 million copies in the United States, read in many of the world's languages and becoming a 1970 film by Mike Nichols." Joseph Heller was born in the Coney Island section of Brooklyn in 1923, the son of Isaac Donald Heller, who drove a delivery truck for Messinger's Bakery, and Lena Heller, a seamstress. Isaac Heller died when Joseph was four years old. "I never grappled much with the idea of trying to find out about him," wrote Heller about his father. "I preferred not to know more.... I knew him by his absence." His mother barely knew English, preferring Yiddish and some Russian. She "raised her family as best she could, taking in boarders." In the section of Coney Island where Joseph grew up "he was surrounded by Jews and Jewish culture." There was a Young Men's Hebrew Association, the Jewish Community Center and the Coney Island Talmud Torah.[21] During 1941, Heller graduated from Abraham Lincoln High School. "He had worked a bit during his school years, delivering telegrams. But he continued to want to be a writer."[22]

Saul Bellow won the 1976 Nobel Prize for Literature, Isaac Bashevis Singer won the Nobel for Literature in 1978 and Eli Wiesel won the Nobel Prize for Peace in 1986. Singer came to the United States in 1935, and Wiesel arrived in 1955. Other notable authors of Russian-Jewish heritage were Abraham Cahan, Anita Diamond, E.L. Doctorow, Cynthia Ozick and J.D. Salinger.

Saul Bellow's "fictional heroes—and [his] scathing, unrelenting and darkly comic examination of their struggle for meaning—gave new immediacy to the American novel in the second half of the 20th century.... The center of his fictional universe was Chicago, where he grew up and spent most of his life, and which he made into the first city of American letters. Many of his works are set there, and almost all of them have a Midwestern earthiness and brashness. Like their creator, Mr. Bellow's heroes were all head and all body both. They tended to be dreamers, questers or bookish intellectuals, but they lived in a lovingly depicted world of cranks, con men, fast-talking salesmen and wheeler-dealers."

Bellow's 1944 novel *The Victim* deals with anti–Semitism. He also wrote *The Adventures of Augie March* (1953), *Henderson the Rain King* (1959), *Herzog* (1964), *Mr. Sammler's Planet* (1969) and *Humboldt's Gift*. "He was frequently lumped together with Philip Roth and Bernard Malamud as a Jewish-American writer, but he rejected the label, saying he had no wish to be part of the 'Hart, Schaffner & Marx' of American letters.... This most American of writers was born in 1915 in Lachine, Quebec, a poor immigrant suburb of Montreal, and named Solomon Bellow.... His parents had emigrated from Russia two years before, though in Canada their luck wasn't much better. Solomon's father, Abram, failed at one enterprise after another. His mother, Liza, was deeply religious and wanted her youngest child, her favorite, to become either a rabbi or a concert violinist." Bellow was awarded the Nobel for his "exuberant ideas, flashing irony, hilarious comedy and burning compassion."[23]

"Isaac Bashevis Singer's vivid evocations of Jewish life in his native Poland and of his experiences as an immigrant in America won him the 1978 Nobel Prize in

Saul Bellow, Pulitzer Prize winner, and Nobel Laureate for Literature, 1976. He wrote *The Adventures of Augie March, Henderson the Rain King, Herzog, Mr. Sammler's Planet* and other works.

Literature.... The Nobel citation praised his 'impassioned narratives, which, with roots in a Polish-Jewish cultural tradition, bring universal human conditions to life.' Mr. Singer's stories and novels, written in Yiddish, often dealt with his upbringing as a rabbi's son in Warsaw and in a small town in eastern Poland and were redolent of the mysticism of Jewish folklore. But he also wrote about loneliness in drab cafeterias, worldliness in Miami Beach and chance acquaintanceship on the sidewalks of upper Broadway.... Most of his fiction first appeared in Yiddish in *The Jewish Daily Forward.*" Many of his stories appeared in English in *The New Yorker.*

Isaac Bashevis Singer was born in 1904, in a "flour-milling town 15 miles northeast of Warsaw. When he was 4, his family moved to Warsaw, and his father set up a rabbinical court in the shabby building where they lived. As a boy, Isaac received a traditional Jewish schooling.... His parents wanted him to be a rabbi, and he obliged them by enrolling at the Tachkemoni Rabbinical Seminary in Warsaw.... But in his early 20's Mr. Singer made a momentous decision: he would drop his religious studies and become a secular writer." Singer came to the United States in 1935. "My first impression," he wrote, "was that here Yiddish literature was dead. It took me five years to convince myself that Yiddish is still very much alive." *The Family Moskat* was serialized in the *Forward*, and appeared in book form in Yiddish in 1945. It was followed by 30 more books by Isaac Bashevis Singer.[24]

"Elie Wiesel, the Auschwitz survivor, became an eloquent witness for the six million Jews slaughtered in World War II and who, more than anyone else, seared the memory of the Holocaust on the world's conscience.... Wiesel had been liberated from Buchenwald as a 16-year-old with the indelible tattoo A-7713 on his arm. Wiesel was awarded the 1986 Nobel Peace Prize for being 'a messenger to mankind. His message is one of peace, atonement and human dignity. His belief that the forces fighting evil in the world can be victorious is a hard-won belief."

"Eliezer Wiesel was born in 1928, in the small city of Sighet, in the Carpathian Mountains near the Ukrainian border in what was then Romania. His father, Shlomo, was a Yiddish-speaking shopkeeper.... His mother, the former Sarah Feig, and his maternal grandfather, Dodye Feig, a Viznitz Hasid, filled his imagination with mystical tales of Hasidic masters.... His idyllic childhood was shattered in the spring of 1944 when the Nazis marched into Hungary. With Allied troops fast approaching, many of Sighet's Jews convinced themselves that they might be spared. But the city's Jews were swiftly confined to two ghettos and then assembled for deportation." Wiesel survived the Buchenwald concentration camp. On April 11, 1945, "after eating nothing for six days, Mr. Wiesel was among those liberated by the United States Third Army." In 1955 Elie Wiesel settled in the United States.[25]

Chaim Potok was "a scholar and ordained rabbi whose best-selling novels about Hasidic Judaism explored the wrenching decision to forsake a close-knit parochial community for the world outside...." Potok came to international prominence in 1967 with his debut novel, *The Chosen*. Unlike the work of the novelists Philip Roth and Saul Bellow, which dealt largely with the neuroses of assimilated secular Jews, *The Chosen* was the first American novel to make the fervent, insular Hasidic world visible to a wide audience.... Set in the Williamsburg section of Brooklyn just after World War II, *The Chosen* tells the story of a brilliant young man struggling to reconcile his obligation to become a rabbi with his desire for a more secular life.... In his books, he drew readers—Jews and non-Jews alike—into a world that few had ever encountered. There, bearded, black-garbed men kept alive an ecstatic brand of Judaism, born in 18th-century Eastern Europe, that centered both on a charismatic spiritual leader, often called a tzaddik and on an individual's direct relationship to God.... These young men's struggles were Mr. Potok's own.

"Herman Harold Potok was born in the Bronx in 1929. Throughout his life, Mr. Potok was customarily called by his Hebrew name, Chaim. His parents, Benjamin Max and Mollie Friedman Potok, were deeply traditional Hasidic Jews, immigrants from Eastern Europe. For young Chaim, daily life centered, just as it had for Jewish boys in the Old World, on the local yeshiva ... where in addition to state-mandated secular subjects, the primary focus was on the study of Jewish sacred texts."[26]

Bernard Malamud was a "novelist and short story writer who won two National Book Awards and the Pulitzer Prize for his chronicles of human struggle. [His] work showed a regard for Jewish tradition and the plight of ordinary men, and was imbued with the theme of moral wisdom gained through suffering." "In *Angel Levine,* a black, rather seedy-looking angel appears to a retired Jewish tailor; in *The Jewbird*, a Yiddish-accented vagabond makes his way into an urban Jewish household in the form of a crow; in *Idiots First*, the Angel of Death, alias Ginzburg, pursues a desperate Jew trying to scrape together money to send his idiot son to California on the midnight train. For Malamud, Jewishness was more a spiritual than a cultural or a religious quality. 'I was concerned with what Jews stood for,' he said, 'with their getting down to the bare bones of things. I was concerned with their ethicality—how Jews felt they had to live in order to go on living.... Bernard Malamud was born in 1914, in Brooklyn, the elder of two sons of Russian Jewish immigrants, Max Malamud and the former Bertha Fidelman. His father ran a small grocery, working 16 hours a day.... Looking back on his childhood, Mr. Malamud would recall that there were no books in his home, no cultural nourishment at all except that on Sundays he would listen to someone else's piano through the living-room window."[27]

Philip Roth was "the prolific, protean, and often blackly comic novelist who was a pre-eminent figure in 20th-century literature." His work explored "what it means to be an American, a Jew, a writer, a man.... He was drawn again and again to writing about themes of Jewish identity, anti–Semitism and the Jewish experience in America. [He received] two National Book Awards, two National Book Critics Circle awards, three PEN/Faulkner Awards, a Pulitzer Prize and the Man Booker International Prize.... Philip Milton Roth was born in Newark in 1933, the younger of two sons. His father, Herman, was an insurance manager for Metropolitan Life who felt that his career had been thwarted by the gentile executives who ran the company. His mother, the former Bess Finkel, was a secretary before she married and then became a housekeeper.... The family lived in a five-room apartment on Summit Avenue within which were only three books when he was growing up—given as presents when someone was ill."[28]

Ayn Rand (born Alisa Rosenbaum) espoused that "only individual ability and effort account for real achievement and that laissez-faire capitalism provides the optimal environment for talent. Her view of selfishness as a virtue and altruism as a vice was a reversal of the traditional Judeo-Christian ethic...." "My philosophy, in essence," Rand once wrote, "is the concept of man as a heroic being, with his own happiness as the moral purpose of his life, with productive achievement as his noblest activity and reason as his only absolute." Alisa Rosenbaum was born in 1905 into a privileged Jewish family in St. Petersburg, Russia. Her father owned a successful pharmacy and the family lived in a spacious apartment on Nevsky Prospekt. The children were aided by tutors and servants. The Rosenbaum family "observed the major Jewish holidays, holding a Seder each year, but otherwise led largely secular lives.... In their urban sophistication and secularism, the Rosenbaums were vastly different from the majority of Russian Jews who inhabited the shtetls of the Pale of Settlements."[29] The Soviet Revolution of 1917 changed everything. In 1926, Alisa

Rosenbaum, a convinced atheist, "came to the United States and headed for Hollywood to work as a movie extra and junior screenwriter. At that time, she met Charles Francis O'Connor, an artist, on a movie set and married him in 1929." Her novels *The Fountainhead* (1943) and *Atlas Struggled* (1957) presented her view that achievement comes from the ability and motivation of the individual.[30]

12

Broadway and Hollywood

Throughout the 20th century, numerous Americans of Russian Jewish background gained prominence as actors, entertainers, producers, directors, and choreographers. Each youngster developed his/her own talents to take advantages of the manifold opportunities that America offered. Soon after leaving the ghetto, most changed their names to enter the American mainstream. Many of them served in the United States Army in World War II, and a number were caught up in the Red Scare after the War. The abundance of Jewish talent in the arts and entertainment was oddly coupled by a lack of Jewish content on Broadway and Hollywood.

From the Yiddish Theater to Broadway and Hollywood

The Russian Jewish immigrants brought Yiddish theater to America. The theater gave the immigrants an emotional lift from the drudgery of their working lives. The theater offered Jewish plays, burlesque, musicals as well as adaptations of Shakespeare, Ibsen and Chekhov. It reminded them of the Old Country but aided their integration into American ways. Nearly all the Yiddish theaters were in New York City, located mainly on Second Avenue. Chicago had the Glickman's Yiddish Theater on Desplaines Street. The Hebrew Actors Union, founded in 1899 at 31 E. 7th Street, New York, protected the interests of the actors.

Boris Thomashefsky was the greatest actor of the American Yiddish theater. He was born in 1868 as Boruch Aharon Thomashefsky in a Ukrainian shtetl. At age 11 he moved to Berychiv to train for the synagogue choir of cantor Nisan Belzer. In 1881, age 13, he left Russia with his family to settle in New York's Lower East Side. He earned money singing in the choir of the Henry Street Synagogue and working in a cigarette factory. While still a teenager he entered the Yiddish theater in New York, as well as touring the Jewish ghettoes of Philadelphia, Chicago, Boston and Washington, D.C. Boris became a star in New York's Yiddish theater. In 1913, he opened his own 2,300-seat National Theater at Houston and Second Avenue. Despite its large size, the theater "cannot begin to accommodate all the persons who want to see his plays. Every year he plays a season of 38 weeks in his own theater, and then takes his company on tour for six to eight weeks or more. … He is one of the most successful of the world's actor-playwright-managers," wrote *The New York Times* on

March 18, 1918. The Yiddish theater "is concerned with everyday emotions and generally tells a simple story mixing drama and song. The hero, overcome by his emotions, happily bursts into song.... He sings through his tears.... The Yiddish audience is like none other. It lives the plays, it suffers and rejoices with the characters, and it gives full vent to its emotions."

"Night after night I have seen the Yiddish theatres swarmed with men, women, and children largely from the sweat-shops," wrote John Corbin in *Harper's Magazine* in 1898. "Many poor Jewish families spend three, four, five dollars a week at the theater.... Compared with their earnings, this represents a patronage of art infinitely beyond that of the families uptown, who parade their liberality in supporting the Metropolitan Opera House."[1]

Thomashefsky put on Shakespeare—*Hamlet, Romeo and Juliet* and *Richard III*—but "altered the plays to suit the Yiddish audience. The King, for example, becomes a rabbi." The 6-foot-tall handsome Thomashefsky was the idol of the Lower East Side. He strutted around town dressed in fine clothes imported from Europe. In 1918 Thomashefsky took his troupe of 100 actors to a theater uptown to lure back his former Lower East Side patrons who had achieved financial success. Thomashefsky's efforts to move uptown failed. In 1924 he declared bankruptcy, sold his theater and went to Europe. In 1930, he returned to New York, weighing 250 pounds, with the play *The Green Millionaire.* During his long career, he wrote many plays, often based on Shakespeare and the Russian classics, but by the 1930s the magic of the Yiddish stage had vanished. He spent his last years in poverty, back in the Lower East Side, where people still remembered him.

Thomashefsky died on July 9, 1939, at age 71. "Boris Thomashefsky's greatest audience—30,000 strong—paid tribute to the Yiddish actor for more than three hours yesterday afternoon as he made his last public appearance on the Lower East Side which he loved so well." After the service and eulogies, "the funeral procession moved slowly down Second Avenue and the waiting thousands fell in behind." The procession stopped briefly in front of the Jewish Actors' Union. Thomashefsky was buried in the Mount Hebron Cemetery, Flushing.[2] The classic music conductor Michael Tilson Thomas is Boris Thomashefsky's grandson.

Several actors of Yiddish theater successfully moved to Broadway and Hollywood. Menashe Goldenberg was the fifth son of Yeshaya Moshe and Sarah Goldenberg, born 1893 in Eastern Europe. The family moved in 1903 to the United States. "At Ellis Island I was born again," he said. Settling in New York's Lower East Side, Emmanuel (as he called himself), attended Public School 137, determined to quickly learn English and American ways. He celebrated his bar-mitzvah in a synagogue on Rivington Avenue. He attended the Townend Harris High School uptown and briefly, City College of New York. "He loved to perform before people." At age 19, he began his acting career in the Yiddish theater under the tutelage of Rudolph Schildkraut.[3] He changed his name to Edward G. Robinson. Over a 50-year career he acted in 30 Broadway shows and 100 Hollywood movies. In *Little Caesar* (1931), he portrayed "the mobsters who ruled the Underworld during the Prohibition era." So convincing was his performance that real mobsters adapted his style of "chomping down on cigar butts while snarling threats and orders out of the sides of their mouths." Other memorable movies were *Double Indemnity* (1944), and *Key Largo* (1948), one of five movies he made with Humphrey Bogart. Robinson was a man "of great kindness and courtesy, whose generosity knew no bounds." Before and during World War II, he spoke up strongly against fascism and Nazism.[4]

Paul Muni was born in Lemberg (now Lviv) in 1895, the son of Yiddish actors. His birth name was Frederich Meshilem Meier Weisenfreund. The family settled on the Lower East Side in 1903. At age 12, Muni began his career in the Yiddish theater in New York and Chicago's Glickman's Yiddish theater. In the 1930s he moved to Hollywood to star in *Scarface* (1932) and in biographical roles depicting Louis Pasteur, Emile Zola, Clarence Darrow, Benito Juarez, and in gangster roles. Muni had a "sense of dedication to his craft.... Acting was not a career but an obsession.... The Muni style had the warmth of the Yiddish stage." In his private life Muni "enjoyed spending time among books, radios and recordings of broadcasts or music and speech." He also enjoyed playing the violin.[5]

Walter Matthau, born in 1920, "worked his way up from poverty on the Lower East Side." His parents Melas and Rose Matushansky were "impoverished Jewish immigrants." His father abandoned the family when Walter was three. Rose worked as a sweatshop seamstress. "The family moved often because she could not pay the rent for their cold-water flats.... Young Walter sought relief in acting, appearing in theatricals in schools and settlement houses, and reading Shakespeare nearly every day. At 11, he started selling ice cream and soft drinks in the Yiddish theater on Second Avenue, and doing bit parts, earning 50 cents a performance, working seven shows per week, while studying the great Yiddish actors." He acted in 1936 in *The Dishwasher* at the Second Avenue Yiddish theater. In the process, "he immersed himself in Yiddish theater and Yiddishkeit, and became fluent in the language."

Walter and his brother Henry "really hustled to take care of their mother." Walter sold newspapers, and ice cream along the streets of the Lower East Side. Matthau attended elementary school at Public School 25 followed by Junior High Public School 64. He graduated from high school in 1939, to take odd jobs as a floor cleaner, file clerk and gym instructor. During World War II, Matthau served as a radio operator and cryptologist and "rose to staff sergeant and earned six battle stars." Returning to New York, he appeared in many Broadway shows. His breakthrough was playing Oscar Madison, "the slovenly sportswriter," in Neil Simon's 1965 Broadway comedy and 1968 film *The Odd Couple* alongside Jack Lemmon. Walter Matthau was "a lifelong enthusiast of sports and classical music," with a great fondness for Mozart's symphonies and operas. Despite his film persona as irascible and grumpy, he was "one of the nicest of men."[6]

"Eddie Cantor, banjo-eyed vaudevillian whose dancing feet and double-takes brought him stardom in movies, radio and television.... His song-and-dance specialties, his nonstop patter of puns and gags, his farce remained essentially vaudeville through the years of success.... No one could have started to achieve fame and wealth by his own efforts with fewer advantages." He was born in 1892 on Eldridge Street, in New York's Lower East Side as Isadore Itzkowitz, the son of Mechel and Meta, an impoverished couple recently arrived from Russia. Meta died the following year in childbirth and Mechel died in 1894 of pneumonia, leaving Isadore an orphan. His 60-year-old grandmother Esther took care of him. She earned a meagre living, hawking safety pins, and acting as a *shadchan* (marriage broker) to recent immigrants. Esther struggled "to keep some sort of food in our stomachs and a roof over our heads." Eddie was a poor student and dropped out of school early, hanging out at poolrooms and earning a few pennies singing songs at street corners. During his early teens he won talent competitions as a singer and dancer. In one of his early acts, he was accompanied on the piano by Jimmy Durante. Now known as Eddie Cantor, he went into vaudeville, and had a long-run on Broadway with the Ziegfeld Follies. He achieved great fame with *Makin' Whoopee*, *If You Knew Susie* and *Ma! He's Making Eyes at Me*. "More than any other Jewish actor of his stature, Cantor assumed a responsibility to help his co-religionists in America and abroad through offstage activism." Eddie Cantor died in 1964, at age 72.[7]

The Yiddish theater in America had many female stars. The best remembered are Molly Picon, Sophie Tucker, and Bessie Thomashefsky, wife of the great Boris Thomashefsky. Like so many other high achievers Molly Picon began her life on a Lower East Side tenement. She was born in 1898, as Malka Opieken. Her father Louis considered himself too intellectual for menial work. "He was just anti," Molly said, "anti-capitalist, anti-religion, anti-labor.... He just faded out of our lives." Molly began performing at age five, winning children's talent shows. Her mother, who worked as a dressmaker, got Molly a job playing children's parts in Boris Thomashefsky's Yiddish company. After World War I, Molly departed for Europe to act in Yiddish theater and movies. She starred in *Ost und West* (East and West) contrasting life in the Old World with the West. This Yiddish language movie was filmed in 1923 in Vienna, and is the earliest surviving Yiddish movie.

Molly returned to New York to perform in the Yiddish theater. In 1930, New York mayor Jimmy Walker came to see Molly act in *The Little Clown*. He said: "This is the first time I have ever attended a Jewish show. I liked it immensely. I wanted to pay my respects to Miss Picon. She is a splendid actress."[8] She starred in *One in a Million*, a musical comedy at the Second Avenue Theatre. The show "runs for about three hours, which means that Miss Molly Picon is amiably busy for about three hours, trying to please, and pleasing."[9] With Yiddish-speaking audiences declining in the 1930s, Molly began a successful transition into English-language radio, television, theater and movies. Molly Picon continued performing well into her 80s.

"Sophie Tucker, the indefatigable entertainer who was billed as the 'Last of the Red-Hot Mamas,' died of a lung ailment and kidney failure in her apartment on Park Avenue.... For 60 years, Sophie Tucker pushed out songs in her spectacular style—big, brassy and flamboyant. She cried and laughed with such zest, such vigor, that audiences were swept in the irresistible torrent of lush sentiment." Her hit song was *My Yiddishe Momme.* She was born in 1887 as Sonia Kalish, in a farmhouse somewhere in Poland when her mother was on her way to join her husband in America. The family established a kosher restaurant in Hartford, Connecticut. Sophie "discovered she could pick up dimes—sometimes a quarter—singing to the customers when she wasn't serving herring and gefilte fish." At age 16, she eloped with Louis Tuck, bore a son and soon ended the marriage. Leaving the boy in Hartford with her parents, she made her way to New York, singing in bars and nightclubs and then appearing in vaudeville. When her career took off in the 1930s, she entered the vast English-language market to share top billing with the likes of W.C. Fields, Eddie Cantor, Al Jolson, Judy Garland and Jimmy Durante. Feeding off the audience responses, she loved live theater and nightclub performances.[10]

Briche "Bessie" Kaufman was born in Tsarist Russia and emigrated with her family to America in 1879 when she was six. She had a few years of schooling until age 12 when she went to work in a Baltimore sweatshop. Besotted with the theater, at age 15, she ran away from home to join the Thomashefsky Players. At age 19 she married Boris Thomashefsky and they appeared together in Yiddish versions of the plays of Shakespeare, Ibsen, and Chekhov. After they separated, Bessie established the Bessie Thomashefsky People's Theater. She was "an actress who helped popularize Yiddish theater in America early in the [20th] century." During the 1920s she moved to performances in English. She retired from the stage in 1930 and settled to California. Bessie Thomashefsky died at 88 in 1962. She was buried alongside Boris, who had died 23 years earlier.[11]

The Yiddish theater in America was at its height in the 1920s. The cut off of Jewish immigrants from Eastern Europe, the acculturalization of those who came before 1915, the Great Depression, and the move to uptown Broadway theaters, rapidly reduced the size of Yiddish-language audiences. As Yiddish theaters shut down, the lead actors and actresses moved to English-language theater, radio, television and film. The once-great Yiddish theater of America now exists only in memory.

Entertainers

"The Eastern European Jews practically invented mainstream American entertainment."[12] "Although Jews constitute only 3 percent of the U.S. population, 80 percent of the nation's professional comedians are Jewish. Why such domination of American humor?" During the 1970s, psychologist Samuel S. Janus interviewed 76 Jewish humorists and concluded "that Jewish humor is born of depression and alienation from the general culture." For Jewish comedians "comedy is a defense mechanism to ward off the aggression and hostility of others.... Almost all had major traumas in early childhood. The late Totie Fields' mother died when Totie was five; Art Buchwald's mother died shortly after his birth. David Steinberg's older brother died young and the family never stopped mourning.... Most who reached prominence before the 1950s grew up in large, Yiddish-speaking immigrant families in Brooklyn or on Manhattan's Lower East Side. About 80 percent came from kosher homes and 90 percent later anglicized their names." The Jewish comedians "are bright, sensitive and relatively stable. But they are not happy guys."[13]

Among the many famous joke writers, script writers, composers, lyricists and entertainers of Russian-Jewish heritage in vaudeville, Broadway, radio, television and movies were the following: George Burns (Naphtali Birnbaum), The Three Stooges—Larry (Louis Fine), Moe (Moses Horwitz) and Curly (Jerome Horwitz)—Jack Benny (Benjamin Kubensky), Milton Berle (Mendel Berlinger), Red Buttons (Aaron Chwatt), Sid Caesar (Isaac Sidney Zisner), Rodney Dangerfield (Jacob Rodney Cohen), Zero Mostel (Samuel Joel Mostel), Don Rickles (Donald Jay Rickles), Phil Silver (Phillip Silver), George Jessel (George Albert Jessel), Mel Brooks (Melvin James Kaminsky), Mel Tolkin (Shmuel Tolchinsky), Karl Reiner, Alan King (Irwin Alan Kniberg), Woody Allen (Allan Stewart Konigsberg), Jerry Lewis (Joseph Levitch), Alan Arkin (Alan Wolf Arkin), Gene Wilder (Jerome Silberman) and Totie Fields (Sophie Feldman). (The Ritz Brothers and the hilarious Marx Brothers were of German-Jewish heritage.)

Seventeen-year-old Herschel Rabinowitz left his Russian shtetl and arrived at Ellis Island in January 1905. "Soon after, he began calling himself Harry, because he was now an American." With his brothers he bought a delicatessen on upper Madison Avenue. Lena Rips' family settled in Jersey City, where her immigrant parents helped establish Congregation Mount Sinai and the Hebrew Home for Orphans and Aged. Harry and Lena married in 1911 and moved into an apartment in Manhattan near his business. Harry next went into the garment business making corsets. Their son Jerome Wilson Rabinowitz was born 1918 in the Jewish Maternity Hospital, Lower East Side, where the food was kosher and the doctors spoke Yiddish. They called him Jerry. His middle name was chosen in honor of Woodrow Wilson, president of the United States at that time. "The family was on its way up.... Music was part of the family life for the Rabinowitzes: there was always a piano and stacks of classical phonograph records, and even before he could read Jerry could pick out his favorite Chopin recordings and put them on the gramophone."[14]

Jerry dropped out of New York University, joined a modern dance troupe, and took the surname Robbins. In 1940, he was a soloist for the American Ballet Company. Turning to choreography, he arranged the dances for *On the Town* (1944), *Call Me Madam*, *The King and I*, *West Side Story* (1957), *Gypsy* (1959) *Funny Girl* (1964) and *Fiddler on the Roof* (1964). Jerry Robbins was among America's leading dancers, choreographers and producers, working for the stage, cinema and television. He died in 1998, age 79.

Elieza "Lippa" and his wife Hadassah "Dorah" Birnbaum had an arranged marriage in a Polish shtetl. They had five children before they arrived in New York, where seven more children were born. Lippa and Dorah were strictly Orthodox. Lippa aspired to be a cantor in a synagogue, but supported his large family working in a sweatshop and later supervising kosher foods. Their ninth child Naftali, called "Natty" was born in 1896. The large family crammed into three squalid rooms of third-floor apartment of a tenement on Rivington Street in the Lower East Side of New York. Tragedy struck in 1903, when 47-year-old Lippa died, leaving the family destitute. Natty dropped out of Public School 22 without completing the fourth grade. He could hardly read or write. "Young Natty tried to make money in any way he could. He sold papers. He shined shoes" and he stole from pushcarts. He found a job at Rosenzweig's candy store "for five cents a day making syrup for ice cream sodas."[15]

Learning that people would tip better when the service was accompanied by a song, Natty formed a harmony group with his brother Heshy, Mortzy Weinberger and Moishe Friedman. Their singing caught the attention of Lou Feingold, a letter carrier and aspiring impresario.

> We were all about the same age, six and seven, and when we were bored making syrup, we used to practice singing harmony in the basement. One day our letter carrier came down to the basement. His name was Lou Farley. Feingold was his real name, but he changed it to Farley. He wanted the whole world to sing harmony. He came down to the basement once to deliver a letter and heard the four of us kids singing harmony. He liked our style, so we sang a couple more songs for him. Then we looked up at the head of the stairs and saw three or four people listening to us and smiling. In fact, they threw down a couple of pennies. So, I said to the kids I was working with: no more chocolate syrup. It's show business from now on. We called ourselves the Pee-Wee Quartet. We started out singing on ferryboats, in saloons, in brothels, and on street corners. We'd put our hats down for donations.[16]

George Burns in 1961. Getting his start selling newspapers and shining shoes, he had a 75-year career as a comedian and singer, spanning vaudeville, radio, movies and television. He died in 1996, at age 100.

Changing his name to George Burns, he began a career as singer, comedian and actor that spanned vaudeville, radio, the movies and television, usually with a cigar in his mouth or in his hand. He acted with his wife in the George Burns and Gracie Allen Show and starred in *The Sunshine Boys* (1975) and *Oh, God* (1977). George Burns died at age 100 years old in 1996.

Jerry Lewis was a "comedian, actor and filmmaker who was adored by many, disdained by others, but unquestionably a defining figure of American entertainment in the 20th century. [He] knew success in movies, on television, in nightclubs, on the Broadway stage and in the university lecture hall. His career had its ups and downs, but when it was at its zenith there were few stars any bigger. And he got there remarkably quickly." He was born in 1926 in a Jewish neighborhood of Newark, New Jersey, much like New York's Lower East Side "with pushcarts, trolleys, peddlers, and urchins, ethnic Jewish stores and storefront synagogues."[17] He was the son of Daniel, a song-and-dance man and Rae, a pianist, who performed in vaudeville and the Borscht Belt circuit. Jerry craved the attention the stage offered him. Over 40 years, Jerry Lewis raised $2 billion for the Muscular Dystrophy Foundation.[18]

Isaac Sidney Zisner was born in 1922 in Yonkers where his parents operated a luncheonette. As Sid Caesar he gained fame with two hit radio shows: *Your Show of Shows* (1950–1954) and *Caesar's Hour* (1957–1960). To keep the laughs flowing, he employed talented writers included Mel Brooks, Woody Allen, Neil Simon, Carl Reiner, Mel Tolkin, Joseph Stein, Michael Stewart, Murry Joseph Schisgal and Larry Gelbart. They often collaborated on other ventures for the stage, movies and television. Mel Brooks, born in 1926, went on to create *The Producers* with Zero Mostel and Gene Wilder (1968), and *Blazing Saddles* (1974) with Gene Wilder—a film he described as "A Jewish Western with a Black Hero."[19] Woody Allen wrote and starred in many movies, including *Manhattan* (1979), *Hannah and Her Sister* (1986), *Crimes and Misdemeanors* (1981), *The Purple Rose of Cairo* (1985), *Radio Days* (1987) and *Midnight in Paris* (2011). Larry Gelbart developed the smash television show *M*A*S*H* and wrote the screenplay for *Tootsie*. Joseph Stein wrote the book, Jerry Bock the music, Sheldon Mayer Harrick wrote the lyrics for *Fiddler on the Roof*. Michael Stewart wrote the lyrics for the musicals *Bye Bye Birdie* (1960), *Hello! Dolly* (1964) and *42nd Street* (1980). Jerry Herman wrote the lyrics for *Mame* (1966) and *La Cage aux Folles* (1984).

Aaron Chwatt was born in 1919 in Manhattan to a Jewish immigrant family. His acting career began while working as a bellhop in the Bronx where his Red hair and shiny bellhop Buttons gave his stage name. His career went on to the hotels of the Borscht Belt to Broadway and, in 1952 his own *The Red Buttons Show* on television. Mendel Berlinger began life in 1905 in a fifth-floor walk-up apartment on W. 118th Street, Harlem, then a Jewish immigrant neighborhood. As Milton Berle he acted alongside Douglas Fairbanks, Charlie Chaplin and other stars of the silent movie era. He had a decades long career on the state, movies and television, where he hosted the *Milton Berle Show*.

Harry Houdini was one of the great stunt performers of the early 20th century.

Born Erich Weisz in Eastern Europe in 1874, the son of rabbi Mayer Samuel and Cecelia Weisz who settled in Appleton, Wisconsin. Houdini's acts included escaping from chains, ropes or straitjackets, often underwater or buried alive.

John Garfield, Kirk Douglas, Peter Falk, James Caan, Tony Curtis, Alan Arkin, Eli Wallach, Richard Dreyfus and Dustin Hoffman; and Sylvia Sidney, Lauren Bacall and Barbra Streisand, among many others, are descendants of Eastern European Jewish immigrants, and went on to become Hollywood, stage and television stars. For most, the stage was their first love but the big money was in film, leading to accusations of "selling out" to Hollywood. Coming from ghetto backgrounds, a fair number had leftist values. There are many other Jewish-American achievement stories as lyricists, composers, screenwriters, actors, producers and managers.

The Red Scare of the 1940s to 1950s, led by Senator Joseph McCarthy and his Un-American Activities Committee, exacted a fearful price on those who refused to testify. Alvah Cecil Bessie, Herbert Joseph Biberman, John Howard Lawson (originally Levy), Albert Maltz and Samuel Ornitz were members of the Hollywood Ten who were imprisoned and then blacklisted. During the Red Scare, some 300 writers, musicians and actors were blacklisted from employment in Hollywood. Among them were such eminent Americans as Aaron Copland, Lillian Hellmann, Arthur Miller, Dorothy Parker (born Dorothy Rothschild), and Orson Welles and Samuel Dashiell Hammett.

Here are snippets of the careers of prominent actors, screenwriters, and directors of Russian Jewish heritage, drawn from the obituary pages of *The New York Times*, and from biographies and autobiographies.

"His husky physique, shock of dark hair and truculent manner made John Garfield a natural choice for the gangster, criminal of grown-up Dead-End Kid." He was born 1913 Jacob Julius Garfinkle in the Lower East Side, New York City. He said: "My father was a presser in a clothing factory during the week, but a cantor on weekends and holidays." His mother died when he was seven and he was expelled from several schools for unruly behavior. He joined gangs and got into street fights. He settled down at Public School 45, a special school for problem children, where he learned boxing and took up oratory and dramatics. He developed acting skills. "I get my kicks from Broadway," yet in 1938 he signed a contract with Warner Brothers. He received Academy Award nominations for his performance in *Four Daughters* (1938) and *Body and Soul* (1947). Notwithstanding his Hollywood success, he returned often for brief appearances on the Broadway stage. John Garfield starred in Clifford Odets' play *Golden Boy* in 1952. He died at age 39 of a heart disorder.[20]

"Eli Herschel Wallach was one of his generation's most prominent and prolific character actors in film, onstage and on television for more than 60 years." Wallach was born in 1915, his immigrant parents owned a candy store. Wallach was "one of the few Jewish children in his mostly Italian-American neighborhood in Brooklyn, made both his stage and screen breakthroughs playing Italians.... The versatile Mr. Wallach appeared in scores of roles, often with his wife, Anne Jackson. No matter the part, he always seemed at ease and in control, whether playing a Mexican bandit in the 1960 western *The Magnificent Seven*, a bumbling clerk in Ionesco's allegorical play *Rhinoceros*, a henpecked French general in Jean Anouilh's *Waltz of the Toreadors*, Clark Gable's sidekick in *The Misfits* or a Mafia don in *The Godfather: Part III*.... His first love was the stage. Mr. Wallach and Ms. Jackson became one of the best-known acting couples in the American theater."[21]

Tony Curtis "drew on his startlingly good looks. With his dark, curly hair worn in a sculptural style later imitated by Elvis Presley and his plucked eyebrows framing pale blue eyes and full lips, Mr. Curtis embodied a new kind of feminized male beauty that came into vogue in the early '50s." Born 1925 as Bernard Schwartz, he was the product of a "Dickensian childhood in the Bronx." His parents were Eastern European Jewish immigrants. His father "Emanuel operated a tailor shop in a poor neighborhood, and the family occupied cramped quarters behind the store; the parents in one room and little Bernard sharing another with his two brothers, Julius and Robert." Mother Helen Schwartz and brother Robert suffered from schizophrenia.

"In 1933, at the height of the Depression, his parents found they could not properly provide for their children, and Bernard and Julius were placed in a state institution. (Julius was hit by a truck and killed in 1938.) Returning to his old neighborhood, Bernard became caught up in gang warfare and the target of anti–Semitic hostility. He learned to dodge the stones and fists to protect his face, which he realized even then would be his ticket to greater things." After he completed public school in the Lower East Side, Bernard began acting in the Borscht Belt theaters. Moving to Hollywood he starred as an escaped convict in Stanley Kramer's *The Defiant Ones*. His great success came in comedies, in particular Billy Wilder's *Some Like It Hot*, co-starring Jack Lemmon and Marilyn Monroe (1959). In 1951 he married Janet Leigh. "Highly photogenic, the couple became a favorite of the fan magazines." This was the first of Curtis's six marriages.[22]

James Edmund Caan was born 1940 in the Bronx, the son of a kosher meat butcher. He took up acting while a student at Hofstra University, Hempstead, New York. He portrayed the "quick-tempered, skirt-chasing" Sonny Corleone in the blockbuster movie *Godfather* (1972). Acting the role of a violent hoodlum, driven by family loyalty, Caan "had all the right Italian gestures as Sonny, [yet] he was the son of Jewish parents." Caan said: "They called me a wise guy. I won Italian of the Year twice in New York, and I'm Jewish, not Italian." His performance won an Oscar for Best Supporting Actor. During 1975, he acted with Barbra Streisand in *Funny Girl*. James Caan died in 2022.[23]

Peter Falk "had a wide-ranging career in comedy and drama, in the movies and onstage, before and during the three and a half decades in which he portrayed the unkempt but canny lead on Columbo. [He] marshaled actorly tics, prop room appurtenances and his own physical idiosyncrasies to personify Columbo, one of the most famous and beloved fictional detectives in television history.... Falk had a glass eye, resulting from an operation to remove a cancerous tumor when he was 3.

The prosthesis gave all his characters a peculiar, almost quizzical squint. And he had a mild speech impediment that gave his L's a breathy quality, a sound that emanated from the back of his throat." Peter Falk was born 1927 in New York to an immigrant Jewish couple who owned a clothing store. He died in 2011.[24]

Lee Cobb was born in 1911 in the Bronx into a Russian-Jewish family as Leo Jacoby. His father Benjamin was a compositor of the Yiddish-language newspaper *The Forward*. Trained as a Method actor he starred in Clifford Odets' *Waiting for Lefty* and *Golden Boy* (1935), he originated the role of Willy Lowman in Arthur Miller's 1949 drama *Death of a Salesman*. He had a long career in Hollywood, acting in 80 films including *On the Waterfront* with Marlon Brando, screenplay by Budd Schulberg (1954), and *12 Angry Men* (1957). In 1969 Lee Cobb returned to the New York stage in Shakespeare's *King Lear*.[25]

Leonard Nimoy was "the sonorous, gaunt-faced actor who won a worshipful global following as Mr. Spock, the resolutely logical human-alien first officer of the *Starship Enterprise* in the television and movie juggernaut *Star Trek*.... His religious upbringing also influenced the characterization of Spock. The character's split-fingered salute had been his idea: He based it on the kohanic blessing, a manual approximation of the Hebrew letter *shin*, which is the first letter in Shaddai, one of the Hebrew names for God.... His zeal to entertain and enlighten reached beyond *Star Trek* and crossed genres. He had a starring role in the dramatic television series *Mission: Impossible* and frequently performed onstage, notably as Tevye in *Fiddler on the Roof*. His poetry was voluminous, and he published books of his photography." Leonard Simon Nimoy was born in Boston in 1931, "the second son of Max and Dora Nimoy, Ukrainian immigrants and Orthodox Jews. His father worked as a barber." More than most Jewish actors, Leonard Nimoy embraced Jewish life. His 1991 movie *Never Forget* is based on the Holocaust. His 2002 book *Shekhina* is "devoted to photography with a Jewish theme."[26]

"I grew up in Brooklyn," wrote Alan Arkin in his 2011 autobiography. "By age seven or eight, I was completely obsessed with performing. Theater, movies, music—I was obsessed with all of them."[27] "Alan Arkin, who won a Tony Award for his first lead role on Broadway, received an Academy Award nomination for his first feature film, and went on to have a long and diverse career as a character actor who specialized in comedy but was equally adept at drama." Alan Wolf Arkin was born 1934, in Brooklyn to Jewish immigrants, "David Arkin, a painter and writer, and Beatrice (Wortis) Arkin, a teacher whom he later remembered as 'a tough old Depression-style lefty.'"[28]

Dustin Hoffman was born 1935 in Los Angeles. His parents were of Russian-Jewish background but Dustin's upbringing was non-religious. "I don't have any memory of celebrating holidays growing up that were Jewish." His first career choice was to be a concert pianist. Instead, he launched his movie career with the highly-successful *The Graduate* (1967), followed by *Midnight Cowboy* (1969), *Papillon* (1973), *All the President's Men* (1976), *Kramer vs. Kramer* (1979), *Tootsie* (1982) and many other films, winning him two Academy Awards and other honors.

Richard Dreyfuss, born 1947, began his acting career in the arts center of Temple Emanuel of Beverly Hills. He gained stardom for his performance in *Jaws* (1975), followed by *Close Encounters of the Third Kind* (1977), and *Goodbye Girl* (1977) for which he received the Academy Award for Best Actor.

Jewish-born Elisabeth Bergner, Luise Rainer, Hedy Lamarr, Sylvia Sidney and Lillian Roth were leading Broadway and Hollywood actresses during the period between the two world wars. Bergner, Rainer and Lamarr began their careers in Germany, and fled to the United States with the rise of Nazism. Elisabeth Bergner starred in *All About Eve*. Luise Rainer received Oscar awards for her roles in *The Great Ziegfeld* (1936) and *The Good Earth* (1937). Sylvia Sidney was born in the Bronx as Sophie Kosow. Her Russian-Jewish father was a clothing salesman. During her long movie career, Sidney appeared with Gary Cooper, Spencer Tracy, Henry Fonda, Fredric March, Gary Cooper and George Raft. Among her many films were *City Lights* (1930), Alfred Hitchcock's *Sabotage* (1936) and Fritz Lang's *Fury* (1936).

Lillian Roth was born in 1910 in Boston the daughter of Arthur and Katie Rothstein, both Russian-Jewish born. At age 6, Lillian was "dragged into show business" by her star-struck parents. She acted in vaudeville and the Broadway stage before heading for Hollywood at age 18 years. She starred in *The Love Parade* (1927) with Maurice Chevalier, and in 1930 in the Marx Brothers' movie *Animal Crackers*. Her 1954 autobiography *I'll Cry Tomorrow*, details her life in Boston, her tragic love life, depression and addiction to alcohol. Her life story was made into a 1956 movie starring Susan Haywood.[29]

Lauren Bacall was "the actress whose provocative glamour elevated her to stardom in Hollywood's golden age and whose lasting mystique put her on a plateau in American culture that few stars reach.... Lauren Bacall was born Betty Joan Perske in the Bronx in 1924, the daughter of William and Natalie Perske, Jewish immigrants from Poland and Romania. Her parents were divorced when she was 6 years old, and her mother moved to Manhattan and adopted the second half of her maiden name, Weinstein-Bacall." In her autobiography, Lauren Bacall tells that after landing at Ellis Island, grandfather Max "borrowed enough money from United

Bronx-born Sylvia Sidney had a long career on the stage and in film (*Argentinean Magazine*, January 1, 1932).

Hebrew Charities to live in a ghastly apartment and set up a pushcart with all sorts of household goods for sale." Soon, the family had enough money to move to the Bronx and purchase a candy store. Lauren resented "the purity of a Jewish upbringing—the restrictions are carried through life being a 'nice Jewish girl'—what a burden. You had it drummed into you by your mother, grandmother, uncles, that nice Jewish girls didn't smoke—weren't fast—didn't chase a boy, ever—'if he wants to see you, he'll call: if not, forget him.'"[30] Bacall's movie career began in 1944 in *To Have and Not Have* opposite Humphrey Bogart. When they married, Bogart was 45 and Bacall 20. She felt "'totally Jewish and always would' and that it was Bogart who thought the children should be christened in an Episcopal church because 'with discrimination still rampant in the world, it would give them one less hurdle to jump in life's Olympics.'" Other film successes were *Key Largo* with Humphrey Bogart and Edward G. Robinson (1948), and *Designing Woman* with Gregory Peck (1957).[31]

The Streisand grandparents were from Galicia. Barbra Streisand's father Emanuel taught English in New York schools while working towards his doctorate at City College. A few months after Barbra Streisand's birth in 1942, Emanuel "died of respiratory failure brought on by a morphine injection intended to alleviate an epileptic seizure." Her mother, Diane, worked as a secretary. "Overwhelmed with debt, she had taken her children and moved into her parents' small apartment in Williamsburg. For the next eight years, Barbra's grandparents' living room was her bedroom. Barbra and her mother shared a bed, while her brother slept in a rollaway cot next to them." The family was not religious. "Barbra's mother rarely lit candles or kept kosher." At her grandparent's insistence Barbra attended the Brooklyn Orthodox Yeshiva, where "she had learned to read Hebrew, even though she didn't understand a word of what she was saying."[32] She attended Public School 89 and Erasmus Hall High School, with Neil Diamond as a fellow student. Her great desire was to get out of Brooklyn and move to Manhattan as a singer and actress. Despite setbacks she was determined to become a star. She sang in nightclubs and on the Broadway stage and was soon headed to Hollywood. Her movie breakthrough was in *Funny Girl,* earning her an Oscar for the Best Actress. In 1983, she starred as a yeshiva boy in the film *Yentl,* based on a short story by Isaac Bashevis Singer. Barbra Streisand is one of the world's best-selling recording artists with her distinctive voice in the mezzo-soprano vocal range.

Hollywood Moguls

Marcus Loew, Adolph Zukor, Samuel Goldwyn, Lewis Selznick, William Fox, Louis B. Mayer, and the Warner Brothers Harry, Albert, Sam and Jack, were all of Eastern European Jewish heritage. As young children they accompanied their Yiddish-speaking parents to the New World. Growing up in the Lower East Side, they helped support their poor families by blacking shoes and selling newspapers. Despite the lack of a formal education, they soon learned English, established successful businesses as clothing manufacturers, furriers or scrap metal dealers. Great risk takers, they entered the nascent movie business, built studios and chains of movie theaters, and established the star system. Adolph Zukor built the Paramount movie studio, Louis B. Mayer and Samuel Goldwyn built Metro Goldwyn Mayer, 20th Century–Fox was named for William Fox, and Jack Warner and his brothers established Warner Brothers. Jack Cohn was a founder of Columbia Pictures. These men shaped American movie-making for much of the 20th century.

In his 1988 book *An Empire of Their Own*, Neal Gabler concludes that "through their movies, the Jewish patriarchs painted an idealized portrait of an American society to which they were denied access. For Jews, one of the lures of the industry was simply that it let them in.... They had come out of hard times and oppression in Eastern Europe, and also shared a heritage of strong mothers and weak fathers. It became the common drive among these men to break with the past."[33] "There were no social barriers in a business as new and faintly disreputable as the movies were in the early years of this century. There were none of the impediments imposed by loftier professions and more firmly entrenched businesses to keep Jews and other undesirables out." The Jewish movie moguls so gloried in the American dream as to "create a new country—an empire of their own, so to speak ... an America where fathers were strong, families stable, people attractive, resilient, resourceful, and decent."[34]

The founders of the Hollywood studios largely hid their Jewish identity. Ben Hecht said in 1954 of the Jewish movie moguls: "Hollywood Jews ... are eager to support Jewish orphanages and hospitals.... This eagerness is the product of guilt that blossoms in the soul of the immigrant Jew who turns into an American nabob. He finds it convenient to forget his Jewishness in the high-class world into which he has vaulted. He is thus eager to prove his Jewishness secretly by donations to Jews in distress. He will support a synagogue with large gifts for 30 years without ever entering it. The closest he comes to this secret Judaism to which he stubbornly lays claim is observing a few religious principles, such as not going to the races on Jewish holidays, or arranging for a rabbi to officiate (in English) at his funeral."[35]

Adolph Zukor was born in an Eastern European shtetl. "My father had built a small store with his own hands. The store he operated with the help of my mother, for it was necessary also for him to cultivate nearby fields to gain a living for us. One day he lifted a heavy box or barrel and broke a vein or vessel in his body. Home remedies failed and finally a doctor was called. Blood poisoning had set in and he soon died. My mother, who was well educated, being the daughter of a rabbi, was left to fend for my brother Arthur, three years old, and for me, one year old. She was delicate and could not hope to run the store and till the fields.... I knew that she had never recovered from the loss of my father. She died when I was eight."

The orphan boy went to work as an apprentice in a store. "All the while, letters were coming to the village from emigrants to America. These, speaking glowingly of freedom and opportunities, were passed from hand to hand." At age 15, Zukor left for America. In New York he found work knitting furs, earning $4 a week. In 1893 he left New York for the boom city of Chicago, then celebrating its World's Columbian

Exposition. Zukor opened a fur shop in Chicago and his timing coincided with interest in this new fashion accessory. Hiring 25 workers, he was soon "swimming in money," having saved $8,000 (about $280,000 in 2024). In 1902, the ambitious 29-year-old Zukor "first began to think about going into the motion picture business."[36] Adolph Zukor formed the Paramount Pictures Corporation and signed on Mary Pickford, Douglas Fairbanks, Gloria Swanson and Rudolph Valentino. He built a nationwide chain of 2,000 movie theaters that thrived until the Great Depression.

Lazar Meir was born 1884 in a shtetl near Minsk in the Russian Empire. His parents Jacob and Sarah were Yiddish-speaking and religious. Coming to Saint John, New Brunswick, in 1886, Jacob eked out a living, collecting and selling scrap metal. At age 12, Lazar dropped out of school and joined his father as J. Meir & Son, junk dealers. Father and son roamed the streets collecting discarded locks, nails, copper trimmings, and other scrap metal. Young Lazar learned to dive into the ocean, and hold his breath long enough to salvage bits of metal from ship wrecks, and drag them to shore. Moving to Boston he set up as a scrap metal dealer. Changing his name to Louis B. Mayer, he entered the nascent movie business.[37] At the height of his career, Mayer "was the czar of the Hollywood movie producers. He was the leading practitioner of the system of building films around stars. He made Greta Garbo famous" and boosted the careers of Norma Shearer, Joan Crawford, Hedy Lamarr, Robert Crawford, Clark Gable and Robert Taylor. "He liked glittering scenes and dramatic stories that could be popular as sheer mass entertainment."[38]

Louis B. Mayer joined fellow Russian-born Jew Samuel Goldwyn (born Samuel Gelbfisz) to form Metro-Goldwyn-Mayer (MGM), Hollywood's most prestigious movie company. Goldwyn was born 1882 in Warsaw. Both his parents died when he was still a boy. At age 12 he left Poland and landed up in Gloversville, New York, sweeping floors in a glove factory. By age 19 he began a career as a highly successful glove salesman and was soon caught in the allure of the movies. Among the 70 movies he produced were such gems as *The Best Years of Their Lives, The Pride of the Yankees, Dodsworth, Guys and Dolls* and *Porgy and Bess*. Despite reaching a high status in the film industry, his elegantly tailored suits and his large mansion, he was mocked for his Yiddish-inflected Goldwynisms, such as "Include me out," "An oral agreement is not worth the paper it is written on," and "A man who goes to a psychiatrist should have his head read."

Louis B. Mayer's son-in-law David O. Selznick led RKO Radio Pictures and produced film versions of *David Copperfield, The Tale of Two Cities* and *Anna Karenina* (all in 1935). Selznick's *Gone with the Wind* (1939) and *Rebecca* (1940) each earned an Academy Award for best picture.

Movie Directors

A sizeable number of the leading American movie directors were of eastern European Jewish descent. Between them they directed many of the great American movies. Sidney Lumet "preferred the streets of New York to the back lots of Hollywood.... In his first film, *12 Angry Men* (1957), he took his cameras into a jury room where the pressure mounted as one tenacious and courageous juror, played by Henry Fonda, slowly convinced the others that the defendant on trial for murder was, in fact, innocent." Lumet also directed the movie classics *A View from the Bridge* (1962), *The Pawnbroker* about a Holocaust survivor (1964), Agatha Christie's *Murder on the Orient Express* (1974), *Serpico* about police corruption (1973), *Equus* (1977), and *The Verdict* with a script by David Mamet (1982). Sidney Lumet was born in 1924, the son of Baruch and Eugenia Wermus, stars of the Yiddish theater.[39]

Billy Wilder was born in 1906 as Samuel Wilder in a Polish shtetl. In the 1920s he made his way to Berlin to become a leading director in the German film industry. With the rise of Hitler, he moved to the United States to become one of Hollywood's most gifted and versatile film makers, directing such memorable films as *Double Indemnity* (1944), *Sunset Boulevard* (1950), *Stalag 17* (1953), *The Seven Year Itch* (1955), *Witness for the Prosecution* (1957), *Some Like It Hot* (1959), *The Apartment* (1960) and *Irma la Douce* (1963).

Ernst Lubitsch was born 1882 in Germany of Russian-Jewish parents. He did not follow his father into the garment business but instead became a film maker. In 1922, he came to Hollywood where he directed Greta Garbo in *Ninotchka* (1939), *A Shop Around the Corner* starring Maureen Sullivan and James Stewart (1940) and *Heaven Can Wait* (1943). Lubitsch "began directing in the silent era but transitioned with apparent ease into talkies. [His] movies still sparkle with urbanity and sly wit."[40] Ernst Lubitsch died in 1947 following a heart attack.

Stanley Earl Kramer was born 1913 in New York City. Abandoned by his father, he grew up in a dingy apartment in New York's Hell's Kitchen. He found his way to Hollywood as producer of the classic Western movie *High Noon* (1952) and *The Caine Mutiny* (1954), and then he directed many movies including *The Deviant Ones*, starring Tony Curtis and Sidney Poitier (1958), *Inherit the Wind* (1960), *Judgment at Nuremberg* (1961), and *Guess Who's Coming for Dinner* starring Sidney Poitier, Katherine Hepburn and Spencer Tracy (1967).[41]

Alan Jay Pakula was born 1928 in the Bronx, the son of a Polish-Jewish immigrants. He was the "director of many psychologically penetrating and celebrated films," including *To Kill a Mockingbird* starring Gregory Peck (1962), *Klute* with Jane Fonda (1971), *All the President's Men* (1976) and *Sophie's Choice* with Meryl Streep (1982). Several of the stars in Pakula movies won Oscars for best actor.[42]

Arthur Hiller Penn directed Warren Beatty in the 1967 hit movie *Bonnie & Clyde,* followed by *Alice's Restaurant* (1969) and *Little Big Man* (1970). In the 1990s, Penn was the producer of the television crime series *Law & Order.* Born 1922, Penn was the son of Sonia (Greenberg), a nurse and Chaim Michelsohn, a watchmaker, who left their Russian shtetl to settle in Philadelphia. To better fit into America, Chaim changed his name to Harry William Penn.

William David Friedkin (1935–2023) was the director of the 1971 film noir *The French Connection* about two narcotic detectives in hot pursuit of a suave French heroin smuggler. The film received Academy Awards for best picture, best actor (Gene Hackman), best film editing, best adapted screenplay and best cinematography. Friedkin's "parents and grandparents came from Kiev in the Ukraine, during a pogrom in the first years of the 20th century. [They] escaped to America in steerage. They spoke no English and were tradespeople and shop workers. Their apartments smelled of gefilte fish, cabbage, smoked herring and stale clothes.... My father owned nothing and made 50 dollars a week, until he was laid off. Then we went on welfare in a one-room apartment with a kitchenette, one toilet, a small closet, and a bed that came out of the wall, next to a cot for me, on North Sheridan Road in uptown Chicago."[43]

Stanley Kubrick "directed coldly brilliant films that explored humanity's baser instincts with great visual flair and often savage wit." Kubrick directed *Paths of Glory* (1957), *Spartacus* (1960), *Lolita* (1962), *Dr. Strangelove* with Peter Sellers (1964), *2001: A Space Odyssey* (1968), and *A Clockwork Orange* (1971).[44] Born 1928 in the Bronx, Stanley Kubrick was the grandson of Hersh Kubrick who arrived at Ellis Island in 1899.

Woody Allen (born Allan Stuart Konigsberg) began his career in the 1950s as a comic writer. His long list of films includes such delights as *Annie Hall* (1977), *Manhattan* (1979), *Hannah and Her Sisters* (1986), *Radio Days* (1987), *Crimes and Misdemeanors* (1989) and *Midnight in Paris* (2011). Mel Brooks (born Melvin Kaminsky) was a comic writer for Sid Caesar's *Your Show of Shows*. Brooks directed *The Producers* (1967), *Blazing Saddles* (1974) and *High Anxiety* (1977). Steven Spielberg's grandparents came to the United States from Tsarist Russia. Among Spielberg's many films are *Jaws* (1975), *E.T. the Extra-Terrestrial* (1982), *The Color Purple* (1985), *Jurassic Park* (1993) and the World War II epic *Saving Sergeant Ryan* (1998). His *Schindler's List* (1993) won seven Academy Awards, including best director.

Bernard Herrmann (born 1911 in New York as Maximilian Herman) came from a family of Russian-born Jews. He wrote the musical scores for many movies including Alfred Hitchcock's *The Man Who Knew Too Much*, *Vertigo*, *North by Northwest*, *Psycho* and *The Birds* as well as the film score of Orson Welles' *Citizen Kane*. Hermann's last film score was for Martin Scorsese's *Taxi Driver* (1976).

With the abundance of Jewish movie producers, directors, actors and screenwriters, Hollywood produced only a small number of Jewish-themed movies. Among them were *Gentleman's Agreement* (1947) with Gregory Peck and John Garfield, *The Pawnbroker* (1964) directed by Sidney Lumet, *Funny Girl* (1968) with Barbra Streisand and directed by William Wyler, *Fiddler on the Roof* (1971) starring Chaim Topol, *Hester Street* (1975) directed by Joan Micklin Silver, *The Chosen* (1981) starring Kirk Douglas, *Crossing Delancey* (1988) directed by Joan Micklin Silver, daughter-in-law of Rabbi Abba Hillel Silver, and the haunting *Schindler's List* (1993) directed by Steven Spielberg.

Playwrights, and Theater Directors and Producers

Arthur Miller, Neil Simon, and David Mamet are listed with Tennessee Williams, Eugene O'Neill, Thornton Wilder and August Wilson, as America's greatest playwrights. Ben Hecht, Paddy Chayefsky and Clifford Odets occupy honored places among the second-tier playwrights. Lillian Hellman was of German-Jewish heritage.

Ben Hecht was born in 1894 to Russian-Jewish immigrants on the Lower East Side of New York. The family moved to Racine, Wisconsin. His uneducated father "purchased for Ben's bar mitzvah gift, four crates of books with Shakespeare, Dickens, Twain, great orations and a multi-volumed world history." Hecht moved to Chicago and found abundant material as a newspaper crime reporter during the Prohibition era. He "chronicled high life and low life in Chicago, New York, and Hollywood in novels, short stories, plays and a stream of memoirs. [To get at these stories] he haunted the streets, whore houses, police stations, courtrooms, theater stages, jails, saloons, fires, murders, riots, banquet halls and bookshops." He gained a great success with his 1930 play *The Front Page*, later made into a successful film, starring Jack Lemmon and Walter Matthau. Ben Hecht was a sought-after Hollywood script writer.[45]

Clifford Odets was born Clifford Gorodetsky in 1906 in Philadelphia. His father, a printer, moved the family to the Bronx in New York. Clifford left school early, determined to become a writer and playwright. His 1935 Broadway play *Waiting for Lefty* earned him the accolade of "the most promising young American playwright." It was followed by *Awake and Sing* "about a Bronx Jewish family whose homelife is volcanic."[46]

Arthur Miller's plays "exposed the flaws in the fabric of the American dream." His play *Death of a Salesman*, reflecting on the Great Depression, opened on Broadway in 1949 when Miller was 33. "It won the triple crown of theatrical artistry that year: the Pulitzer Prize, the New York Drama Critics' Circle Award and the Tony." *The Crucible*, about the Salem witch-trials, was "inspired by his virulent hatred of McCarthyism." His 17 plays "often reflected or reinterpreted the stormy and very public elements of his own life—including a brief and rocky marriage to Marilyn Monroe, and his staunch refusal to cooperate with the red-baiting House Un-American Activities Committee."[47]

In his autobiography Arthur Miller tells how the family came from Poland to America. His grandparents and their six older children came ahead, leaving behind the youngest child, Isadore, with relatives in Poland. When Isadore was seven a ticket arrived for the "lone-boy to cross Europe and the ocean.... He was put on a train with a tag around his neck asking that he be delivered to a certain ship sailing for New York on a certain day." Young Isadore spent three weeks in steerage, "the bottom deck where the light of day never shone." His parents were too busy to welcome him at Castle Garden and sent Isadore's brother to bring him to the Lower East Side "tenement where, in two rooms, the eight of them lived and worked, sewing the great long many-buttoned coats that were then in fashion." Isadore was allowed to attend school "for several months and was then removed to take his place at one of the sewing machines in the apartment, never to see the inside of a school again. By the time he was 12 he himself was employing two other boys to sew sleeves alongside him in some basement workshop, and at age 16, he was sent off as a salesman by his father Samuel." Arthur Miller's immigrant father Isadore never learned to read or write English, yet he rapidly moved from the sweatshops to owning a large coat manufacturing business in the Seventh Avenue garment district.[48]

"Arthur Miller was born on West 110th Street in Manhattan on Oct. 17, 1915, to Augusta and Isadore Miller." His father was a coat manufacturer and so prosperous that he rode in a chauffeur-driven car from the family apartment overlooking the northern edge of Central Park to the Seventh Avenue garment district.... The Depression changed everything for the family.... The crash meant the collapse of the coat business and a move from the apartment overlooking Central Park to considerably reduced circumstances in the Flatbush section of Brooklyn, where the teenage Arthur worked as a bakery delivery boy.[49] "My Brooklyn," wrote Miller, "consisted of Jews, some Italians, a few Irish."[50]

Neil Simon is "the playwright whose name was synonymous with Broadway comedy and commercial success in the theater for decades, and who helped redefine popular American humor with an emphasis on the frictions of urban living and the agonizing conflicts of family intimacy." He began his career writing jokes for Sid Caesar's *Your Show of Shows.* "Beginning with the breakthrough hits *Barefoot in the Park* (1963), and *The Odd Couple* (1965) and continuing with popular successes like *Plaza Suite* (1968), *The Prisoner of Second Avenue* (1971) and *The Sunshine Boys* (1974), Mr. Simon ruled Broadway." In the 1980s, "Simon wrote the semi-autobiographical trilogy, *Brighton Beach Memoirs* (1983), *Biloxi Blues* (1985) and *Broadway Bound* (1986). These comedy-dramas were admired for the way they explored the tangle of love, anger and desperation that bound together—and drove apart—a Jewish working-class family."[51] Marvin Neil Simon was born 1927 in the Bronx, New York. His parents had a tempestuous marriage, worsened by the financial chaos of the Great Depression.[52]

David Alan Mamet's grandparents were Russian-Jewish immigrants. He was born 1947, into a professional family living in Chicago. His father Bernard, a lawyer, and mother Lenore, a school teacher, divorced when David was 11 years. His success as a playwright came with *Glengarry Glen Ross* (1984), followed by *American Buffalo*, that premiered in the Goodman Theater, Chicago (1985). He wrote the screenplay for the heist movie *House of Games* (1987).

Paddy Chayefsky won three Oscar Awards. "His most famous play was *Marty*, the story of a fat, unhappy butcher. First done on television, it became a movie and won an Oscar, starring Ernest Borgnine, in 1955. His second Academy Award, starring George C. Scott and Diana Riggs, came in 1971 for *The Hospital* and his last in 1976 for the screenplay of *Network*, starring Faye Dunaway and Peter Finch, a grim satire on the high-pressure world of New York City television.... The playwright's real first name was Sidney. His parents, Russian-Jewish immigrants, lived in the Bronx, where he was born in 1923. He attended DeWitt Clinton High School and graduated from City College with a bachelor of science degree in 1943. He then entered the Army, where he reportedly acquired the name Paddy after asking to be excused from K.P. to attend mass. He served in the 104th Infantry Division and was injured in Aachen, Germany, by a mine explosion." Paddy Chayefsky died in 1981, aged 58, of cancer.[53]

Theater Directors and Producers

David Szemanski with his wife and three sons arrived from Russia in 1882 to settle in America. Plagued by alcoholism, David could not support his family and the boys, Levi (later Lee), Sam and Jacob went out on the streets selling newspapers. Changing their last name to Shubert, the brothers leased and bought theaters on Broadway and across the nation. In 1912, David T. Nederlander took a 99-year lease of the Detroit Opera House and built the nation's second largest theater organization. During the first half of the 20th century, the Shubert Organization and the Nederlander Organization were the leading managers and producers of legitimate theater in America.[54]

"Joseph Papp was born on June 22, 1921, in the Williamsburg section of Brooklyn to Shmuel and Yetta Papirofsky. His parents spoke Yiddish, and Yosl Papirofsky, as he was named, began to learn English only when he was old enough to play in the streets and go to school." His childhood was spent in poverty, "surrounded by terror.... I got beat up regularly," he said. His father was a trunk maker. "To help the family make a living, Yosl would shine shoes, pluck chickens and, with his father, sell peanuts from a pushcart. His family would move several times a year, often in the middle of the night, because they could not pay the rent. He rose from a childhood in the slums of Brooklyn to found the New York Shakespeare Festival, through which he presented free Shakespeare in Central Park for more than three decades. In the 1960's, he took over the old Astor Library and turned it into the Public Theater, a huge six-theater complex in which he presented and championed the work of many young playwrights." Joseph Papp was "one of the most influential producers in the history of the American theater."[55]

Lee Strasberg was "the father of Method Acting in America, artistic director of the Actors Studio, stage director, film actor and a major figure in world theater. [He] guided several generations of actors, including Marlon Brando, James Dean, Marilyn Monroe, Al Pacino and Robert De Niro.... Among the many other actors who have worked at the Studio are Julie Harris, Paul Newman, Joanne Woodward, Geraldine Page, Maureen Stapleton, Anne Bancroft, Dustin Hoffman, Patricia Neal, Rod Steiger, Mildred Dunnock, Eva Marie Saint, Eli Wallach, Anne Jackson, Ben Gazzara, Sidney Poitier, Karl Malden, Shelley Winters and Sally Field.... He revolutionized the art of acting and had a profound influence on performance in American theater and movies.... The Method, a system of vocal, physical and emotional exercises, was initiated in Russia by Constantin Stanislavsky; it encouraged the actor to use his psyche and subconscious in preparing for a role. Mr. Strasberg adapted it to the American theater, imposing his refinements, but always crediting Stanislavsky as his source," wrote Mel Gussow in *The New York Times* in 1982.

He was born Israel Strassberg in 1901, in Bodzanow, Poland, the youngest of three sons of innkeepers Baruch and Ida Strassberg. Baruch migrated first, leaving his family behind with an uncle who was a rabbinical teacher. With his meager earnings as a sweatshop presser on the Lower East Side Baruch managed, over several years, to send for his family. Israel was 7 years old when he arrived in America. Dropping out of high school, young Israel joined the drama club of a settlement house. His acting debut was on the Yiddish stage. Along the way he changed his name to Lee Strasberg. In 1923 Konstantin Stanislavsky and his Moscow Art Theater visited the United States to present Anton Chekhov's *Uncle Vanya* and Maxim Gorky's *The Lower Depths*. Strasberg was so moved by Stanislavsky's method that he determined to establish a similar theater company in America that would shift theater from light entertainment to dramatize real life during the Depression.

Strasberg, together with Harold Clurman and Cheryl Crawford, formed the Group Theater. They assembled 28 like-minded people, among them Joseph Edward Bromberg (born Josef Bromberger), Stella Adler, Morris Carnovsky, Pearl Miller, John Garfield, Lee Cobb, Elia Kazan and Clifford Odets, with the aim to bring "together actors, directors and writers in search of a theater that would be responsive to society" and reflect the times, including the hardships of the Great Depression. After the Group Theater folded in 1941, Strasberg turned from acting to teaching, and developed Method Acting requiring "that an actor in preparing for a role delve not only into the character's life in the play, but also, far more importantly, into the character's life before the curtain rises. In rehearsal, the character's prehistory, perhaps going back to childhood, is discussed and even acted out. The play became the climax of the character's existence." Strasberg's Method Acting had a profound impact on his notable students and helped shape American theater and movie acting. In 1952, Elia Kazan gave Senator Joseph McCarthy's House Un-American Committee the names of eight members of the Group Theater he claimed had joined the Communist Party 18 years earlier.[56] Lee Strasberg died in 1982, at age 80.[57]

Harold Clurman's "versatility as a man of the theater was perhaps unequaled—he was an outstanding director, critic, author and teacher." His interest in theater began as a little boy accompanying his parents to Yiddish theater on the Lower East Side. In his early 20s he moved to Paris to study acting and theater. While there he shared an apartment with Aaron Copland. Returning to America, he founded the Group Theater, with Lee Strasberg and directed several of its plays including Clifford Odets' *Awake and Sing* (1935) and *Waiting for Lefty* (1935). Between puffs on his cigar, Curwin was a great story-teller and conversationalist. In a career of over 60 years, he directed many plays and taught and wrote about the theater.[58]

Mike Nichols was born in 1931 as Mikhail Igor Peschkowsky, the son of a Russian-Jewish physician. With his "gift for communicating with actors and keen comic timing," he was one of America's most celebrated movie and theater directors. Nichols directed Dustin Hoffman in *The Graduate*, and Richard Burton and Elizabeth Taylor in *Who's Afraid of Virginia Woolf* (1966, a film that won five Academy Awards). On Broadway, he directed many plays including Neil Simon's *Barefoot in the Park* and *The Odd Couple*, Chekhov's *Uncle Vanya* and Arthur Miller's *Death of a Salesman*.[59]

George S. Kaufman was born 1898 into a middle-class Pittsburgh Jewish family. Dropping out of college, he moved to New York where he became a drama editor and then a playwright. During the Golden Age of Broadway—between the Great Wars—Kaufman "had at least one hit on Broadway, either as author or director, or both, nearly every year.... Eighteen of his plays had 200 or more performances and more than 20 sold to the movies." He earned Pulitzer Prizes for *Of Thee I Sing*, lyrics by Ira Gershwin (1931), and *You Can't Take It with You* by Moss Hart (1936). In 1950 he had another great success directing Frank Loesser's *Guys and Dolls* that ran 1,200 performances on Broadway.[60] Kaufman frequently collaborated with Moss Hart, born in New York to a cigar maker of English-Jewish lineage.

Norman Milton Lear died in 2023, at age 101. He was born in 1922 in New Haven, Connecticut, the son of Jeanette and Hyman Lear, immigrants from the Russian Empire. He grew up in the Jewish ghetto of Chelsea, Massachusetts. During World War II, Lear flew 52 combat missions in the Mediterranean theater as a gunner on B-17 Flying Fortress bombers. Norman Lear created or developed 100 television shows, including such hits as *All in the Family* featuring the bigot Archie Bunker (1971–1079), *Sanford and Son* (1972–1977) and *Good Times* (1974–1979), winning him six Emmys, two Peabody Awards, and the National Medal of Arts.[61]

"Though Jews had been an integral part of mainstream theater for decades—creating, presenting, teaching and consuming it—and had found in it the ultimate and most enduring expression of their artistry, seldom was the product Jewish on the surface," wrote theater critic Jesse Green in November 2023 in *The New York Times*. "Like many Jewish playwrights of the period, [Arthur] Miller, barely a generation away from a Polish shtetl himself, erased the Jews if not the Jewishness from almost all his reputational works.... The American theatrical canon—starting in the 1920s for musicals and the 1960s for plays—is disproportionately the work of our tiny minority. [The] invisibility of Jewishness ... is the result of a fear of offense or habit of disguise that evolved as a kind of protection for Jews both onstage and off."

In Hollywood, the Russian-Jewish movie moguls aimed at assimilation. "William Fox, Louis B. Mayer, Jack Warner and the rest rarely made movies with juicy Jewish roles." Assimilation, writes Green, "is never just a reaching toward something; it's a turning away from something else." Green calls for an open expression on the stage of Jewish content and Jewish values so that "we can celebrate that success in the names of Broadway theaters: the Friedman, the Jacobs, the Schoenfeld, the Hirschfeld, the Gershwin, the Simon, the Rodgers, the Sondheim. But having given so much to the world, we should let the world take it."[62]

13

The Sciences

In 1920, British-born William McDougall, Fellow of the Royal Society, was appointed professor of psychology at Harvard College. The following year he delivered six lectures at the invitation of Harvard president, A. Lawrence Lowell, on the topic: "Is America Safe for Democracy?" McDougall claimed that America's open immigration policy was flooding the country with fast-breeding inferior stock that was diluting "the nation's innate mental endowment" causing America to speed "down the road to destruction." McDougall advocated the use of "eugenic methods [of] sterilization and institutional segregation ... to increase the birthrate among the intrinsically better part of the population, and its decrease among the inferior part." Harvard and other leading universities, claimed McDougall, would soon be overwhelmed by the sons "of recent immigrants and the less effective descendants of earlier immigrants."[1]

History has shown how foolish and dangerous were the statements of William McDougall and his ilk. The Russian-Jewish immigration of 1881–1914 yielded a rich crop of scientists with such profound discoveries as vaccines against poliomyelitis and hepatitis B, the birth control pill, anti-depressant medications, and streptomycin, the first effective treatment against tuberculosis. Nobel Prizes were first awarded in 1901, well before the flowering in America of Eastern European Jewish immigrants. Between the 1940s and 1980s, at least 40 Nobel Prize winners were the first or second-generation offspring of Russian Jewish immigrants to the United States. Here are a number of them: The Chemistry award went to Melvin Calvin (1961), Paul Berg and Walter Gilbert (1980), Ronald Hoffman (1981), Jerome Karle (Karfunckle) and Hebert Hauptman (1985). The Medicine award went to Selman Waksman (1952), Joshua Lederberg (1958), George Wald (1967), Marshall Warren Nirenberg (1968), Julius Axelrod (1970), and Roslyn Sussman Yalow (1977). The Physics award went to Israel Isaac Rabi (1960), David Glaser, Robert Hofstadter and Richard Feynman (1961), Sheldon Glashow and Steven Weinberg (1979) and Arthur Leonard Schawlow (1981). The Economics prize went to Paul Samuelson (1970), Simon Kuznets (1971), Milton Friedman (1976), Lawrence Klein (1980), and Harry Miller (1990). One in four of the 954 Nobel laureates between 1901 and 2022 were Jews, who excelled in particularly chemistry, physics, medicine and economics.

Rose Herwitz and Elias Calvin left Tsarist Russia and opened a grocery store in

St. Paul, Minnesota. Their son Melvin, born in 1911, earned his doctorate at the University of Minnesota and went, in his mid–20s, to the University of Manchester as a post-doctoral student. Using carbon-14 isotopes as radioactive tracers, Calvin discovered how plants combine carbon dioxide and hydrogen to form sugar. The process of photosynthesis is known as the Calvin Cycle, earning Melvin Calvin the 1961 Nobel Prize in Chemistry.[2] Samuel Ruben (birth name Charles Rubenstein) from California and Martin David Kamen (birth name Menachem David Kamestsky), raised in Chicago—two other sons of Russian-Jewish immigrants—are credited with the synthesis of the isotope carbon-14.

In 1971, Paul Berg "was already a well-known researcher at Stanford University when he oversaw the artificial introduction of DNA from one virus into another, creating the first recombinant DNA, or rDNA. The achievement was the first link in the chain of advances that has led to the genetic engineering of new therapeutic treatments for diseases and of vaccines, like the messenger RNA versions used to counter the virus that causes Covid-19."[3] Brooklyn-born Paul Berg shared the 1960 Nobel Prize for Chemistry with Boston-born Walter Gilbert, who did pioneering work in the sequencing of nucleic acids.

Selman Abraham Waksman was born 1888 in a Ukrainian shtetl. After he was denied admission to a Russian university he sailed to America, settled in Philadelphia and entered Rutgers University to begin a career as a biochemist. Over a 40-year period, he painstakingly studied 10,000 chemicals produced by microbes, searching for those that caused disease in humans. In 1949, he discovered streptomycin, the first potent medication against tuberculosis. Waksman coined the word antibiotic, which he described as "a chemical substance produced by a microbe which has the capacity to inhibit the growth of and even to destroy other microbes." Forty years after he arrived in America, without connections or knowledge of English, Waksman was awarded the Nobel Prize in 1952.[4]

"A prodigy as a youth, Dr. Joshua Lederberg was 33 when he won the Nobel for Physiology or Medicine for discovering that bacteria can mate and exchange genes. He was one of the youngest Nobelists. [His discoveries] created new understandings of how bacteria evolve and acquire new traits, including resistance to antibiotic drugs. A founder of the field of molecular biology, he helped lay the foundations for many biological revolutions, including biotechnology."[5] The son of rabbi Zwi and Esther Lederberg, Joshua was born in Montclair, New Jersey. The family moved to New York and Joshua graduated Stuyvesant High School at age 15 and then enrolled in Columbia University. Joshua Lederberg served from 1978 through 1990 as president of Rockefeller University.

George Wald was born 1906, on the Lower East Side of Manhattan to Jewish immigrant parents "who were working in the garment industry." His chief scientific contribution, leading to his 1967 Nobel Prize in Medicine, "was to help understand how light activates photo-receptive cells in the retina, causing the molecular changes that lead to impulses along the optic nerve to the brain."[6] Marshall Warren

Nirenberg, the son of a Jewish immigrant shirtmaker, was 34 years old in 1961 when he conducted crucial experiments to solve the genetic code by demonstrating "the rules by which the genetic information in DNA is translated into proteins, the working parts of living cells. The code lies at the basis of life, and understanding it was a turning point in the history of biology. Dr. Nirenberg identified the particular codons (a codon is a sequence of three chemical units of DNA) that specify each of the 20 amino acid units of which protein molecules are constructed."[7]

Julius Axelrod was born 1912 in the Lower East Side of New York to Polish-Jewish immigrants Molly and Isadore Axelrod, a basket weaver. "Though he hoped to become a physician, medical schools in that era maintained strict quotas on accepting Jews, and his applications for admission were rejected." Instead, he worked in biochemistry laboratories. In the 1940s, "Dr. Axelrod played a major role in identifying acetaminophen as the pain-relieving chemical in a common headache treatment. [Later he] helped to discover how chemicals released by nerve cells in the brain regulate mood and behavior… [His work] was essential to the development of psychiatric drugs and led directly to the development of selective serotonin reuptake inhibitors, the class of antidepressants that includes Prozac, Zoloft and Paxil." Julius Axelrod shared the 1970 Nobel Prize in Medicine.[8]

Baruch Samuel Blumberg "the Nobel Prize–winning biochemist and medical anthropologist who discovered the hepatitis B virus, showed that it could cause liver cancer and then helped develop a powerful vaccine to fight it, saving millions of lives."[9] Born in 1925 in Brooklyn to Ida and Meyer Blumberg, Baruch attended a Yeshivah in Flatbush before entering Far Rockaway High School (where fellow Jewish immigrant boys and future Nobel laureates in Physics, Burton Richter and Richard Feynman, also studied). Baruch Blumberg won the Nobel Prize in Medicine in 1976.

Rosalyn Sussman was born in the South Bronx in 1921. "Her father, Simon Sussman, who had moved from the Lower East Side of Manhattan to the Bronx, was a wholesaler of packaging materials; her mother, the former Clara Zipper was a homemaker." She was the first physics major at All-Women Hunter College. "Yet she struggled to be accepted for graduate studies. In one instance, a skeptical Midwestern university wrote: 'She is from New York. She is Jewish. She is a woman.' Undeterred, she went on to carve out a renowned career in medical research, and in the 1950s became a co-discoverer of the radioimmunoassay, an extremely sensitive way to measure insulin and other hormones in the blood." In 1977, Rosalyn S. Yalow received the Nobel Prize in Medicine.[10]

"It's a miracle," said Israel (Isidor) Isaac Rabi, "how a sickly child from a Lower East Side poverty-stricken family moved in one generation to where I am." He was born in 1898 in the Eastern European shtetl of Rymanow, and brought the next year to America. His father found work in a dressmaking sweatshop. "If my father did not work, the family went hungry."[11] He studied physics at Columbia University and earned a Ph.D. in 1927. Awarded "an International Education Board Fellowship, he spent two years in Europe which included two months with Niels Bohr in Copenhagen; a year with Wolfgang Pauli and Otto Stern in Hamburg; two months with Werner Heisenberg in Leipzig and half a year with Pauli in Zurich. In Hamburg he became interested in molecular beam." He returned to New York to take a faculty position at Columbia, where he developed a method to measure the magnetic properties of atoms, molecules and atomic nuclei. "In November 1940 he joined a group of physicists to set up the Radiation Laboratory of the Massachusetts Institute of Technology in Cambridge. This laboratory was devoted to the development of radar for military purposes. During most of this period, he was also a consultant for the Manhattan District Atomic Energy Project." Isidor Rabi was awarded the Nobel Prize for Physics in 1944 for his discovery of nuclear magnetic resonance. This discovery led to the convenience of microwave ovens. Isidor Rabi served, 1955–1957, as chairman of the science advisory committee to President Dwight D. Eisenhower.[12]

Dr. Rosslyn Yalow at her Bronx Veteran Administration Hospital, October 1977 (U.S. Information Agency).

"Donald A. Glaser, who won the Nobel Prize in Physics in 1960 for inventing, at 25, an ingenious device called the bubble chamber to trace the paths of subatomic particles. Dr. Glaser's bubble chamber generated data that enabled physicists to figure out that most particles of matter, like protons and neutrons, are composed of even smaller particles known as quarks."[13] Glaser was born in 1926 in Cleveland, Ohio, the son of Russian Jewish immigrants. At age 20, he completed his doctorate in physics from the California institute of Technology. He was awarded the Nobel Prize for Physics in 1960 at age 34.

Richard Feynman was "arguably the most brilliant, iconoclastic and influential of the postwar generation of theoretical physicists." He received the 1965 Nobel Prize in Physics.[14] His father Melville migrated from Minsk in 1895, when he was five years old. He tried various jobs, including dry cleaning and selling uniforms to police officers and mailmen. Richard's American-born mother Lucille came from an immigrant family that first settled in the Lower East Side and then found success in the millinery trade. Soon after they married, Melville and Lucille settled in Far Rockaway, then a semi-rural section of the Bronx. By the time of Richard's birth in 1918, the Feynman family had shed Orthodoxy, the observance of the Sabbath, and *Yiddishkeit* and had moved to the Reform Shaaray Tefila Temple, where Richard attended Sunday school and belonged to the youth group. Like most other assimilated Jews in Far Rockaway, the Feynmans were "embedded in a culture that prized learning and discussion" and expecting "to fulfil themselves through their own children, who had to be sharply conscious of their parents hopes and sacrifices."[15] After graduating from Far Rockaway High School, Richard Feynman entered the Massachusetts Institute of Technology, then Princeton University where he received a Ph.D., in 1942. From Princeton he was recruited into the Manhattan Project, to build the atomic bomb at Los Alamos, New Mexico. He spent most of his academic career at the California Institute of Technology.

For his work on quantum electrodynamic, Julian Seymour Schwinger shared the 1965 Nobel Prize for Physics with Richard Feynman. Julian was born in New York in 1918 to Eastern European Jewish immigrants who prospered as garment manufacturers. His academic potential was recognized by Isidor Isaac Rabi who arranged for Julian to enter Columbia University where he obtained his Ph.D. at age 21. Schwinger had a brilliant career as a theoretical physicist. Four of Schwinger's graduate students won Nobel Prizes; Roy Glauber, Benjamin Roy Mottelson and Sheldon Glashow were of Russian-Jewish heritage, and Walter Kohn of Austrian-Jewish heritage.

"Paul A. Samuelson, the first American Nobel laureate in economics and the foremost academic economist of the 20th century. [He] helped build the Massachusetts Institute of Technology into one of the world's great centers of graduate education in economics. In receiving the Nobel Prize in 1970, Mr. Samuelson was credited with transforming his discipline from one that ruminates about economic issues to one that solves problems, answering questions about cause and effect with mathematical rigor and clarity." Paul Anthony Samuelson was born on May 15, 1915, in Gary, Indiana, the son of Frank Samuelson, a pharmacist, and the former Ella Lipton. His family, he said, was "made up of upwardly mobile Jewish immigrants from Poland who had prospered considerably in World War I, because Gary was a brand-new steel town when my family went there."[16]

Simon Kuznets won the 1971 Nobel Prize for Economics "for pioneering the measurement of national income and economic growth.... Probably more than any other person, Dr. Kuznets devised the system of measurement that now results in the Commerce Department's frequent estimates and revisions of growth in the gross national product. The same system is used by private economists and such agencies as the World Bank to calculate the economic progress of industrial and developing nations."[17] Simon Kuznets was born 1901 in Pinsk, then in the Russian Empire. While he had some training in Judaism and Jewish history, his primary interests were secular. He came to the United States in 1922 to escape the turmoil in Russia caused by the Bolshevik revolution. He entered Columbia University, which awarded him a doctorate in 1926. Kuznets spent his academic career at the University of Pennsylvania (1930–1954) and then Harvard University (1960–1971).[18] Simon Kuznets died in 1985 at age 84.

Milton Friedman, the winner of the 1976 Nobel Prize in Economics, was the "grandmaster of free-market economic theory in the postwar era and a prime force in the movement of nations toward less government and greater reliance on individual responsibility." He was born in Brooklyn in 1912, the last of four children of Eastern European immigrant parents who worked in sweatshops before opening a clothing store in Rahway, New Jersey. The family lived in an apartment above the store. The family spoke mostly in English but Milton picked up "a smattering of Yiddish, enough to understand the conversation of adults but not enough to speak it fluently." Milton waited on tables and clerked in stores to supplement a scholarship he earned at Rutgers University. As a graduate student in economics at the University of Chicago, he met and married Rose Director, who was born in a shtetl in Tsarist Russia. "Times were tough and jobs in our chosen field of college teaching were scarce—especially for Jews. We had only ourselves to depend on. Our parents could not help us with expenses at school."[19]

Other Nobel laureates in Economics, Kenneth Arrow (1971), Lawrence Klein (1980), Harry Markowitz (1990), Merton Miller (1990), Garry Becker (1993), Robert William Fogel (1993) Joseph Eugene Stiglitz (2001), Roger Bruce Myerson (2007), Eric Maskin (2007), Leonid Hurwicz (2007), Paul Krugman (2008), Alvin Roth (2012), Michael Kremer (2019) and Ben Shalom Bernanke (2022), were of Eastern European Jewish heritage.

"No disease drew as much attention, or struck the same terror, as polio.... Polio hits without warning. There was no way of telling who would get it and who would be spared. It killed some of its victims and marked others for life, leaving behind vivid reminders for all to see: wheelchairs, crutches, leg braces, breathing devices, deformed limbs."[20]

"An Immigrant and an Immigrant's Son Saved Americans from Polio" ran the headline of an article in *Forbes Magazine*.[21] "They were two young Jewish men who grew up just a few years apart in the New York area during the Great Depression, and though they were both drawn to the study of medicine at New York University School of Medicine, Sabin graduated in 1931 and Salk graduated in 1939. They did not know each other at the time, their names would, years later, be linked in a heroic struggle that played out on the front pages of newspapers around the world. In the end, both Albert Sabin and Jonas Salk could rightfully claim credit for one of humanity's greatest accomplishments—the near-eradication of polio in the 20th century. And yet debate still echoes over whose method is best suited for the mass vaccination needed to finish the job: Salk's injected dead-virus vaccine or Sabin's oral live-virus version."[22]

Poliomyelitis is a highly infectious disease. Epidemics of "the viral illness gripped a fearful nation with images of children doomed to death or paralysis." In 1952 alone, there were 57,000 cases of polio in the United States, causing 3,000 deaths and leaving 21,000 with permanent paralysis. On April 12, 1955, the 40-year-old Dr. Jonas Salk announced "that his new polio vaccine was safe and effective. It was a turning point in the fight against a disease that condemned some victims to live the rest of their lives in tanklike breathing machines called iron lungs.... The Salk vaccine changed medical history, preventing many thousands of cases of crippling illness and saving thousands of lives. In the United States, the vaccine soon ended the yearly threat of epidemics and the toll of paralysis and death.... In the five years before 1955, when mass inoculations with the vaccine began, cases of paralytic polio averaged about 25,000 a year in the United States. A few years after polio vaccination became routine, the annual number of cases dropped to a dozen or so, sometimes fewer. In 1969 not a single death from polio was reported in the nation, the first such year on record, and now the disease is on the verge of being eradicated worldwide." The Salk vaccine was by injection, using killed virus.[23]

Daniel Salk was born in 1890 to a Lithuanian-Jewish family living in the Lower East Side. He worked in the garment district. In 1913, he married Doris Press, a recent immigrant from the Ukraine. Doris knew some spoken English but could read and write only in Yiddish. Doris and Daniel settled first in the Lower East Side but soon moved to Harlem, where her parents had settled. Jonas Edward Salk was born in East Harlem in 1914, the eldest of three sons. Later in his life, Jonas "reviewed his ancestors. None had leapt to fame. None of them had a brilliance that shone above others. Ordinary men and women; they worked hard, raised large families and kept the faith. They were Russian Jews." Daniel, Doris and children were part of a large extended family that shared Sabbath dinners, bar-mitzvahs, Jewish holidays, marriages, and funerals.[24] Jonas went to Public School No. 44, then to the Townsend Harris High School for exceptionally promising students. He graduated from City College in 1934 and enrolled in New York University's medical school. His chosen field of research was virology, employed as professor at the

Jonas Edward Salk developed the first effective poliomyelitis vaccine, taken by injection.

University of Pittsburgh School of Medicine. After the polio vaccine was proved successful in the field trials, Dr. Salk became a hero to the public. "An opinion poll ranked him roughly between Churchill and Gandhi as a revered figure of modern history." In 1963, Salk established the Salk Institute for Biological Studies in La Jolla, California.

Albert Sabin "was best known for developing the live-virus polio vaccine, taken orally." It became generally preferred over the alternative killed-virus vaccine developed by Dr. Jonas Salk.... Its virtues included delivery in syrup or a sugar cube instead of by injection. [The Sabin vaccine] was licensed in 1961 and eventually became the vaccine of choice in most parts of the world. Albert Bruce Sabin was born as Abram Saperstein in 1906, in Bialystok, Poland, then a part of the Russian Empire. He attended *cheder* and went regularly to pray in the synagogue. In 1921, when he was 15 years old, the Sabin family immigrated to the United States. He spoke Hebrew, Yiddish, Russian and German but no English. After taking a six-week cram course in English, he entered high school in the silk-mill town of Paterson, New Jersey. Upon graduation, he went first to dental school but switched to medicine and in 1931 received his medical degree from the University of New York School of Medicine. As head of pediatric research at the University of Cincinnati, he began the quest for a vaccine against the dreaded polio virus. Success came in the late 1950s. Oral Sabin vaccine, using modified and weakened live virus, gives lifetime protection from poliomyelitis, while the injected Salk vaccine needed later booster doses. The Sabin vaccine has become the world standard. "The 1960s would belong to Albert Sabin, the way the 1950s had belonged to Salk," wrote David Oshinsky.

Albert Sabin had a lifelong passion for the Jewish life. He mourned the murder of six million Jews during the Holocaust. He visited Israel in 1959 and admired the rekindling of Jewish life in the Jewish homeland. He received an honorary degree from the Hebrew University. "I became even more strongly influenced by the events in Israel than I ever was before," wrote Albert Sabin. "I wanted to help in whichever way I could." During 1970, Dr. Sabin became president of the Weizmann Institute of Science in Israel but stepped down in November 1972 because of a heart condition.[25] Albert Sabin died in 1993 age 86. His rival in science Jonas Salk died in 1995, age 80.

In 1960, the U.S. Food and Drug Administration approved Enovid as a birth-control pill, giving women, for the first time, control over pregnancy. The use of the pill profoundly changed family life. The father of "The Pill" was Dr. Gregory Goodwin Pincus, working with scientist Min-Chuen Chang and obstetrician Dr. John Rock.[26] Seven years earlier, Margaret Sanger, president of the International Planned Parenthood Federation visited Pincus's Worcester Foundation for Experimental Research, in Worcester, Massachusetts. She discussed with Dr. Pincus the possibility of developing a pill to prevent unwanted pregnancies. Sanger received funding for the project from Katharine McCormick, whose husband Stanley was the son of Cyrus McCormick of International Harvester fame. Soon after their marriage,

Albert Bruce Sabin developed the live-virus poliomyelitis vaccine, taken orally (United States Department of Health and Human Services).

Stanley manifested paranoid schizophrenia and was institutionalized for the rest of his life. Katharine, educated at the Massachusetts Institute of Technology, was convinced that schizophrenia was a chemically-induced disorder. She funded biological research into schizophrenia. After Stanley died, Katharine inherited his millions and agreed to fund Gregory Pincus's research to develop a safe and effective contraceptive pill. Within five years, Pincus and his team had developed and tested the contraceptive pill, and declared it safe and effective.

His parents, Joseph and Elizabeth Lipman Pincus, were immigrants from the Russian Empire. They settled in Connecticut, where Joseph attended the Connecticut Agricultural College. Early in the 20th century, Joseph moved to Woodbine, New Jersey, to teach agricultural methods at the Baron de Hirsch agricultural school, aiming to train inner-city Jewish immigrant boys how to become successful American farmers. Joseph W. Pincus was editor of *The Jewish Farmer*—the world's first Yiddish-language agricultural magazine. Its aim was "to provide the non–English reading Jewish farmer expert advice on agricultural subjects; to supply him with a publication to which he can turn for sympathy and encouragement; to furnish him with a medium for the expression of his feelings and aspirations; and to bring him inspiration through keeping him in touch with his fellow tillers of the soil." At its peak, the journal had a circulation of about 5,000 in the United States and abroad.[27]

After the de Hirsch agricultural school closed, Joseph Pincus began research into seed for vegetables and grain. After Nazi Germany occupied the Ukraine, millions of Russians were at risk of starvation. Joseph Pincus arranged the shipment of one million pounds of vegetable and grain seed to Russia, arguing that seed "take up very little cargo space and does not spoil."[28]

Gregory Goodwin Pincus, the son of Jewish immigrants Joseph and Elizabeth Pincus, was born in Woodbine, New Jersey, in 1903. He excelled at high school and gained a full scholarship to Cornell University. He devoted his life to research into hormone biology. In 1944, he established the Worcester Foundation for Experimental Research that limped along for a decade before it received funding from Katharine McCormick. Gregory Pincus did not long enjoy fame as the Father of the Pill. He developed myeloid metaplasia, a disease of the bone marrow and died in 1967 at age 64.

14

Manufacturing and Business

Arriving in America during the middle of the 19th century, Jews from German-speaking lands worked as peddlers. They fought in the Civil War—on the Union and on the Confederate side. Many went into retailing and established department stores. Nathan and Isidor Straus built Macy's; Abraham Lincoln Neiman and Herbert Marcus opened Neiman-Marcus in Dallas, Texas; William Filene established Filene's in Boston; Andrew and Isadore Saks opened Saks 5th Avenue in New York; Adam Gimbel established Gimbel's; and Benjamin and his brother Lyman Bloomingdale operated Bloomingdale's. Julius Rosenwald built Sears-Roebuck into America's largest catalog company. Levi Strauss established a clothing company that still carries his name. In merchant banking, Marcus Goldman and Samuel Sachs formed Goldman-Sachs; Henry, Emanuel and Mayer Lehman founded Lehman Brothers; Solomon Loeb and Jacob H. Schiff formed Kuhn-Loeb. Paul Moritz Warburg was one of the original members of the Federal Reserve Board of Governors. These successful German Jews funded the welfare agencies to assist the immigrants who arrived in the United States between 1881 and 1914.

Within a few years of arrival, many of the Eastern Jewish immigrants left the ghettoes to begin the climb up the ladder of achievement in manufacturing and business. As early as 1919, the aspiring and entrepreneurial Russian immigrants were fast supplanting German Jews as the most prominent Jewish businessmen in America. Among them were Meyer Solomon Adler of Providence, Rhode Island, who ran a waste-paper company; Sam Beckman of Chelsea, Massachusetts, who operated a wholesale grocery business; Abraham Goldberg of Akron, Ohio, who had a clothing factory; David Kopeman from Creston, Ohio, who owned a junk-metal business; and Bernard Schwartz of Detroit, Michigan, who operated a cigar factory.[1] Most began their careers with little money but with an original idea backed by acumen and the single-minded determination to succeed.

Here are some of the outstanding achievement stories: Sidney J. Weinberg was one of 11 children of Pincus and Sophie Weinberg, immigrants from the Russian Empire. The family was poor and Sidney left school after the 8th grade to sell newspapers, became a janitor's assistant, earning $3 a week, and was then employed in the mail room of the august German-Jewish investment banking house Goldman-Sachs. His intelligence and skills were soon recognized. Sidney Weinberg became known as "Mr. Wall Street" rising to head of the firm from 1930 until his death 39 years later.

Naftali Feuerstein, from an Eastern European deeply Orthodox family, arrived in America in 1893. He started out as a peddler. In 1907, now Henry Feuerstein, he established Malden Knitting Mills. His grandson Aaron Mordechai Feuerstein was educated at Boston Latin School and Yeshiva University, and joined Malden Mills in 1947. During the 1950s Aaron moved the company from Malden to Lawrence, Massachusetts, making the fabric Polartec. On December 11, 1995, Malden Mills was engulfed in flames. "Three days later, most of the plant's 1,400 workers lined up to receive their paychecks, figuring it might be their last from Malden Mills.… Aaron Feuerstein became a national hero when he refused to lay off workers at his textile plant." Instead, he awarded holiday bonuses and paid his idled workers three months' wages. He kept the company aloft by moving production to nearby buildings and spent $130 million to build a new plant. Feuerstein told *Parade Magazine* in 1996: "I have a responsibility to the worker, both blue-collar and white-collar. I have an equal responsibility to the community. It would have been unconscionable to put 3,000 people on the streets and deliver a deathblow to the cities of Lawrence and Methuen. Maybe on paper our company is worth less to Wall Street, but I can tell you it's worth more." Feuerstein, a religious Jew and Talmud scholar, was feted as "The Mensch of Malden," but he was unable to stem the collapse of New England's textile industry. Burdened by its enormous debt, Malden Mills declared bankruptcy in 2001. Aaron Mordechai Feuerstein died in 2021 at age 95.[2]

Cosmetics

Helena Rubenstein, Estee Lauder, Max Factor, Charles Revson, Samuel Rubin and Lawrence Gelb were pioneers in the American beauty business. Born in Cracow, Poland, in 1870, Chaja Rubinstein was the eldest of eight daughters of a well-to-do Orthodox Jewish shop-keeping family. She attended medical school for two years before moving to Australia in 1896, taking several bottles of her mother's beauty creams. Leaving Poland, she changed her name to Helena Juliet Rubinstein. In Australia "she immediately noticed women's complexions looked rough and dried." She sent home for a shipment of face creams made for the women of her family by the Hungarian chemist Jacob Lykusky. The key ingredient was lanolin, available in abundance from the secretions of Australia's merino sheep. Producing her product locally, Rubinstein opened a shop on fashionable Collins Street, Melbourne, and made a small fortune selling the face cream to treat the sun-damaged complexions of Australian women. After 10 years in Australia, she left for London and opened a beauty salon. At the start of World War I, she moved to New York and opened Maison de Beauté at 15 East 49th Street, followed by branches in other American cities. Helena Rubinstein became "a symbol of beauty [and] inspired other women to look their best." Cosmetics, she said, "merely accentuate and enhance innate charm and beauty, never substitute for it." Rubenstein became one of America's wealthiest women. Her art collection included works by Picasso, Matisse, Renoir and Chagall. Helena Rubinstein died in New York in 1965 at age 94.[3]

Josephine Esther Mentzer was born in Corona, Queens, in 1908, the daughter of Rose Schotz Rosenthal and her second husband Max Mentzer, who ran a hardware store. "The Mentzers were hard-working immigrants.... Esther was destined to become known to the world by the diminutive of Estée." While still in high school "she became intrigued by the work of her uncle, John Schotz [who] created a number of beauty products ... concocted over a gas stove in a modest kitchen." Estée was beautiful "with shining blond hair, dark hazel eyes, and a complexion so flawless and radiant that everyone remarked on it." At age 22, she married Joseph Lauter, later changed to Lauder. She called her first beauty product Super Rich All-Purpose Crème and believed that, with the use of cosmetics, "Every woman can be beautiful." Her big break came during the Great Depression when she operated a beauty concession at 39 East 60th Street, New York. Her single-minded determination to succeed "resulted in the establishment of a company estimated to be worth about $5 billion when it went public in 1995 and she was given the title of founding chairwoman. In 2003, it had 21,500 employees and an estimated worth of about $10 billion. Its products are sold in more than 130 countries across five continents." In her desire to be "100 percent American," Estée Lauder moved away from the Jewish and immigrant ways of her parents. She died in 2004 at age 97. Her son Ronald serves as president of the World Jewish Congress.[4]

Max Factor, Sr., invented the term "make-up." He began life humbly in 1877 as Maxsymilian Faktorowicz in a shtetl near Lodz in the Russian Empire. His father was a textile mill worker and part-time rabbi. His mother died when he was seven and he was put to work as apprentice to a wig maker. He displayed great skill, gaining a position at age 14 in Moscow as assistant wig maker and cosmetician to the Imperial Russian Grand Opera Company. Four years later he was conscripted into the Imperial Russian Army. After discharge he opened a cosmetic and hair-styling shop in Moscow and served as cosmetician to members of the Russian royal family. Troubled by rising anti–Semitism, Max, his wife Esther and their children, left Russia in 1904 to join relatives who settled in St. Louis. At Ellis Island the clerk misspelled his last name as Factor and thenceforth he was Max Factor. Max was a small, slightly built man who learned to speak English, but with a heavy Russian-Yiddish accent. He opened a display at the Louisiana Purchase Exhibition to sell his cosmetics and wigs. The fast-developing film industry gave Max Factor his opportunity. In 1908, he moved with his family from St. Louis to Hollywood and opened a beauty salon that attracted the likes of Gloria Swanson, Mary Pickford, Jean Harlow, Claudette Colbert and other glamorous stars of the early years of the movies. Factor made the toupees for John Wayne, Fred Astaire and Rudolph Valentino. In 1909, he established Max Factor & Company, among the early international cosmetic empires.[5]

Frank, the youngest of the four Factor children, "helped his father refine theatrical makeup for the movies and later retailed the glamorous look of Hollywood to ordinary women." After his father died, Frank changed his name to Max Factor, Jr., "When color film was introduced, Factor created 'Pan-Cake' makeup … to prevent actors' faces from looking green on camera.… Soon the public was clamoring for it as well.… By 1950 Max Factor & Company employed 10,000 people." The Factor family sold their business in 1973.[6]

Charles Haskell Revson who "built an empire from colorful nail enamel that a chemist friend heated over a Bunsen burner, was a man of unrelenting drive, unremitting standards, far-ranging imagination and an uncanny ability to spot a trend while it was still a distant breeze." He was born in Boston in 1906, the son of a Russian-Jewish immigrant working as a cigar packer. Charles entered the beauty business selling nail polish. In 1932, he established Revlon Inc., manufacturing nail enamel and selling his products through beauty salons, drug stores and department stores. In 1939, Revson introduced "matching lips and fingertips" offering a wide range of colors for matching lipstick and nail polish. In 1965, he sponsored "The $64,000 Question" television quiz-show that dramatically increased sales. The ever-resourceful Charles Revson expanded his company into cosmetics, shampoos, skin care, fragrances and men's products. In 1966, he entered the pharmaceutical industry. "By 1974 the Revlon product range had grown to more than 3,500 individual items, sold in 85 countries."[7]

Charles Revson, Estée Lauder and Helena Rubenstein were of Russian-Jewish heritage, but remained bitter rivals in business. Revson "was loath to mention the name of his competitors, and it was known as the height of folly to invite the Revlon founder and Estée Lauder … to the same party. When the two did find themselves in the same room, they pretended they weren't, and proceeded, with entourages, to opposite ends." After Helena Rubenstein died, Revson bought her Park Avenue duplex. "Revson fully enjoyed the accouterments of success—the yacht, the triplex, a country estate in Westchester, a chauffeur-driven Rolls-Royce, and the tailors and barbers who came to him." Charles Revson died of cancer in 1975 at age 68. The funeral service was held at Temple Emanu-El in New York.[8] Samuel Rubin was born in Bialystok in the Russian Empire. In 1905, when he was three, he came with his parents to New York. After graduating from City College, he worked as a perfume salesman. In 1937 he founded Fabergé Inc., selling perfumes seductively named "Aphrodesia" and "Tigress." In 1963, he sold the company to devote his time and money to the Samuel Rubin Foundation, supporting hospitals and scholarships for medical students, and funding projects in Israel.[9] Lawrence M. Gelb was born in New York and gained a degree in chemistry at New York University. Observing that middle-aged people were dealing "with drab, faded and graying hair," in 1931 he and his wife Joan Clair, founded Clairol, Inc., to manufacture and sell hair coloring and haircare products.[10]

Household Names

Most of the aspiring Jewish children of Russian-Jewish immigrants sought their opportunities outside the ghetto. They abandoned shtetl life, cut off their beards and earlocks, worked on Saturdays and on minor Jewish holidays, adopted Western dress, cast aside the Yiddish language, and ate non–Kosher foods. A minority remained true to the religion, language and values of the Old World. Dov Behr Manischewitz built a company to offer kosher foods, both for daily use and especially for Passover. He was born in 1857 in a Lithuanian shtetl. He was deeply religious and was trained as a *shochet*, a ritual meat purveyor. In 1886, he settled with his family in Cincinnati, where he began baking matzah at home. When his matzah caught on with friends and other religious Jews, the entrepreneurial Manischewitz built a company, to become a pioneer in the American ethnic food market. He helped design and build the equipment to shift matzah making from hand to entirely machine production, yet adhering fully to Jewish dietary laws. He added Manischewitz wines for Passover.[11] After Dov Behr died in 1914, his family continued to run the business, making Manischewitz the world's largest matzah and kosher-wine company. After the family sold the business in 1990, the Manischewitz Company offered a wider range of kosher products and expanded worldwide.

Born 1870 in Eastern Europe Sandor Herz settled in Chicago. He had little education and supported himself selling newspapers. He changed his name to John Daniel Hertz. With the coming of the automobile, he established a cab company and the Hertz-Drive-Ur-Self System, which became Hertz car rentals. Morris Mirkin was born in 1919 to Russian Jewish immigrants who settled in Sioux City. In 1958, Mirkin, founded Budget-Rent-A-Car.[12] Two years later, Mirkin teamed up with his cousin Jules W. Lederer to develop one of the nation's largest car rental companies. Born in Detroit in 1917, Lederer "dropped out of school in the ninth grade to support his mother and sister after his father had died. He made his living as a salesman, selling everything from pens and pencils bearing advertising slogans, to hats and newspapers." Selling hats in a Sioux City department store in 1939 he met, and later married, Esther Pauline "Eppie" Friedman, who became better known as the syndicated advice columnist Ann Landers. Esther's twin sister Pauline assumed the name of Abigail Van Buren, writing the "Dear Abby" syndicated advice column.[13]

Samuel Glazer was "co-founder of the company that gave the world Mr. Coffee, one of the first and most popular automatic drip coffee makers to appear on American kitchen counters." Glazer and his friend Vincent Marotta "bought a coffee delivery company serving the Cleveland area in the late 1960s.... They hired two former Westinghouse engineers to create a compact, stylish version of the commercial dispenser. Their effort led to Mr. Coffee, in which water enters an electric heating element at the top, then trickles into the coffee grounds in a disposable paper filter before emptying into a glass pot resting on another heating element to keep it warm. To avoid the bitterness that boiling can cause, it heats the brew to only about

200 degrees.... Samuel Lewis Glazer was born in Cleveland on Feb. 24, 1923, to Isador and Yetta Gross Glazer. His father died when Sam was 6, and for years Sam supported his family, first by delivering newspapers and then by selling dog food, and then boots to steelworkers."[14]

Reuben Mattus was born in 1912 in Poland. At age 12, he came to the United States with his widowed mother. "Starting as a teen-ager and working first out of a horse and wagon, Mr. Mattus peddled the Mattus family's homemade ice cream for more than 30 years to small candy stores and neighborhood restaurants in the Bronx, expanding his business gradually. The financial rewards were modest until 1959, when he hit on the idea that would make his fortune. Correctly deducing that a large share of ice cream lovers in New York would be willing to pay for something they perceived as different, even evocative, and maybe better, Mr. Mattus came up with the name Haagen-Dazs, wanting it to sound cold, clear, luxurious and Danish. A map of Scandinavia was printed on its carton."[15]

Born in Winnipeg, Manitoba, in 1917, Irvine Robbins "was the son of Aaron and Goldie Chmelnitsky Robbins, immigrants from Poland and Russia, respectively. When Mr. Robbins was a child, the family moved to Tacoma, Wash., where his father became a partner in a dairy.... Irvine Robbins with his brother-in-law, Burton Baskin, started the Baskin-Robbins chain of ice cream stores, together concocting quirky flavor combinations with names like Daiquiri Ice, Pink Bubblegum and Here Comes the Fudge." Burton Baskin was born 1913 in Streator, Illinois, a town 80 miles southwest of Chicago, where his immigrant father ran a clothing store. Baskin and Robbins opened several ice-cream stores in California and then sold the stores to the managers, and began franchising their "31 Flavors" nationwide. Baskin and Robbins flipped a coin to decide which name came first.[16]

"Nathan Handwerker was co-founder with his wife, Ida, of Nathan's Famous, Inc., the hotdog, fast-food restaurant chain.... Handwerker came to this country in 1912 as a penniless young man from Poland. He went to work as a part-time delivery boy for $4.50 a week at Max's Busy Bee eatery on the Lower East Side. On Sunday afternoons he went to Coney Island and worked as roll-slicer behind the counters of Feltman's German Gardens on Surf Avenue. He became popular with some of Feltman's show-business customers who came there for Feltman's famed 10-cent frankfurters. Two of Mr. Handwerker's customers, Jimmy Durante and Eddie Cantor, who were singing waiters at Coney Island, did not like the idea of paying 10 cents for a frankfurter and urged Mr. Handwerker to open up his own stand and sell them for a nickel. In 1916, Mr. Handwerker took his life savings of $300 and his new bride, the former Miss Ida Greenwald, and opened a small stand at Surf and Stillwell Avenues. He sold hot dogs for a nickel and they were laced with his wife's secret recipe of spice. They caught on immediately with the palates of the thousands who flocked to Coney Island." Nathan's became one of the leading hot dog makers, sold in supermarkets nationwide.[17]

Ida Rosenthal, Lena Himmelstein, Donald and Doris Fisher, Ralph Lauren,

Nathan's Famous Frankfurters stand on the boardwalk, Coney Island, New York, 1954 (Library of Congress, LC-DIG-ds-05430).

Calvin Klein and Les Wexler are innovators in the clothing industry. Ida Rosenthal was the co-founder of Maidenform, "the company credited with changing the shape of American women." She was born Ida Cohen in 1886 near Minsk, her father a Hebrew scholar and her mother ran a small store. At age 19 Ida came to the United States to join her fiancé, William Rosenthal. They married in 1907. Ida worked as a dressmaker and opened a dress shop. Ida and William formed the Maidenform company to manufacture brassieres, lingerie and swimsuits. It became the most successful bra manufacturer in the world. She died at age 87 in 1973.[18]

Another pioneer in women's clothing was Lena Himmelstein. Born 1877 in Lithuania, she was orphaned after her parents were murdered in a pogrom, and was raised by grandparents. She came to Ellis Island where the clerk misspelled her name as Lane. She married a fellow Russian immigrant, but he died young. Lena sold her diamond earrings to buy a sewing machine and supported herself and her son Raphael by making lingerie and dresses for expectant mothers. Her next innovation was to make clothing for larger women. At age 32, she married a fellow Lithuanian-Jewish refugee Albert Malsin, who helped her establish the Lane Bryant chain as the nation's leading producer of ready-made plus-size clothing. Lena Himmelstein Malsin died at age 74 in 1951.[19] After Lena's death, her son Raphael served three decades as chief executive of Lane Bryant.

Donald and Doris Feigenbaum Fisher, Ralph Lauren and Les Wexler established leading clothing emporiums. Donald Fisher's inspirational moment came in the 1960s when he wondered: "What if someone put together all the styles, colors and sizes Levi Strauss had to offer in one store?" In 1969 the Fishers opened their first Gap clothing store in California selling the full range of Levi Strauss jeans, as well as music on tape and records. Catering to the youth market, The Gap, Inc., expanded with the Banana Republic and Old Navy brands. "With the aging of its original primary market, the baby boom generation, the company branched out to reach its offspring, and Baby Gap and Gap Kids stores became fixtures in American malls and city shopping districts." The Gap grew to over 3,000 stores in the United States and 24 other countries.[20]

"I came from nowhere. I had nothing," said Ralph Lauren. "Ralphie Lifshitz grew up sleeping three to a room, the smallest kid in his class … but he dreamed of being a Brahmin."[21] Grandfather Sholomo Zalman Lifshitz accompanied by his son Frank, left Poland in 1920 to settle in the Bronx, New York. Frank, a house painter, married Frieda Cutler. Ralph, born in 1939, was the youngest of four children. In his teen years, he changed his last name to Lauren. He attended the Manhattan Talmudical Academy, studied business administration at City College and found work as a clothing designer. In 1967, he launched the Ralph Lauren Corporation, first making clothing for men, then adding women's clothing and fragrances. His Polo label clothing has become a symbol of casual elegance. Calvin Richard Klein was another ambitious and gifted son of Jewish immigrants who settled in the Bronx. He attended the High School of Art & Design in Manhattan. In 1969, together with his boyhood friend Barry Schwartz, he launched Calvin Klein, Inc., that became "one of the most iconic American fashion designers of all time and went on to lead a global multi-billion-dollar design empire" selling men's and women's clothing.[22]

Leslie Herbert Wexner was born 1937, the son of Bella and Harry Wexner, who owned a clothing store in Columbus, Ohio. In 1963, Wexner launched his first store,

The Limited, selling moderately-priced clothing. By 1976, The Limited grew into a nationwide chain. Wexner's holdings expanded to Victoria's Secret, Abercrombie & Fitch, Express, Inc., and Bath & Body Works. Wexner's philanthropy extends to Jewish causes, Ohio State University and its medical center.

Entrepreneurs

"At the dawn of the cable television industry Ralph Joel Roberts bought a small cable service in Tupelo, Mississippi, and built it into Comcast, today the largest cable television company in the nation...." In 1963, Mr. Roberts was a little-known entrepreneur who had sold Muzak systems and men's belts and suspenders, but he was ambitious and always scouting for new business opportunities. Already in his 40s, he was approached by a Philadelphia acquaintance named Dan Aaron, who alerted him to a 1,200-subscriber cable television system for sale in Tupelo. Intrigued by the nascent cable industry's potential and aided by Mr. Aaron and Julian Brodsky, a Philadelphia accountant, Mr. Roberts built Comcast through a series of acquisitions of cable systems around the country. In 2001, Ralph and his son Brian "made an audacious but successful $45 billion bid to acquire AT&T's cable business. The deal made Comcast the nation's largest cable operator.... In 2011, fulfilling the Roberts's long-held interest in NBC, Comcast acquired a majority stake in NBCUniversal from General Electric for $6.5 billion; in doing so, it became one of the industry's leading content producers.... In February 2013, Comcast paid $16.7 billion to purchase the remaining stake in NBCUniversal." Brian Roberts admired his father's "will to succeed, and to do it with certain core values and integrity. Maybe it was losing both his parents before he was 21, living through the Depression, but somehow, he became an optimist." Ralph Joel Roberts was born in 1920, in New York. His parents Robert Max and Sarah Roberts were Russian-Jewish immigrants "who prospered with a string of pharmacies in the city."[23]

"Laurence A. Tisch, the self-made New York billionaire was hailed as a white knight for saving CBS Inc." Laurence, born 1923, and his brother Preston, born 1926, were the children of Sadye and Al Tisch of Brooklyn, whose parents immigrated from the Russian Empire. Laurence Tisch "was known as a brilliant, contrarian investor who bought failing companies when their share prices were at low ebb and then turned them into profitable enterprises with much higher stock valuations. He and his brother Preston built up and controlled the Loews Corporation, a conglomerate of hotels, insurance, cigarette manufacturing, movie theaters, oil tankers and watchmaking that also was a vehicle for other investments.... He spent his leisure time with his family, in frequent discussions of Jewish traditions with Talmudic scholars, on the boards of leading cultural institutions in New York City and as a philanthropist." At the death of Laurence Tisch in 2003, at age 80 years, New York Mayor Michael R. Bloomberg said: "Larry Tisch made an enormous contribution to the city, and he will be sorely missed. He represented what is best about

New York, and his generosity will leave a legacy that we will all try to build on."[24] Preston Tisch owned a half-share of the New York Giants of the National Football League.

"My fundamental responsibility was as an American," said Max Fisher, "Then as an American Jewish leader. And finally, I had my love for Israel."[25] In 1933 Max Martin Fisher formed the Aurora Gasoline company based in Detroit, Michigan, that "became one of the largest independent oil companies in the Midwest, with nearly 700 Speedway gas stations.... Fisher was a major benefactor of the Detroit Symphony Orchestra. The orchestra's new home, dedicated in October 2003, is called the Max M. Fisher Music Center. He headed several Jewish-American organizations including the United Jewish Appeal, the Council of Jewish Federations and the American Jewish Committee." He served as advisor to several U.S. presidents on Jewish affairs and sought to improve ties between Washington and Jerusalem. In 1975, Fisher assisted Secretary of State Henry Kissinger "to help heal a diplomatic rift between the United States and Israel over relations with Egypt."[26]

Henry Crown's life "exemplified the Horatio Alger rags-to-riches story of American industrialists." He was one of Chicago's great entrepreneurs. At his death in 1990 he was the "patriarch of one of America's greatest fortunes [that] includes hotels, buildings, railroads, meat packing, coal, sugar, recreation and the aerospace industry." In 1951, he bought a controlling interest in New York's iconic Empire State Building but sold it 10 years later. "Crown was named Henry Krinsky at birth in 1896, the third of seven children of a Lithuanian immigrant sweatshop worker, Arie Krinsky, and his wife Ida. His father changed the family name to Crown while Henry was a boy." Henry left school after the eighth grade to work as an errand boy earning $4 a week. He went into business with his brothers selling sand, gravel, lime and coal. This evolved into the Material Services Corporation. In the 1960s, Crown acquired a controlling interest in General Dynamics, a leading military contracting company. The Henry & Gladys Crown Charitable Trust Fund helped Northwestern, Stanford and Brandeis universities.[27]

Solomon Isadore Neuhaus was born 1895 in a Lower East Side tenement, the oldest of eight children of impoverished immigrants from the Russian Empire. After his father abandoned them, his mother moved the family to Bayonne, New Jersey. Armed with a business diploma, Solomon found work with the failing local newspaper. He raised the paper to profitability by cutting expenses, and increasing circulation and advertising revenue. Over the years he acquired 30 other newspapers, including the New Orleans *Times-Picayune* and the Portland *Oregonian*. In 1959, he bought Condé Nast, the publishers of *Vogue*, *Glamour*, *Mademoiselle*, *Brides*, and *House & Home* magazines to become "one of the country's largest communication empires." Along the way, he changed his name to Samuel Irving Newhouse. He died at age 84.[28] His sons Samuel Jr., and Donald added to the company holdings by purchasing *The New Yorker*, *Vanity Fair* and *Architectural Digest* as well as several more newspapers.[29]

Real Estate

Russian-heritage Jews were some of the largest builders in New York. Irwin Salmon Chanin, was born 1891 in Brooklyn. He graduated with a degree from Cooper Union in civil engineering. His company "built some of New York's most eye-catching structures in the late 1920's and early 30's ... including the 56-story office skyscraper at 122 East 42d Street, and two twin-towered structures that epitomize Central Park West: the Century Apartments, between 62nd and 63rd Streets, the Majestic Apartments, between 71st and 72d Street, and six legitimate theaters: the 46th Street, Biltmore, Mansfield, Theatre Masque, Royale and Majestic. They also built New York's ultimate movie palace, the Roxy." "His company also built the Lincoln Hotel, the Beacon Hotel, and the World Apparel Center on Broadway, between 39th and 40th Streets."[30]

Born Abraham Elias Lefkowitz in 1876 in the Lower East Side, he began his career as a newsboy and bootblack. Starting with $200, and now named A.E. Lefcourt, he went on to build "more skyscrapers than any other individual." In his determination to end sweatshops, he shifted clothing manufacture from the Lower East Side to Midtown. Lefcourt demolished many historic but obsolete buildings and replaced them with "towering modern buildings.... In 1924, he was the largest individual owner of property" in the new garment district. He liked to put his name on his buildings, including the Lefcourt-Colonial, Lefcourt-National, Lefcourt-Marlborough and the Lefcourt State Building. He died at age 55 of a heart attack. His funeral was held at Temple Emanu-El, Fifth Avenue and 65th Street.[31]

"Henry H. Minskoff was president of Sam Minskoff & Sons, one of the New York area's largest building concerns [that] produced dozens of office buildings ... including 1 Astor Plaza on Times Square; the MGM Building at the Avenue of the Americas and 55th Street, the Rolex Building at Third Avenue and 42d Street, and at 250 Broadway, opposite City Hall, apartment houses and shopping centers in Manhattan, Queens and Westchester County, as well as projects in Baltimore, Philadelphia and Detroit." Minskoff was born in New York City, the second of six children of Russian-Jewish immigrants. After graduating from Lehigh University, Henry joined his father's real estate company. The Sam Minskoff Theater on Broadway was named for his father.[32]

Abraham Levitt was born in Brooklyn. His father was a rabbi in Russia before coming to the United States. Abraham was a real-estate lawyer who established Levitt & Sons, a real estate development company, that was passed on to his son William, born in 1907. Serving in the United States Navy, William foresaw the need for affordable housing after World War II. In 1947, buying land cheaply, using prefabricated materials and assembly line methods, he began building 17,000 identical 800 square foot homes at Levittown, on Long Island, each costing $6,900, with low down payments. Levittown was soon followed by similar vast housing schemes in Pennsylvania, New Jersey, and Maryland. William Levitt became known as the "King of Suburbia." He died at age 88.[33]

Usher Selig Goldman was born 1917, the son of a Brooklyn grocer. He "came into wealth by ignoring the advice of his mother: 'Never leave the store, Sol. It's a gold mine.'" Instead, he left the family grocery business to a younger brother, dropped out of Brooklyn College after a matter of months and at the age of 18 went into the business at which he became one of the most celebrated practitioners. During the Great Depression, he bought foreclosed properties. Over a 50-year career he "built one of New York City's great fortunes buying and selling real estate," including the Chrysler Building. Despite the volatile New York real estate market, at the time of his death, he owned over 600 buildings. Sol Goldman died at age 70. The funeral service was held at Temple Emanu-El, Fifth Avenue and 65th Street.[34] Temple Emanu-El, New York's first Reform Temple, was established in 1845 in the Lower East Side by German-Jewish immigrants. With the success of its community, the Temple moved uptown. In the 20th century, the funeral services of many highly successful Jews of Russian-Jewish heritage were held at Temple Emanu-El.

Second generation Jews of Eastern European heritage were active in real estate construction in cities across the nation. Carl Sandburg called Chicago "the city of big shoulders," wrote the *Chicago Tribune*. "For years, some people believed those shoulders belonged to Arthur Rubloff, whose name, in giant letters, appeared on billboards on so many buildings." He was born in Duluth, Minnesota, to parents who immigrated from Russia. In 1930, with $330, he started his career to become "a giant in Chicago real estate development and once ranked by *Forbes* magazine as one of the nation's top five developers.... Among projects he was involved in were One Magnificent Mile, a glittering retail and residential complex on Michigan Avenue; Carl Sandburg Village, a self-contained network of high-rise apartment buildings; and continuing redevelopment projects north of Chicago's downtown Loop." Rubloff donated large sums to the Art Institute of Chicago, Northwestern University and the University of Chicago.[35]

Yakov Pritzker was the founder of the Pritzker family in America. He came to Chicago from the Ukraine in 1881, graduated in law from DePaul University and set up a law practice. His son Abram Nicholas, born 1896, graduated from Harvard Law School and joined his father as Pritzker & Pritzker, specializing in business law. In the 1930s, Abram branched out into real estate. The Pritzker family is best known for owning the Hyatt hotel chain, as well as "casinos, a law firm, cable television systems and companies that make items ranging from railway boxcars to aluminum forgings for missiles."[36] The wealthy Pritzker children and grandchildren have engaged in philanthropy and public service, among them Penny Pritzker, who served as United States secretary of commerce and J.B. Pritzker, Democratic governor of the State of Illinois.

Jack Buncher was born in Pittsburgh in 1911. Though he graduated having studied medicine, in 1931 he joined his father in the scrap metal business. The Liberty Scrap Company grew with the great demand for metal during World War II. After the war, Buncher entered the real estate market to become one of Pittsburgh's largest property owners. Buncher supported the United Jewish Federation of Greater Pittsburgh. His "Buncher Leadership Program was an all-important tool in the development of Jewish leaders on every continent [enabling] more than 220 lay and professional leaders to acquire the skills they need to help their communities flourish."[37] Also, in Pittsburgh, Joseph Soffer and Sydney Gumberg were leading shopping mall developers.

Matthew Bucksbaum was born in 1926 in Marshalltown, Iowa, where his family owned three grocery stores. He served with the Army Air Force in the Southwest Pacific Theater during World War II. Returning home, he established General Growth Properties that "built dozens of open-air shopping centers and later enclosed malls. Taking advantage of an increasingly automobile-based culture, the company's projects both fueled and fed on the growth of American suburbs.... At Matthew Bucksbaum's retirement, the company's holdings numbered more than 200 malls encompassing more than 200 million square feet of space, and the family was one of the country's wealthiest." He funded the Bucksbaum Institute of Clinical Excellence at the University of Chicago. He died at age 87.[38]

Sherman W. Dreiseszun was born in 1920 in Kansas City, the son of Polish-Jewish immigrants. During World War II, he served as a gunner whose B-17 was shot down over the Mediterranean. "When he was struggling to survive in the water, he promised G-d that upon his return to civilian life, he would dedicate himself to his synagogue and Jewish causes.... Mr. Dreiseszun was a two-time past President and President for Life of Kehilath Israel Synagogue, member of its Men's Club; past President of the Menorah Medical Center Board of Directors; Chairman Emeritus of the Menorah Legacy Foundation Board; Chairman of Israel Bonds Campaign; founding board member and officer of the Jewish Heritage Foundation; member of the Jewish Federation Board of Governors and Board of Directors; founding Board Member, past President and Board Member of the Jewish Community Campus Board."[39] He built shopping malls in Kansas, Missouri, Colorado, and Michigan. His Town Pavilion and One Kansas City Place are two of the city's tallest buildings and helped transform the landscape of Kansas City.

Sam Eig and Morris Cafritz—both immigrants—were leading builders in Washington, D.C., and Maryland. Sam Eig was born 1899 near Minsk in the Russian Empire and came to the United States in 1914. He worked as a busboy and butcher's assistant before opening a liquor store in Washington, D.C. Starting in 1946, he used the profits to buy and build real estate. He was "board chairman of Eig Enterprises and one of Montgomery County's leading builders and land developers.... Mr. Eig developed and built the 26-story Washingtonian Towers apartment building in Gaithersburg in 1966. Ten years before that, he had developed the Washingtonian Motel and Country Club nearby. He built the Shady Grove Music Fair. He also donated land to synagogues and Protestant and Catholic churches, hospitals, and Red Cross facilities. He was a cofounder and trustee of the Camp Echo Lake for underprivileged children.... He was past president and a life member of the board of governors of B'nai Israel Synagogue. He also had served on the boards of several Maryland banks and had been chairman of the United Givers Fund campaign.... In 1952, *Fortune* magazine named him one of the country's top 10 self-made men who had made outstanding contributions to their profession and communities."[40]

Morris Cafritz was born in Lithuania, then part of the Russian Empire. He came to the United States with his family in 1898, settling first in New York and later, Washington, D.C. He began his career in real estate in 1904 at age 17 when he borrowed $1,400 from his father, a grocer, to purchase the Star Coal & Coke Company. Buying bowling alleys, he became known as the bowling king of Washington. He helped raise the money to build the Washington, D.C., Jewish Community Center. In the 1920s he bought a large tract of land to build 3,000 houses. The Cafritz Construction Company built the Universal Building, the 1,600-unit River House Apartments and several hotels, to become the largest private property developer in Washington, D.C. With his wife he established the Morris and Gwendolyn Foundation to support the arts and community services in Washington, D.C. Morris Cafritz died in 1964, aged 77 years.[41]

Malcolm Irving Glazer, born in 1928, was the fifth of seven children of Abraham and Hannah Glazer, immigrants from Lithuania. Raised in Rochester, New York, Malcolm learned watch repair from his father, who ran a pawnshop. He was 15 years old when his father died, leaving the family $300 kept in a cigar box. Malcolm was a "small man with a reddish beard—sometimes referred to in the news media as the leprechaun.... In the 1950s, he dropped out of college to run a watch repair and jewelry business and then expanded into real estate, buying duplexes and mobile homes in Rochester. Mr. Glazer became the chief executive of First Allied Corporation, a holding company for his family investments. He had interests in shopping centers, restaurants, food packaging and supplies, broadcasting, nursing homes, banking and natural gas." In 1999 he purchased the Tampa Bay Buccaneers National Football League team and, in 2005, gained control of renowned English soccer team Manchester United. Malcolm Glazer died in 2014 at age 85.[42]

Jerry J. Moore "was the shopping center king of Texas," wrote *Texas Monthly* in 1998. "Moore has always had a flair for turning real estate into gold. Born in Houston in 1927 to Polish-Jewish immigrants (his father was a plumber), he dropped out of San Jacinto High School after the tenth grade and hawked vacuum-cleaners door-to-door. In 1958 he founded his company, Jerry J. Moore Investments, and bought his first piece of real estate—a three-room shotgun house in North Houston.... By 1989 Moore was the biggest individual shopping-center developer in the U.S., with more than 160 properties encompassing 19 million square feet of space around Texas, 70 percent of which was in the Houston area.... He also owns about 700 antique cars, one of the largest collections in the world, including 30 rare Duesenbergs. In 1991 *Texas Monthly* ranked him third on its list of that year's one hundred wealthiest Texans." Jerry Moore died in 2008 and was buried at Beth Yeshurun Cemetery.[43]

In 1855 the English poet Robert Browning published *Andrea del Sarto* about the life of the 16th-century Italian painter. A line of the poem reads: "A man's reach should exceed his grasp." The sons and daughters of the poor Russian-Jewish immigrants were driven to achieve in the New World. As manufacturers and entrepreneurs, many succeeded beyond the wildest dreams of their youth; both for themselves, and for the benefit of the nation.

15

World War I

World War I began in Europe in 1914. On August 19, President Woodrow Wilson said the United States should stay out of the conflict and "must be neutral in fact, as well as in name, during these days that are to try men's souls. We must be impartial in thought as well as in action." Over the next 30 months, the United States was drawn into the war by unrestricted German submarine aggression. In January 1916, Meyer London and Morris Hillquit, both Jews born in Tsarist Russia who immigrated to the United States in their teens, met with President Wilson in an attempt to avoid a war with Germany. Their political base was the Lower East Side of New York, with many regarding Russia (then an ally of France and Great Britain), rather than Germany, as their enemy. Meyer London was born 1871 in a Lithuanian shtetl. He came to the Lower East Side of New York in 1891, found work as a librarian, while attending night classes at New York University law school. He joined the Socialist Part of America and set up practice in labor law, and served as legal counsel to the International Ladies Garment Workers Union (ILGWU). He served from 1915 through 1991 and from 1921 through 1923 in the United States House of Representatives.

Morris Hillquit, born Moishe Hillkowitz, organized garment workers and ran in 1917 for mayor of New York City on a socialist, anti-war platform, gaining 22 percent of the votes. After the passage of the Selective Service Act on May 18, 1917, London called upon his fellow Jews to comply with the military draft. "No republic can last unless its laws are obeyed," said London.[1] The Yiddish-language *Daily Forward* "preaches faithful and loyal citizenship.... Every man between the ages of 21 and 30 must do his duty."[2] In February 1917, Tsar Nicholas III abdicated and eight months later, the Bolsheviks seized power. On April 6, 1917, the United States declared war against Germany. "The world," President Woodrow Wilson declared, "must be made safe for democracy." In March 1918, Soviet Russia withdrew from World War I.

Emma Goldman was born 1869 into an Orthodox Jewish family in Kovno, Lithuania, then part of the Russian Empire. At age 16 she immigrated to the United States, and found work in clothing factories. An outspoken anarchist, she campaigned for free speech, and birth control. Anarchism, she wrote, is "based on liberty unrestricted by man-made law [and that] all forms of government rest on violence, and are therefore wrong and harmful, as well as unnecessary."[3] She founded

Meyer London, U.S. representative from New York's 12th District, 1916 (Library of Congress, LC-DIG-ggbain-22813).

Emma Goldman, pictured here in 1910, was an anarchist and anti-war activist. She was deported to Russia in 1919 (Library of Congress, LC-DIG-ppmsca-02894).

the *Mother Earth* magazine. In 1917, with her partner, Alexander Beckman, she organized protests against the entry of the United States into World War I. Goldman was arrested under the Espionage Act of 1917 and was sentenced for two years for "counseling young men not to register" for the military draft.[4] On her release from prison, Emma was deported to Russia, on December 21, 1919, with 248 other anarchists and radicals. At first, she supported the Bolshevik revolution but turned against it and left Soviet Russia in 1924.

The Jewish Welfare Board sought to reassure Jewish immigrants that their sons would be well-cared for by the United States Army. A poster shows a smiling Jewish doughboy off to training camp, with his possessions, including a Torah scroll and his books—ready to pray, study, read, play music and fight for his country.

Jewish Welfare Board poster, 1918. This Yiddish language poster encouraged Jews to join the Army. "He Has Everything He Needs," including a Torah scroll, Yiddish books and a violin (National Archives, NARA-512486).

A Yiddish-language poster shows an old-world Jewish man touring a military camp. A kind officer reassures him that the Army is taking good care of the Jewish recruits. Another poster shows a caring Army officer telling a traditional Jewish couple: "Don't worry; he will be alright."

A quarter million American Jews, one-third of them foreign born, served in the United States Army during World War I. They were drawn largely from New York, Illinois, Pennsylvania, and Massachusetts, but also from every other state of the Union. (In 1919, the Jewish communities of Florida, Arizona, and Nevada were small.) Most were the children of Russian Jews who had immigrated to the United States. An analysis conducted by the American Jewish Committee showed that "The Jews of America have contributed their full quota to the winning of the war, and a generous margin beyond their quota; that they enlisted cheerfully, fought gallantly and died bravely for the United States."[5] Congressman Julius Kahn, from California, served as chairman of the House Military Affairs Committee, U.S. Congress. He wrote: "I desire to congratulate my co-religionists on the splendid showing they are making in the matter of serving our country in this war. Many of the boys who go down to the front will be wounded. Many of them will be killed [but they] have been ready to make the supreme sacrifice whenever the land that gives them shelter demands it. [American Jews] will do our share toward keeping Old Glory floating proudly in the skies."[6]

Morris Morrison from Brooklyn volunteered. "My mother didn't want me to

***Left:* The Jewish Welfare Board campaign reassured Jewish immigrants in this November 1918 poster that their sons would be well looked after by the U.S. Army (National Archives, NARA-45538774). *Right:* Jewish Welfare Board poster, 1918, reassuring Old World parents. "Don't Worry. He Is All Right" (National Archives, NARA-45538782).**

go," he explained, "but I figured this country was different from Russia, and it is worth fighting for." Michael Shalinsky wrote: "When my turn came to be drafted it didn't bother me at all. If I hadn't been drafted, I would have gone anyway. Both my parents are Jewish immigrants from Europe, and this country has been good to our family."[7]

In August 1917, the 77th Division's Camp Upton training camp at Yaphank, Long Island, New York, was ready "to mold into soldiers thousands of civilians little used to Army discipline." The recruits represented all races and creeds—some who had recently been subjected to the pogroms in Russia, gunmen and gangsters.... Italians, Chinamen, the Jews and the Irish; a heterogeneous mass representing the study of American manhood.[8] Between 25 and 35 percent of the 20,000 soldiers in the 77th Division, known as the Melting Pot Division, were Jewish.

The 77th Division completed military training in April 1918 and was shipped to France. The Meuse-Argonne Offensive, in October 1918, pitted 200,000 Americans against entrenched German forces. The 77th Division suffered 10,000 casualties, with many Jewish soldiers listed as killed, severely wounded or died from illness; among them were Harry Abromowitz, Isador Ackerman, Jacob Danilowitz, Hyman Jacob, Jack Garfinkel, Jacob Goodman, Harry Greenblatt, David Klein, Jacob Levine, Moses Lowenstein, Alan Slomovitz, Max Silverman and Hyman Shapiro.

During the battle in the forest a battalion of 550 men was surrounded by German forces. The situation for the Lost Battalion was desperate, with food, water and ammunition running short, and many men shot dead. After several patrols and runners had been shot down, private Abraham Krotoshinsky volunteered to try to break through the German lines and carry a message to the main body of the 77th Division. Krotoshinsky was born in Plotsk, then part of the Russian Empire. "I ran away from Russia and came to America to escape military service. I hated Russia, its people, its government, in particular its cruel and inhuman treatment of Jews. Such a Government I refused to serve." He came to New York in 1912, at age 20, and found work as a barber in the Bronx. Not yet a citizen, he willingly joined the U.S. Army.

Abraham Krotoshinsky recalled: "Our situation appeared and was desperate and hopeless. The morning of the fifth day they called for volunteers for courier. I volunteered and was accepted. I went because I thought I ought to. First of all, I was lucky enough not to be wounded. Second, after five days of starving, I was stronger than many of my friends who were twice my size. You know, a Jew finds strength to suffer. I started out at daybreak, but it did not take me long to be aware that I was a target for the Germans. I ran across an open space, down a valley and into some bushes. I remember crawling, lying under bushes, digging myself into holes. Somehow or other, I found myself at nightfall in German trenches. I saw several of them smoking cigarettes. I hid under some bushes, lying prone and acting dead. A German stepped on one of my fingers, but I kept myself from making any outcry. Later I crawled into another deserted German trench. You can imagine the thrill I got when I heard good English words spoken. No music ever sounded better."[9] Krotoshinsky's bravery saved 194 lives. For his valor, private Abraham Krotoshinsky was awarded the Distinguished Service Cross by General John J. Pershing, commander-in-chief of the American Expeditionary Force.

On October 14, during the rescue of the Lost Battalion, Sergeant Benjamin Kaufman of Company K, 308th Infantry, 77th Division "took out a patrol for the purpose of attacking an enemy machine gun which had checked the advance of his company." Several members of Kaufman's troop were killed or wounded. "Before reaching the gun, he became separated from his patrol and a machine gun bullet shattered his right arm. Without hesitation he advanced on the gun alone, throwing grenades with his left hand and charging with an empty pistol, taking one prisoner and scattering the crew, bringing the gun and prisoner back to the first-aid station."[10] For valor, Kaufman was awarded the Medal of Honor. Born 1894 in Buffalo, and raised in Brooklyn, New York, Kaufman was one of eight children of Russian-Jewish immigrants. He was a student at Syracuse University before he was drafted into the U.S. Army.

Lee J. Levinger served as a Jewish chaplain during the Great War. In his 1921 book *A Jewish Chaplain in France* he records the condescending comments of Army officers towards Jewish soldiers, especially those foreign-born. Colonel Charles W. Whittlesey, a graduate of Williams College and Harvard Law School, was the commander of the Lost Battalion. "As to the Jewish boys in the Battalion," Whittlesey noted, "I cannot recall many of them by name, but certain figures stand out simply because they are so unexpected. The ordinary run of soldiers, whether Jews, Irish, or Americans—the big, husky chaps who simply do what they are expected to do—naturally pass from our memory. It is the odd figures who stick in your mind. There was one chap for example (Herschkowitz was his name) who seemed the worst possible material from which to make soldier-stuff. He was thick-set, stupid looking, extremely foreign, thoroughly East Side, and yet, one day when we were holding the bank of the Vesle, and it became necessary to send runners to communicate with our commands, Jack Herschkowitz was the *only man* who volunteered for the job. It was a nasty physical job. It would have been a difficult thing even if it had not been under fire, because it meant cutting through under-brush, uphill and downhill. Under fire this became almost impossible, and the boys knew it, so none of them cared for the job, but Herschkowitz made the trip four times that day. What was it? Well, just plain pluck, that's all. There were a great many fellows of this type—East Siders of whom the regular Army men expected nothing at all—but the 77th Division just seemed equal to anything."

Born in Eastern Europe, Jack Herschkowitz worked in a New York grocery store before conscription into the U.S. Army. His Distinguished Service Cross (DSC) citation reads: "Near Binarville, France, 29 September 1918. In order to obtain ammunition and rations, Private Herschkowitz, accompanied an officer in an effort to reestablish communication between battalion and regimental headquarters. They were attacked by a small party of Germans, but drove them off, killing one. When night came, they crawled unknowingly into the center of a German camp, where they lay for three hours undetected. Finally discovered, they made a dash to escape. In order to protect the officer, Private Herschkowitz deliberately drew the enemy fire to himself, allowing the officer to escape. Private Herschkowitz succeeded in getting through and delivering his message the next morning."

Captain William Harrigan led soldiers to rescue the Lost Battalion. Later he said: "I wish to say a special word for the Jewish members of the 77th Division, and they were 40 percent of that division. They were put to as hard a test of modern warfare when they walked 35 miles through the Argonne Forest."[11] Major General Robert Alexander, commander of the 77th Division, "found that Hebrew names on the Honor Roll of the division were fully up to the proportion that they should have been; in other words, the Hebrew boy paid his full share of the price of victory. When the time came for recommendations to go in for marks of distinction which we were able to give, I found there again that the names of the Hebrews were as fully represented on that list as the numbers in the division warranted, by long odds." A lieutenant colonel "was rather nervous the first time under fire because I had a number of foreign boys in one company and didn't know how they might behave. Among them was a little Jew who was medical man of the company, carrying bandages instead of weapons, but going over the top with the others. A restless fellow, always breaking orders and getting into trouble of some kind or another."

During a battle, "I saw that little Jew jumping out of a shell hole and starting for the rear as fast as he could run. I pulled my revolver, ready to shoot him rather than have an example of cowardice set for the rest. But I was surprised to see him turn aside suddenly and jump into another shell hole, and when I went over there, I found him hard at work bandaging up another wounded soldier. He was simply doing his duty under fire, absolutely without sign of fear as he tended the boys who were hurt. I was sorry I had misjudged him so badly and watched his work after that, with the result that I was later able to recommend him for a decoration."[12]

Abel Davis was born 1874 in Kaunus (Kovno), Lithuania, one of eight children of Pesach and Keile Davis. When he was six years old his family moved to Chicago. Abel started as an errand boy in a department store, and went on to Northwestern Law School, to establish a flourishing law practice in Chicago. In the First World War, Colonel Abel Davis was commander of the 132nd Infantry of Illinois, serving with the British Fourth Army. He was awarded the Distinguished Service Cross for "extraordinary heroism in action in France, October 9, 1918. Upon reaching its objective, after a difficult advance, involving two changes of directions, Colonel Davis's regiment was subjected to a determined enemy counterattack. Disregarding the heavy shell and machine-gun fire, Colonel Davis personally assumed command and by his fearless leadership and courage the enemy was driven back."[13]

Hyman Silverman was the son of Russian Jews who settled in Chelsea, Massachusetts. He was in his third year of study at Northeastern University when he was drafted into the U.S. Army. On October 27, 1918, German fire ignited an ammunition dump, killing and wounding many American soldiers. Private Silverman jumped into the dump to remove the ammunition even while more exploded around him. Despite his own wounds, he pulled injured comrades away from the dump. Only after they were safe did he accept treatment for himself. Private Abraham Cohen of Needham, Massachusetts, showed exceptional courage on November 9, 1918, by going out "under terrific machinegun fire to administer help to a wounded soldier." For their exceptional bravery, Private Hyman Silverman and Private Abraham Cohen were awarded the Distinguished Service Cross.

The immigrant Fleshner family, of Springfield, Massachusetts, sent four of their six sons to serve in the war. The oldest, only 23, lost an arm and an eye while carrying ammunition through a barrage, but exclaimed later in the hospital: "I'm the luckiest Jew in the Army. Any other man in my place would have been killed." The Rosenberg family of North Bergen, New Jersey, also sent six sons into military service. Russian-born Liba Goldstein, of Cambridge Springs, Pennsylvania, had 20 grandsons in the allied armies. The colony of 300 immigrant Jewish farming families of Woodbine, New Jersey, sent 43 men to the service.

Sergeant William Sawelson of Newark, New Jersey, was posthumously awarded the Medal of Honor "for conspicuous gallantry and intrepidity above and beyond the call of duty in action with the enemy at Grandpré, France, October 26, 1918. Hearing a wounded man in a shell-hole some distance away calling for water, Sergeant Sawelson upon his own initiative left shelter and crawled through heavy machine-gun fire to where the man lay, giving him the little water he had in his own canteen. He then went back to his own shell-hole, obtained more water and was returning to the wounded man, when he was killed by a machine-gun bullet." On August 9, 1918, Sergeant William Shemin left cover to cross open ground, exposing himself to heavy fire, to rescue wounded soldiers. After other officers were wounded, 19-year-old Shemin, the son of Russian-Jewish immigrants, took command and led his troop to safety. For his courage and leadership, Shemin received the Distinguished Service Cross. Ninety-three years later, President Obama signed the National Defense Authorization Act to present the Medal of Honor to William Shemin's descendants.

The New York–based 27th Division had around 1,000 Jewish soldiers, including Lieutenant Colonel Morris Liebman, killed in action in Flanders. Chaplain Lee Levinger records that 65 other Jews "of the 27th who were killed in action or died in hospitals in France, their full proportion of the nearly 2,000 dead of the division." The Jewish dead included private Robert Friedman of the 102nd Engineers. "Most of our losses were incurred in the terrific fighting at the Hindenburg Line, and most of our men were buried there in the great divisional cemeteries of Bony and Guillemont Farm.... I can still see the Magen Davids standing here and there among the rows of crosses.... The Jews of the 27th won their full share of decorations. Nine of them wear the Distinguished Service Cross conferred by the American command; seven, the British Military Medal; one received the French Croix de Guerre with star; and one, the Belgian Order of the Crown.... Major Emanuel Goldstein, Medical Corps, was decorated for showing exceptional bravery and courage while remaining in the most exposed positions under heavy shell and machine-gun fire, to render first aid to several wounded men."[14] After his platoon had suffered heavy casualties and all the sergeants were wounded, "Corporal Abel J. Levine collected the remaining soldiers to form a platoon and continued the advance. He was wounded but he refused assistance until his men had been cared for and evacuated." For his bravery under fire, Corporal Levine received the Distinguished Service Cross (D.S.C.).

"Private Morris Silverberg, a stretcher bearer in the 108th Infantry, displayed extreme courage on September 29, 1918, by repeatedly leaving shelter and advancing over an area swept by machine-gun and shell fire to rescue wounded comrades. Hearing that his company commander had been wounded, he voluntarily went forward alone, and upon finding that his officer had been killed, brought back his body." Private Silverberg received the D.S.C.

"I asked a boy from one of our machine gun battalions," wrote Lee Levinger, "why he had led a group of volunteers in bringing from an exposed position some wounded men of another regiment, an act in which the only other Jew in the company had been killed and for which my friend was later decorated. He answered me: 'There were only two Jewish boys in the company and we'd been kidded about it a little. We just wanted to show those fellows what a Jew could do.' A dying Jewish boy sent his last message to his parents: 'Tell them I did my duty as a soldier and brought honor to the Jewish name.'"[15]

In the early years of the 20th century, the American Jewish community swelled in size to more than three million, about 250,000 of whom enlisted in the armed forces, eager to defend their country and to end the bloodshed in Europe.

In his book *A History of the Jews in the United States*, first published in 1930, Rabbi Lee Levinger summarizes the Jewish contribution to the United States forces in the Great War: "Of the Jewish soldiers, 48 percent were enrolled in the infantry, the hardest and most dangerous branch of all. … The Jews had a larger proportion than the non-Jews in infantry, medical corps, and signal corps; a smaller proportion in cavalry and engineers; about the same proportion as the non-Jews in the quartermaster corps and the ordnance corps. Ten thousand Jews were commissioned officers … and 1,000 of these were in the Navy.… Almost all of them entered the service for the war directly from the various walks of civil life.… About 2,800 Jews died in service, and 10,000 others were wounded. The Jewish graves were designated by the Magen David, the six-pointed star, instead of the Cross. Over 1,100 citations for valor were conferred on American Jews, 750 of these by the American command and 350

Matzah deliveries for soldiers of the Jewish faith of the 77th Division, American Expeditionary Force, France, 1919 (Library of Congress, LC-USZ62-127594).

by other allies; 177 American Jews can wear the Distinguished Service Cross, 174 the Croix de Guerre, four the Medaille Militaire, and three the Medal of Honor, the rarest of all decorations."[16]

Many college students of the classes of 1916–1920, including the Jewish students, interrupted their studies to serve their country during World War I. Ralph Horween of the Harvard Class of 1918, proudly listed that he served as "seaman 1st class U.S. Naval Force when United States entered the war; called to active duty, April 13, 1917, and assigned to patrol boat *Talofa*; promoted to quartermaster 2nd class in May; entered Cadet School, Massachusetts Institute of Technology, June 1; appointed ensign Sept. 26; assigned to the USS *Connecticut,* Atlantic Fleet, Oct. 15; commissioned ensign U.S. Navy March 1, 1918; assigned to destroyer *Maury* July 1; promoted lieutenant September 1; transferred to destroyer *Gregory,* Mediterranean Squadron, April 2, 1919; resignation accepted July 1, 1919." Karl Blaustein reported: "Enlisted private Quartermaster Corps June 20; ordered to Fort Jay, New York; promoted corporal Aug. 3; transferred to Fort Dupont, Delaware, in August; to Camp Quartermaster Detachment, Camp Meade, Maryland, Sept. 22; promoted to sergeant Oct. 23; attached to Engineers, 79th Division, July 5, 1918, as private; assigned to Company B, 304th Engineers, July 7; sailed for France July 8; discharged June 6, 1919. Engagement: Meusc-Argonne offensive."

Maurice Saunders Burstein was born in Russia and came to the United States as a child. He "enlisted as a private to the Ordnance Department, Nov. 17, 1917; called to active duty March 4, trained at Fort Slocum, New York; detailed to Ordnance Training School, Dartmouth College, New Hampshire; March 21; to Camp Hancock, Georgia, April 27; assigned to 103d Ordnance Company, Camp Devens, Massachusetts, June 14; promoted sergeant in October; detailed to Field Artillery Central Officers' Training School, Camp Zachary Taylor, Kentucky, Nov. 4; discharged Dec. 6, 1918."[17]

Abraham Lincoln Green, Class of 1920, served in France with the medical corps. Aron Seth Steuer, 21, sailed for France in October 1917, to serve in the tank corps of Company B, 304th Battalion. Discharged in May 1919, he returned to Harvard and graduated in 1920. Steuer went on to Columbia Law School and in 1932 he was elected to serve on the Supreme Court of the State of New York. Born in Odessa, Hyman Bernard Horovitz served in the Massachusetts Coast Artillery, then was called to federal service at Fort Andrew, Massachusetts. Later, he sailed for France to serve in the Marne-Aisne, Aisne-Oise and Meuse-Argonne offensives. After his discharge from the Army in February 1919, Horovitz returned to his studies, graduated in 1920 and went on to Harvard law school.[18] Morris Iphraim Stern, prepared at Boston Latin School and a member of the Harvard Class of 1915, and Benjamin Joseph Ginsburg, Harvard Class of 1917, were killed in action. Louis A. Kline, Columbia extension school Class of 1916, was a corporal in the 4th Infantry of the United States Army. He was killed in action in France on October 1, 1918.

Apart from the 77th, Jews were thinly spread among the divisions of the

American Expeditionary Force during World War I. In the military camps and in the battles, these Jews rubbed shoulders with their fellow Americans from all walks of life and across the length and breadth of the land. These encounters hastened the process of Americanization. They returned to an unsettled America. During 1919 there were labor strikes in Seattle, Boston and Los Angeles, and race riots in Chicago and Omaha. The Ku Klux Klan was on the march; anti-immigration and anti–Jewish forces were fast gaining strength. J. Edgar Hoover warned of a high risk of communist insurrection. To quell dissent, U.S. Attorney General A. Mitchell Palmer authorized the search and seizure, arrests, detentions and deportation of persons considered a threat to society. The socialist leader Eugene Debs was sent to prison for opposing the draft.

Emma Goldman and 248 others were rounded up and deported to Russia. In 1919, five socialist New York State assemblymen were expelled from the New York legislature. Louis Waldman, Charles Solomon, Samuel Orr and Samuel Aaron DeWitt were Jewish and represented heavily Jewish neighborhoods in New York City. German Jews led by Louis Marshall, Jacob Schiff, Julius Rosenwald and Felix Warburg were determined, through the American Jewish Committee, to check the spread of radicalism and communist influences among Eastern European Jews.[19] Still, American Jews had their allies. Addressing a 1926 interfaith meeting, General John D. Pershing said: "Jews are an essential part of America. As citizens among us they have always done their full share. When the time came to serve their country under arms, no class of people served with more patriotism or with higher motives than the young Jews who volunteered or were drafted and went overseas with our other young Americans to fight the enemy. [They were] patriotic, well disciplined, well behaved young Jews, whose commanders spoke of them in the highest terms."[20]

16

The Remarkable Achievements of the Second Generation

"The future of American Jewry is indissolubly bound up with the future of the Russian Jews," wrote Israel Friedlander in 1915. "There is no more urgent and no more fruitful task before the Jewry of America than that of conserving the immense Jewish energy of her immigrant population and of infusing it into the growing organism of American Judaism."[1]

"At arrival the Russian Jewish immigrants in the first large wave had relatively poor English language skills and earnings but quickly experienced rapid increases in language skills, their earnings and occupational status. They quickly reached parity with, and then surpassed, those of other immigrants and even of the native born. And their U.S.-born children achieved even higher levels of success in education, earnings and occupations."[2]

Anzia Yezierska, the daughter of a Talmud scholar, left her shtetl in 1893, at age 13, to settle in the Lower East Side of New York City. Like the majority of Russian-Jewish immigrants, her family was religious, spoke and wrote in Yiddish, knew hardly a word of English and arrived dirt-poor. They were desperate to find any work to pay for rent and to feed and clothe the family. Yet "like all people who have nothing, I lived on dreams." In her 1921 story *America and I*, Anzia Yezierska wrote:

As one of the dumb, voiceless ones I speak. One of the millions of immigrants beating, beating out their hearts at your gates for a breath of understanding. From the other end of the earth from where I came, America was a land of living hope, woven of dreams, aflame with longing and desire. Choked for ages in the airless oppression of Russia, the Promised Land rose up—wings for my stifled spirit—sunlight burning through my darkness—freedom singing to me in my prison—deathless songs tuning prison-bars. I arrived in America. My young, strong body, my heart and soul pregnant with the unlived lives of generations clamoring for expression. What my mother and father and their mother and father never had a chance to give out in Russia, I would give out in America. The hidden sap of centuries would find release; colors that never saw light—songs that died unvoiced—romance that never had a chance to blossom in the black life of the Old World. In the golden land of flowing opportunity, I was to find my work that was denied me in the sterile village of my forefathers. Here I was to be free from the dead drudgery for bread that held me down in Russia. For the first time in America, I'd cease to be a slave of the belly. I'd be a creator, a giver, a human being! My work would be the living job of fullest self-expression.

> But from my high visions, my golden hopes, I had to put my feet down on earth. I had to have food and shelter. I had to have the money to pay for it. I was in America, among the Americans, but not of them. No speech, no common language, no way to win a smile of understanding from them, only my young, strong body and my untried faith. Only my eager, empty hands, and my full heart shining from my eyes![3]

Between the years 1881 and 1914, two million Jews departed the Russian Empire. Most of them boarded ships in German ports and crossed the Atlantic Ocean to settle in the United States. Some 100,000 settled in Canada, 40,000 (mainly from Lithuania) ventured to South Africa, and 150,000 departed to Argentina; 70,000 were inspired by Zionism to settle in Ottoman Palestine (The First and Second Aliyot). Among them were David Ben Gurion, Yitzhak Ben-Zvi, Moshe Sharett, Joseph Trumpeldor and David Remez who would guide the Jewish population to nationhood. The first five presidents of the State of Israel were born in the Russian Empire. About 100,000 Russian Jews settled in Germany, and 100,000 settled in France. About 150,000 Russian Jews came to Great Britain, with most of them crowding into Whitechapel, in London's East End to establish a Jewish ghetto. They were not welcomed. Under the Alien Act of 1905, Russian Jews were declared "undesirable immigrants" and denied further entry into Great Britain.

Wherever they settled, the children of Russian Jewish immigrants displayed high levels of achievement and contributed greatly to the well-being of their adopted country. Born in South Africa, Brian Josephson, Michael Levitt, Sidney Brenner, Aaron Klug and Nadine Gordimer were Nobel Prize winners. Most of the signers of the Israeli Declaration of Independence in 1948 and nearly all Israeli Nobel Prizewinners were children of Eastern European Jews. Zelman Cohen, the 19th governor-general of Australia, came from an Eastern European Jewish family. John Monash, Australia's most revered Army commander, was born in 1865 in Melbourne, of Eastern European Jewish parents. The philosopher Isaiah Berlin, historian Lewis Bernstein Namier, theater director Jonathan Miller, Michael and Simon Marks of Marks & Spencer, Jack Cohen the founder of Tesco, Isaac Wolfson, and numerous other distinguished British academics, physicians, writers, artists, civil servants, lawyers, judges, businessmen, manufacturers and newspaper editors were the children of the once "undesirable" Eastern European Jewish immigrants.

The great majority of the Russian-Jewish immigrants to the United States left Ellis Island to settle first in the squalid and overcrowded Jewish ghetto of the Lower East Side of New York or in the Jewish neighborhoods of Boston, Philadelphia, Chicago, Baltimore and Cleveland. On their arrival in America, most of the Russian-Jews "were engaged in a really difficult struggle for existence."[4] They worked long-hours for low pay in the garment sweatshops, cigar and cigarette factories, or selling goods off pushcarts, to form an "industrial Jewish working class."[5] To help support the family, their children, as young as six or seven, earned extra pennies by selling newspapers or shining shoes at street corners. Family and social difficulties increased. Many fathers abandoned their families, children dropped out of school

"The Alien Invasion: Searching Baggage of Immigrant Jews in the Transit Shed at Port of Tilbury, on the River Thames, near the City of London," 1891 newspaper cartoon.

and got into trouble, and people succumbed to tuberculosis and other infectious diseases. The social services established by German Jews, who arrived in America a half-century earlier, were stretched to their limits. The public schools in the ghettoes, welcomed the children of the Russian-Jewish immigrants, and fostered their desire for knowledge and their powerful wish to become Americans.

On arrival in the United States, Russian Jews were viewed as genetically inferior in body and in mind, likely to degrade the American stock, and an unwelcome burden on society. They were deemed unlikely to make a successful adjustment to the fast-industrializing United States. William Zebina Ripley served as professor of political economy at Harvard College. His appointment in 1901 was largely based on the publication of his book two years earlier entitled *The Races of Europe: A Sociological Study.* Ripley wrote: "The Jew betrays an inherent dislike for manual or outdoor labor, as for physical exercise or exertion in any form.... The European Jews are all undersized; not only this, they are more often absolutely stunted. [They are] narrow-chested and deficient in lung capacity.... These people are prone to nervous and mental disorders; insanity, in fact, is fearfully prevalent among them."

About one Jew in 10, wrote Ripley, has a hooked nose, but many have a "tucking up of the wings [that] renders a nose concave in profile, to be immediately recognizable as Jewish." Carrying the stereotype even further, Ripley found that the eyebrows of Jews "appear to be nearer together than usual, arching smoothly into the lines of the nose. The lids are rather full, the eyes large, dark, and brilliant." Another alleged Jewish peculiarity was the "separation of the teeth, which seem to stand well apart from one another." Ripley expressed his alarm about the "horde of Russian exiles, this great swamp of miserable human beings, terrific in its proportions, that threatens to drain itself off into our country unless we restrict its ingress."[6]

Fearing that the children of the Russian-Jewish immigrants would follow their parents into the garment trades and remain in the ghettoes, the German Jewish elite set up trade schools to guide them into productive trades as plumbers, carpenters, electricians, house painters and factory workers. But these children set higher goals for themselves. Like Anzia Yezierska, they rapidly learned English and American ways and discovered their individual talents. Many excelled in school. Others excelled in sports, as boxers, basketball and football players. Still others established businesses. Within a decade of arrival, the Russian-Jewish immigrants and their families left the Jewish ghettoes to settle in brighter neighborhoods. Until Jewish immigration haltered at the start of World War I, new arrivals—"greeners"—took their places in the Jewish ghettoes.

Many authors have commented on the high achievements of the great wave of Russian-Jews who came to America during the years 1881 to 1914. Stephen Birmingham contrasted the achievements of the German Jews who arrived in the United States during the middle of the 19th century, and the Russian Jews who arrived 50 years later: "It had taken the Germans two and in some cases three generations to reach their status in wealth and almost assimilation. It had taken the Russians barely one. Was it possible that the Russians were of all things, cleverer?" By the 1920s, the Russian Jews showed that they were enterprising but they were still "brash, aggressive, pushy, argumentative. They had not yet acquired the fine sheen of social polish the Germans had striven so hard, and so long, to possess."[7]

"The Ghetto boy is making use of his heterogeneous opportunities with the greatest energy and ambition," wrote the journalist Hutchings Hopgood in 1902, "The public schools are filled with little Jews; the night schools of the east side are practically used by no other race. City College, New York University, and Columbia University are graduating Russian Jews in numbers rapidly increasing.... It is a mistake to think that the young Hebrew turns naturally to trade. He turns his energy to whatever offers the best opportunities for broader life and success. Other things besides business are open to him in this country, and he is improving his chance for the higher education as devotedly as he has improved his opportunities for success in business. It is easy to see that the Ghetto boy's growing Americanism will be easily triumphant at once over the old traditions and the new socialism."[8]

"Probably among no nationality does the economic condition change more rapidly than among the Russian Jewish people in the United States. The transition period from the junk peddler to the iron yard owner, from the dry goods peddler to the retail or wholesale dry goods merchant, from the cloak maker to the cloak manufacturer, is comparatively short."[9] In 1919, Paul Douglas noted that "the Jews are the most highly skilled of all the newer races" arriving in America.[10]

In 1981, Deborah Dash Moore wrote that the 1920s saw "the entry of the Eastern European Jew into the small business enterprises and then his son into the university and the professions. Secure within the ethnic boundaries of their middle-class neighborhoods the second-generation Jews went on to scale the walls of a larger American society."[11]

Steven Pearse wrote: "Higher levels of education including advanced degrees from the best of schools allowed Jews to practice demanding scientific, literary, education, artistic, professional and entrepreneurial careers."[12]

Using data from the 1900 United States population census, Barry R. Chiswick of Georgetown University compared the occupational status of adult Jewish immigrants "with other immigrants and native-born white men. On arrival the Jewish immigrants had a low occupational status but they experienced very rapid improvements with duration. Occupational parity was reached with Western European and Canadian immigrants (5-years after immigration) and the native born (14 years). Their high level of attainment reflected large human capital investments (at home and in school) and an emphasis on decision making skills."[13] In a later report, Chiswick wrote: "Russian Jewish immigrants from the late 19th and early 20th centuries experienced high levels of human capital accumulation and economic success. … And their U.S.-born children achieved even greater successes compared to other native-born children."[14]

Most of the children of the Russian Jewish immigrations—both those born in Russia and those born in the United States—were raised in the Jewish ghettoes where they attended elementary school. Early in their lives many of these children displayed talent. Irving Berlin, Walter Matthau, Molly Picon, Sophie Tucker, and George Burns learnt in their pre-teen years that they could earn a little extra money by singing and performing, and honed their talent by winning talent competitions. Others were encouraged by their public-school teachers to sit the examinations for elite high schools. In time, these smart children entered elite colleges and went on to graduate school to train as physicians, dentists, accountants, lawyers, researchers and academics.

By 1920, the children of the "undesirable" immigrants faced a new set of prejudices. They were accused of being overly ambitious, pushy, uncouth, unathletic, too smart, and crowding non–Jews out of the Ivy League colleges. Abbott Lawrence Lowell, president of Harvard College, claimed in 1922 that Jewish students were "not easily assimilated.… It is the duty of Harvard to receive just as many boys who have come, or whose parents have come to this country without our background, as it can effectively educate.… If every college in the country would take a limited proportion of Jews, I suspect we should go a long way toward eliminating race feeling among the students." Anti-Semitism increased, wrote Lowell, "with the immigration from the Old World." Lowell called on Jews "to help us" by agreeing to lower Jewish college applications, especially to Harvard.[15] In the 1920s, Harvard and other leading colleges imposed a hidden quota on the admission of Jews. Character rather than academic excellence became the leading criterion for college admission.

This work, *Children of the American Jewish Ghetto*, describes the remarkable achievements of the children of allegedly un-assimilable Russian-Jews who arrived in America in the years 1881 to 1914. Despite overt anti–Semitism, they entered the professions of medicine, accounting, law and academia, established successful businesses, and helped shape America's intellectual, musical and literary identity. At least 40 of these children became Nobel laureates, many others won Pulitzer Prizes, Oscars, Academy Awards and other laurels of high achievement. Many succeeded in the boxing ring, the basketball court and on the athletic field. Jacob Koppel Javits, Abraham Alexander Ribicoff, Diana Feinstein and Bernard Sanders were prominent politicians. Ruth Bader Ginsburg was a beloved Supreme Court justice, Hyman Rickover was the father of America's nuclear Navy. Abraham Beame, Michael Rubens Bloomberg and Ed Koch each served as mayor of New York City. George Gershwin, Aaron Copland and Leonard Bernstein helped establish a distinctive American musical style. Numerous men and women of Russian-Jewish heritage were prominent in business and manufacturing; among them Helena Rubinstein, Max Factor, and Estée Lauder in cosmetics, Henry Crown of General Dynamics, Leon Hess in oil refining, Les Wexner in retailing, William Levitt the developer of Levittown, and Ralph Lauren and Calvin Klein in clothing. Success came largely through individual initiative and merit.

In 1972, the year after he won the Nobel Prize for Economics, Simon Kuznets analyzed the economic structure of the Jews of America. The great migration from 1881 to 1914 transformed the Jews of America overwhelmingly into a community of Russian origin. By 1908 "one-third of the Jewish immigrants were already in small retail businesses. Their children were being prepared by intense education for a phenomenal advance in their social position. During the period between 1920 and 1940 a great change was underway that would transform a community that was largely made up of workers into one that was largely of middle-class people: white collar, businessmen and professionals" (p. 18). By 1957, one third of Jewish men were self-employed physicians, lawyers, accountants, or businessmen, compared with 10 percent for the general population. American Jews were largely congregated in cities (88 percent for Jews against 37 percent for the general population). Jews had long since departed the inner-city ghetto and moved to the suburbs. By entering the American mainstream, Jews had become much more secular and were intermarrying at an ever-greater rate.[16]

Factors That May Account for Jewish Achievement

In 1911, the prominent German economist Werner Sombart issued his book *The Jews and Modern Capitalism* (translated two years later into English). Jews helped fashion modern capitalism, based on unfettered competition and the desire to offer goods pleasing to the customer. Sombart believed that "Intellectual interests and intellectual skills were more strongly developed in the Jew than physical (manual) powers.... No other people has valued the learned man, the scholar, as highly as the

Jews. The Jewish mind is an instrument of precision [that has] made the Jews prominent chess-players, mathematicians and skilled at all calculating thought.... Jews have a special kind of imagination ... their calculating, dissecting and combining minds work like lightning, illuminating dark places in a flash. Once the Jew has made up his mind what line he will follow, the rest is comparatively easy, and his mobility only makes his success more so." Being "perennial strangers" and less than full citizens increased their desire to succeed.[17]

"The Jewish mind-set behind the waves of genius has not been successfully explained," wrote Norman Lebrecht in 2020. He does not believe that Jews are "genetically gifted above the average in mathematics, entertainment and money" but postulates that "Jews learned from adversity to think differently from others.... Among Jews, anxiety is a primary motivating factor for the engine of fresh thinking." Anxiety over their place in the wider society has motivated Jews to think "outside the box." Lebrecht offers Gustav Mahler, Modigliani, Marcel Proust, Sigmund Freud, Karl Marx, Albert Einstein, Felix Mendelsohn, Franz Kafka and Heinrich Heine as examples of "out of the box" Jewish genius.[18]

Other writers have attributed Jewish achievement to their close family life and the high value they place on education, their skills in reading, writing and speaking, self-discipline, and the strong desire to succeed.[19] Robert Eisen believes that generations of rabbinic study prepared Jews for success when Western society opened to them.[20] Maristella Botticini at Università Bocconi in Milan, and Zvi Eckstein at Tel Aviv University, argue that Jewish skills in speaking and writing equipped them for survival in a hostile world.[21] Another theory suggests that Jewish workers formed powerful trades unions, made sure their children would not remain factory workers, but instead would enter the professions. Eli Lederhendler argues that the strong work ethic and middle-class values that the Russian Jews passed on to their children were acquired not in the Old Country but developed after they came to the United States.[22]

"As far as Jews are concerned," wrote Hans Eysenck of the University of London, in 1975, "there is no question that they score very highly on IQ tests.... Whether these differences are genetic ... or whether they are mainly due to infant care and environmental stimulation ... cannot be answered with any degree of confidence at the moment."[23] In their paper *Natural History of Ashkenazi Intelligence*. Gregory Cochran, Jason Hardy, and Henry Harpending from the Department of Anthropology, University of Utah, postulate that high Ashkenazi "verbal and mathematical intelligence but not spatial ability" are compensation for such Jewish genetic diseases as Tay-Sachs and Gaucher's Disease. "Other Ashkenazi disorders are known to increase intelligence."[24]

Theories abound to explain the achievements in America of Jews who came from the Russian Empire. I once asked the wife of a billionaire to account for his success. She answered with the Yiddish word *bashert;* that it was pre-ordained, it was his destiny. Examining the lives of children of Russian-Jewish immigrants, I believe that many were able to think beyond the accepted wisdom, were risk-takers, and were individually motivated to give thanks and repay the country that took them in. In 1918, a quarter-century after he arrived as a little boy in the Lower East Side, and the year he acquired American citizenship, Irving Berlin wrote *God Bless America*. The song became America's second national anthem. It was "an expression of gratitude for what this country has done for its citizens, of what home really is." Berlin said he "first heard the title phrase from his mother, who frequently spoke the words ... despite their poverty. His daughter Mary Ellin Barrett later wrote that Berlin meant every word: 'It *was* the land he loved. It *was* his home sweet home. He, the immigrant who had made good, was saying thank you.'"[25] Numerous Jewish immigrants to America, and their children have acted in accordance with President John F. Kennedy's 1961 inaugural address: "Ask not what your country can do for you—ask what you can do for your country."

The Great Depression

The path of the Russian-Jewish immigrants to achievement was not smooth. The quotas imposed in the 1920s kept Jews out of Ivy League colleges, forcing many to seek other colleges to graduate as professionals and enter the middle class. The collapse of Wall Street and the Great Depression of 1929–1939 put millions out of work. American Jews were greatly affected. "A large list of American university and college scientific schools have found more and more doors of many important industrial firms being closed to their technical graduates who are Jewish."

Employment agencies and companies frequently stated that they sought only "Christian" or "Anglo-Saxon" job applicants. "There are in New York City about 369,000 Jewish youth, between the ages of 16 and 24. They are almost wholly native born, predominantly second-generation Americans. They continue their schooling for a longer period and have four times as many college graduates, relatively, as the non–Jewish group.... Thirty-one percent of Jewish youth—115,000—were unemployed; 40,000 of them never had a job.... Unemployment among Jewish youth in New York City is greater, especially in the case of the males, than among the white Protestant workers.... The figures show that it is hard for Jews, as Jews, to get jobs."[26]

Jewish Immigration to the United States After 1921

The 1921 Emergency Quota Act reduced immigration to the United States. The Immigration Act of 1924 (Johnson-Reed Act) limited all immigration to America to 153,000 persons a year. This Act gave preference to "desirable" immigrants from Great Britain (with 65,721 places each year) and Germany (with 25,957 places each year). The quotas for Poland and Russia numbered together 9,308, virtually halting "undesirable" Jewish immigration to America. During the Great Depression, immigration was further reduced. The rise of Hitler and his Nazi party led to a rush of

German Jews seeking to emigrate using the German quota. By 1939 over 300,000 Germans, mainly Jews, had applied for the limited number of places. On March 13, 1939, the German liner *St. Louis* sailed from Hamburg with 937 passengers. Nearly all were Jews fleeing Nazi Germany. They hoped to settle in Cuba to await entry to the United States on the German quota. The Cuban government refused to allow the passengers to land. Likewise, the United States government turned the ship away, forcing the desperate refugees to return to Europe. Most of them found sanctuary in Britain and France, but 254 of them perished in the Holocaust. Six million Jews—from Poland, Soviet Russia, Hungary, Rumania as well as France, Holland, Belgium, Italy and Greece—were killed in the Holocaust. The Russian Jewish immigrants of 1881–1914 and the German-Jewish refugees of 1933–1940 greatly enriched American life. One can only imagine the benefits to our country of continued immigration from Southern and Eastern Europe that was so severely reduced by the Johnson-Reed Act of 1924.

During World War II, over half a million American Jews joined America's armed forces to fight Japan in the west and Nazi Germany in the east. The 1950s witnessed the move of Jews from the inner cities to the suburbs. Generation after generation, Jews have entered ever deeper into the American mainstream. The Pew Report of 2020 gives a snapshot of American Jewry of the sixth and seventh generation after their forebears left the Russian Empire. Jews comprise two percent of the total population of the United States. About a quarter of American-Jewish adults "do not identify with the Jewish religion: They consider themselves to be Jewish ethnically, culturally or by family background and have a Jewish parent or were raised Jewish [and describe] themselves as atheist, agnostic or 'nothing in particular' rather than as Jewish. Among Jewish adults under 30, four in 10 describe themselves this way." Over half of marriages are with non–Jewish partners. Most American Jews identify with the Conservative or the Reform branches of Judaism. "At the same time, younger Jewish adults are much more likely than older Jews to identify as Orthodox." Secular Jews say they have little in common with Orthodox Jews. American Jews in 2020 are still moved by stories of the Holocaust and strive for justice and equality. American Jews "are culturally engaged, increasingly diverse, politically polarized and worried about anti–Semitism."[27]

Writing in *The New York Times,* Senator David Aiken Reed, co-author of the restrictive Johnson-Reed Immigration Act of 1924, announced: "America of the Melting Pot Comes to an End." He claimed that "Americans are beginning to smart under the irritation of her foreign colonies—these groups of aliens, whether in the city slums or country districts, who speak a foreign language, and live a foreign life, and want neither to learn our common language or to share our common life." Reed wanted to keep "American stock up to the highest standard—that is, the people who were born here."[28] The Immigration and Naturalization Act of 1965 replaced the Johnson-Reed Act of 1924. Instead of giving high priority to immigrants from Western Europe, the 1965 Act produced a large migration from war-torn Vietnam and

Cambodia as well as immigrants arriving from Korea, the Philippines, China and India. By the 1990s only one in eight immigrants to America came from Europe; three in eight came from Asia. Large numbers of Spanish-speaking immigrants came from Mexico and other Central and South American counties. Since the 1970s, half a million Jews from the former Soviet Union have come to America. Refugees are arriving from Haiti, Cuba, Venezuela and Guatemala. In the process, the United States has increasingly become a multi-lingual and multi-ethnic nation. A new melting pot.

Each flow of immigrants brings its own culture, language, cuisine, mode of dress, and outlook. Like earlier immigrants from Ireland, the Russian Empire and Italy, the newcomers settle first in their own ghettoes. Each wave of immigrants evokes accusations that the newcomers are unassimilable and are leading the nation to ruin. It takes a generation for the new immigrants to learn English and adjust to American ways. Their American-born and American-educated offspring rapidly find a comfortable and proud home in America. The Russian-Jewish immigration of 1881–1914 was a shining example of an impoverished community that found a safe haven in the United States of America. Since then, generation after generation of America's Jews have been successful, both individually and by making valuable contributions to the nation as a whole.

Chapter Notes

Chapter 1

1. Franklin D. Roosevelt addressing members of Daughters of the American Revolution, April 21, 1938.
2. Israel Zangwill, *The Melting Pot*, 1908.
3. Morris Raphael Cohen, *A Dreamer's Journey* (Boston: Beacon Press, 1949), p. 95.
4. *The International Jew: The World's Foremost Problem*. Reprint of a series of articles appearing in the *Dearborn Independent* from May 22 to October 2, 1920. Owned by Henry Ford, the weekly *Dearborn Independent* expressed his views.

Chapter 2

1. Charles Hirschman and Elizabeth Mogford, "Immigration and the American Industrial Revolution from 1880 to 1920," *Social Science and Research* 38, no. 4 (2009), pp. 897–920.
2. Chaim Weizmann, *Trial and Error: The Autobiography of Chaim Weizmann, Book One* (Lexington, MA: Plunkett Lake Press, 2013).
3. Abraham Cahan, "The Russian Jew in America," *The Atlantic Magazine*, July 1898.
4. Simon M. Dubnow, *History of the Jews of Russia and Poland, Volume III* (Philadelphia: Jewish Publication Society, 1920), pp. 31–33, 54. Simon Dubnow was murdered along with many thousand others by the Nazis in the Riga ghetto on December 8, 1941.
5. "Jewish Massacre Decried," *New York Times*, April 28, 1903, p. 6.
6. Eli Lederhendler, *American Jewry: A New History* (Cambridge: Cambridge University Press, 2017), pp. 63–68.
7. Norma F. Pratt, *Morris Hillquit: A Political History of an American Jewish Socialist* (Westport, CT: Greenwood Press, 1979,) pp. 5–6.
8. Morris Raphael Cohen, *A Dreamer's Journey* (Boston: Beacon Press, 1949), pp. 60–62.
9. Mary Amtin, *The Promised Land* (Leipzig: Bernhard Tauchnitz, 1913), pp. 173–189.
10. "Help for the Needy Refugees; Appeal for Russian Jews," *New York Times*, December 22, 1891.
11. Boris Bogen, *Jewish Philanthropy* (New York: Macmillan, 1917), pp. 90–91.

Chapter 3

1. *School Physiology Journal* 14 (1898).
2. Jacob A. Riis, *How the Other Half Lives: Studies Among the Tenements of New York* (New York: Charles Scribner's Sons, 1890).
3. Jacob Riis, *Review of Reviews* 13 (1896), pp. 58–62.
4. Louise Ware, *Jacob A. Riis: Police Reporter, Reporter, Useful Citizen* (New York: Appleton, 1938), p. 141.
5. Rose Cohen, *Out of the Shadow* (New York: Doran, 1918), p. 69.
6. Abraham Cahan, "The Russian Jew in America," *Atlantic Magazine*, July 1898.
7. Charles E. Bernheimer, ed., *The Russian Jew in the United States: Studies of Social Conditions in New York, Philadelphia and Chicago* (Philadelphia: Winston, 1905), p. 32.
8. Edmund James, *The Immigrant Jew* (New York: Buck, 1907), p. 6.
9. "Vast Crowds Honor Sholem Aleichem," *New York Times*, May 16, 1916, p. 13.
10. Albert Fried, *The Rise and Fall of the Jewish Gangster* (New York: Columbia University Press, 1993), p. 25.
11. Maurice H. Knight, "The Chicago Ghetto Re-Surveyed," *Social Studies* 6, no. 2 (December 1927), pp. 242–252.
12. Irving Cutler, *The Jews of Chicago: From Shtetl to Suburb* (Urbana: University of Illinois Press, 1996), p. 58.
13. Edmund J. James, ed., *The Immigrant Jew in America* (New York: Buck, 1907), p. 59.
14. Charles S. Bernheimer, ed., *The Russian Jew in the United States: Studies of Social Conditions in New York, Philadelphia and Chicago* (Philadelphia: Winston, 1905), pp. 135–136.
15. *The Presbyterian* LIX, no. 9 (March 2, 1889).
16. Charles S. Bernheimer, ed., *The Russian Jew in the United States: Studies of Social Conditions in New York, Philadelphia and Chicago* (Philadelphia: Winston, 1905), pp. 122–125.
17. Greg Hand, Cincinnati Construction Recalls Cincinnati's Long-Vanished Jewish Ghetto," *Cincinnati Magazine*, November 14, 2018.
18. Nathan Glazer, *Social Characteristics of American Jews, 1654–1954* (New York: American Jewish Committee, 1955), p. 25.

19. Judith B. Kramer and Seymour Leventman, *Children of the Gilded Ghetto: Conflict Resolution of Three Generations of American Jews* (New Haven: Yale University Press, 1961), pp. 7–22.

Chapter 4

1. Edwin Markham, *Children in Bondage* (New York: Hearst, 1907), p. 216.
2. James Kaplan, *Irving Berlin: New York Genius* (New Haven: Yale University Press, 2019).
3. Laurence Bergreen, *As Thousands Cheer: The Life of Irving Berlin* (New York: Da Capo, 1996), p. 11.
4. Lawrence Bergreen, *As Thousands Cheer: The Life of Irving Berlin* (New York: Da Capo, 1996).
5. Charles S. Bernheimer, ed., *The Russian Jew in the United States: States: Studies of Social Conditions in New York, Philadelphia and Chicago* (Philadelphia: Winston, 1905), p. 26.
6. *New York Times*, July 22, 1899.
7. Alexander Fleisher, *The Newsboys of Milwaukee: The Effect of Working on Newsboys' Home Lives* (Milwaukee: Milwaukee Bureau of Economy and Efficiency, Bulletin No. 8, November 1911).
8. *Washington Post*, April 2, 1908.
9. Lewis Hine, *Child Labor at the National Capital, 1912*, National Child Labor Committee publication 264.
10. Jane Addams, *Newsboy Conditions in Chicago* (Chicago Federation of Settlements, 1903).
11. Maurice B. Hexter, superintendent of United Jewish Charities; reported in *Studies of the Helen S. Trounstine Foundation* 1, no. 1 (1919), p. 157.
12. Vincent DiGirolamo, *Shouting the News: A History of America's Newsboys* (New York: Oxford University Press, 2019).
13. Anna Reed, *Newsboy Services: A Study of Educational and Vocational Guidance* (New York: World Book, 1917).
14. Allen DuPont Breck, *The Centennial History of the Jews of Colorado, 1859–1959* (Denver: University of Denver Press, 1960), p. 114.
15. Nettie P. McGill, *Children in Street Work*, Department of Labor publication No. 138 (Washington, D.C.: U.S. Government Printing Office, 1928).
16. Harry E. Burroughs, *Boys in Men's Shoes: A World of Working Children* (New York; Macmillan, 1944).
17. *New York Times*, June 16, 1929.
18. *New York Times*, December 19, 1946.
19. Susan Campbell, *Frog Hollow* (Middletown, CT: Wesleyan University Press, 2010).
20. Glen Fowler, "Harry Weinberg, 82, Businessman in Transit and Real estate, Is Dead," *New York Times*, November 6, 1990. Also, *New York Times*, June 1, 1980.

Chapter 5

1. Melech Epstein, *Jewish Labor in the USA: An Industrial, Political, and Cultural History of the Jewish Labor Movement; 1882–1914* (New York: Trade Union Sponsoring Committee, 1950), p. 103.
2. Eugene Lyons, *David Sarnoff: A Biography* (New York: Harper& Row, 1986), p. 27.
3. *New York Times*, April 16, 1886.
4. *New York Times*, September 25, 1900.
5. Samuel Gompers, *Seventy Years of Life and Labor: An Autobiography* (New York: Dutton, 1925).
6. Leonard Rogoff, *Homelands: Southern Jewish Identity in Durham and Chapel Hill, North Carolina* (Tuscaloosa: University of Alabama Press, 2001), pp. 39–51.
7. Scott Eyman, *Lion of Hollywood: The Life and Legend of Louis B. Mayer* (New York: Simon & Schuster, 2005).
8. Robert Berkvist, "Kirk Douglas, a Star of Hollywood's Golden Age, Dies at 103," *New York Times*, February 12, 2022, front page.
9. Eli Lederhendler, *Jewish Immigrants and American Capitalism 1880–1920* (New York: Cambridge University Press, 2009), p. 46.
10. Abraham Rogoff, *The Founding of the Jewish Trade Unions in the United States; 1880–1900* (New York, 1945), p. 109.
11. Nettie P. McGill, *Children in Street Work*, U.S. Children's Bureau, Publication #183 (Washington, D.C.: U.S. Government Printing Office, 1928).

Chapter 6

1. Howard Sachar, *A History of Jews in America* (New York: Vintage Books, 1993).
2. Jean B. Elshtain, *The Jane Addams Reader* (New York: Basic Books, 2020).
3. Florence Kelly, *The Sweating System Hull House Maps and Papers*, 1895, pp. 27–45.
4. Consumers' League, *The Sweatshops: Blight of the Tenements* (New York, 1904).
5. Rose Cohen, *Out of the Shadow: A Russian-Jewish Childhood in the Lower East Side* (New York: Doran, 1918), pp. 122–124.
6. Daniel Katz, *All Together Different: Yiddish Socialists, Garment Workers, and the Labor Roots of Multiculturalism* (New York: New York University Press, 2011), p. 4.
7. "May 1, 1895: New York State Investigates Labor Conditions for Women and Children," https://feminist.org/news/may-1-1895-new-york-state-investigates-labor-conditions-for-women-and-children/.
8. Bernard Weinstein, *The Jewish Unions of America* (Cambridge: Open Book, 2018). "B. Weinstein Led the Labor Movement," *New York Times*, April 26, 1946, p. 21.
9. Morris Hillquit, *History of Socialism in the United States* (New York: Funk & Wagnalls, 1903), pp. 276–287.
10. Norma F. Pratt, *Morris Hillquit: A Political History of an American Jewish Socialist* (Westport, CT: Greenwood, 1979).

11. Meagan Day, How poor, mostly Jewish immigrants organized 20,000 and fought for workers' rights," *New York Times*, March 8, 2018.
12. ILGWU website, Kheel Center, Cornell University.
13. "David Dubinsky, 90, Dies; Led Garment Union," *New York Times*, September 18, 1982, p. 1. Louis Levine, *The Ladies Garment Workers Union* (New York: Huesch, 1924), pp. 105–110.
14. "Rose Schneiderman Dies at 88; Pioneer Women's Union Leader," *New York Times*, August 12, 1972, p. 26.
15. Matilda Rabinowitz, *Immigrant Girl, Radical Woman: A Memoir from the Early Twentieth Century* (Ithaca: Cornell University Press, 2017).
16. Steven Fraser, *Labor Will Rule: Sidney Hillman and the Rise of American Labor* (New York: Free Press, 1991).
17. "Hillman Dies at 59 of a Heart Attack," *New York Times*, July 11, 1946, p. 1.
18. "Hillman Union Picks His Wife as Official," *New York Times*, August 27, 1946.
19. "Born in Strife 50 Years Ago; Amalgamated Union Prospers," *New York Times*, December 27, 1954, p. 47. "Jacob Potofsky, Long the Head of Clothing Workers, Dies at 84," *New York Times* August 6, 1979.
20. Phylis Dillon and Andrew Godley, "The Evolution of the Jewish Garment Industry, 1840–1940," in *Chosen Capital: The Jewish Encounter with American Capitalism,* edited by Rebecca Kubrin (New Brunswick: Rutgers University Press, 2012), 35.
21. Andrew S. Dolkart, "From the Rag Trade to Riches," in *Chosen Capital: The Jewish Encounter with American Capitalism,* edited by Rebecca Kubrin (New Brunswick: Rutgers University Press, 2012), pp. 62–66.
22. Dolkart, p.73.

Chapter 7

1. Jane Addams in an address to the annual meeting of the National Education Association, July 1, 1908.
2. Deborah Dash Moore, *At Home in America* (New York: Columbia University Press, 1981), pp. 101–103.
3. Mary Antin, *The Promised Land* (Boston: Houghton Mifflin, 1912), pp. 209–211.
4. Rose Cohen, *Out of the Shadow* (New York: Doran, 1918), pp. 194–195.
5. Bertha Proskauer was Julia's sister.
6. Bertha Proskauer, *Julia Richman* (New York: Julia Richman High School Association, 1916).
7. Selam Berrol, "When Uptown Met Downtown: Julia Richman's Work in the Jewish Community of New York, 1880–1912," *American Jewish History* 70, no. 1 (September 1980), pp. 35–51.
8. Julia Richman obituary, *New York Times*, June 26, 1912, p. 12.
9. Charles S. Bernheimer, ed., *The Russian Jew in the United States: States: Studies of Social Conditions in New York, Philadelphia and Chicago* (Philadelphia: Winston, 1905), pp. 186–221.
10. See Chapter 9: From Public School to Ivy League College.
11. Hilda Satt Polacheck, *I Came a Stranger: The Story of a Hull-House Girl* (Urbana: University of Illinois Press, 1989).
12. Rose Cohen, *Out of the Shadow* (New York: Doran, 1918), pp. 180–182.
13. Lillian Wald, *New York Times*, March 11, 1938, p. 18.
14. Lillian Wald, *The House on Henry Street* (New York: Henry Holt, 1924).
15. Rose Cohen, *Out of the Shadow* (New York: Doran, 1918), pp. 231–232.
16. Edward J. James, *The Immigrant Jew in America* (New York: Buck, 1906).
17. Julius B. Maller, "Juvenile Delinquency Among the Jews of New York," *Social Forces* 10, no. 4 (May 1932), pp. 542–549.
18. William Kvoraceus, *Juvenile Delinquency and School* (New York: World Books, 1945), p. 120.
19. John A. Garraty, *Henry Cabot Lodge: Biography* (New York: Knopf, 1953), p. 611.
20. Frank Moss, *The American Metropolis*, Chapter Nine, "New Israel: A Modern Source of Crime" (New York: Collier, 1897), pp. 154–160.
21. Theodore Brigham, "Foreign Criminals in New York," *North American Review* 188 (September 1, 1908).
22. Mia Brett, "Ten Thousand Bigamists in New York," The Gotham Center for New York History, online, October 27, 2020.
23. William Z. Ripley, *The Races of Europe: A Sociological Study* (New York: Appleton, 1899), pp. 366–400.
24. Report of the Immigration Commission, Senate Document #633, 61st Congress, 2nd Session (Washington, D.C.: Government Printing Office, 1911), p. 360.
25. U.S. Immigration Commission, *Dictionary of Races or Peoples*, Vol. 5, 1911, pp. 73–75.
26. Madison Grant, *The Passing of the Great Race* (New York: Charles Scribner's Sons, 1916), p. 81–82.
27. Timothy W. Ryback, "A Disquieting Book from Hitler's Library," *New York Times*, December 7, 2011.
28. *The International Jew: The World's Foremost Problem*: Based on Reports in the *Dearborn Independent*, May 22 to October 2, 1920, pp. 39–40, 214.
29. Kenneth M. Ludmerer, "Genetics, Eugenics, and the Immigration Restriction Act of 1924," *Bulletin of the History of Medicine* 46, no. 1 (January–February 1972), pp. 59–81.
30. David A. Reed, "America of the Melting Pot Comes to End," *New York Times*, April 27, 1924, Section XX, p. 3.
31. Zvi Gitelman, "Exiting the Soviet Union," *Michigan Journal of International Law* 3, no. 1 (1982).
32. H.S. Linfield, *The Jewish Population in the*

United States, 1927 (American Jewish Year Book, 1928).

Chapter 8

1. *Report of the United Hebrew Charities of Chicago, 1891–92*. Chicago, 1892, p. 8.
2. *Twenty-Fifth Anniversary of the Educational Alliance, March 21, 1915* (New York: Educational Alliance, New York).
3. "Henry Rice Dead in His 80th Year: Was Head of the United Hebrew Charities," *New York Times*, June 8, 1914, p. 7.
4. *Fifty Years of Social Service: The History of the United Hebrew Charities of the City of New York* (New York, 1926).
5. Hebrew Sheltering and Immigrant Aid Society, Annual Report (New York, 1909).
6. *Fifty Years of Learning Thru Doing, 1884–1934: The Fiftieth Anniversary of the Founding of the Hebrew Technical Institute, Stuyvesant and East Ninth Streets, New York, Hebrew Technical Institute* (New York, 1934).
7. *First Annual Report of the Chicago Jewish Training School*, 1890.
8. O.J. Milliken, "The Jewish Training School of Chicago," *The Elementary School Teacher* 6, no. 6 (February 1906), pp. 278–280. In 1953, the Chicago Jewish Training School was destroyed by fire.
9. Gerald Sorin, *A Time for Building: The Third Migration, 1880–1920* (Baltimore: John Hopkins University Press, 1992), p. 149.
10. Barbara A. Solomon, *Pioneers in Service: A History of the Associated Jewish Philanthropies of Boston* (Boston, 1956), pp. 22–25.
11. *Catalogue of the Baron de Hirsch Trade School*, 1900.
12. "De Hirsch Trade School Diplomas Awarded," *New York Times*, June 10, 1903, p. 5.
13. "53 de Hirsch graduates told there was a Great Future in Farming," *New York Times*, February 21, 1905, p. 10.
14. Boris Bogen, *Jewish Philanthropy* (New York: Macmillan, 1917), p. 133.
15. Baron de Hirsch Agricultural School, Annual Report, 1908.
16. "Nathaniel Myers Dies: President of the Hebrew Technical School for Girls for 21 Years," *New York Times*, May 31, 1921, p. 9.
17. Annual Reports for the Hebrew Technical School for Girls, 1901–1910.
18. *Directory of Social Service of the City of New York* (New York: Columbia University Press, 1919), p. 86.
19. "Mrs. N.T. Phillips, a Figure in the City, '79, Was a Force in Jewish Affairs," *New York Times*, February 7, 1946, p. 22.
20. *Twenty-Fifth Anniversary of the Educational Alliance, March 21, 1915* (New York: Educational Alliance, New York).
21. Boris Bogen, *Jewish Philanthropy* (New York: Macmillan, 1917), p. 234.
22. Settlement Houses, Jewish Virtual Library, online.
23. Chicago Jewish Institute, *Program of Celebration During Lincoln Week*, 1909.
24. "Chicago Hebrew Institute," *The Electronic Encyclopedia of Chicago*, online.
25. Alexander M. Dushkin, *Jewish Education in New York City* (New York: New Yok Bureau of Jewish Education, 1915).
26. "Jewish School Quits the Lower East Side as Perilous," *New York Times*, May 14, 1972, p. 49.
27. Boris D. Bogen, "The Jewish Boy Criminal," *Jewish Charity* IV, no. 4 (January 1905).
28. Boris Bogen, *Jewish Philanthropy*, pp. 173–175, 223, 234.
29. Reena Sigman Friedman, "Send Me My Husband Who Is in New York: Husband Desertion in the American Jewish Immigrant Community, 1900–1926," *Jewish Social Studies* 44, no. 1 (Winter 1982), pp. 1–18.
30. Ari Lloyd Fridkis, "Desertion in the American Jewish Immigrant Family: The Work of the National Desertion Bureau in Cooperation with the Industrial Removal Office," *American Jewish History* 71, no. 2 (December 1981), pp. 285–299.
31. Rob Edelman and Audrey Kupferberg. *Matthau: A Life* (Lanham, MD: Rowman & Littlefield, 2000), p. 5.
32. *Fourth biennial session of the National Conference of Jewish Charities in the United States, held in the city of Philadelphia, May 6 to 8, 1906* (Philadelphia, 1906), pp. 100–101.
33. Bogen, *Jewish Philanthropy*, p. 298.
34. *Sixth Annual Report of the Jewish Board of Guardians for Year Ending December 31, 1926* (Albany: Lyon, 1927).
35. Reena Friedman, Shalvi/Hyman, *Encyclopedia of Jewish Women*, online.
36. "Jews Plan to Train Young Delinquents," *New York Times*, July 2, 1923, p. 8.
37. Jewish Telegraph Agency, August 7, 1933.
38. Michael Shnayerson, *Bugsy Siegel: The Dark Side of the American Dream* (New Haven: Yale University Press, 2020). "Siegel, Gangster, Slain on Coast," New York Times, June 22, 1946, p. 7.
39. "Meyer Lansky is Dead at 81. Financial Wizard of Organized Crime," *New York Times*, January 16, 1983, p. 29.
40. "Lepke Surrenders to FBI," *New York Times*, August 25, 1939, p. 15.
41. Richard Johnston, "Lepke Shows Fear as He Goes to the Chair," *New York Times*, March 5, 1944, p. 30. Irving Lehman was at that time chief justice of the New York Court of Appeals.
42. "Gang Leader Shot as He Leaves Court," *New York Times*, June 14, 1912, p. 3.
43. "Gangsters Kill 2 Lined Up at Wall. Enemies Trap Joseph Amberg," *New York Times*, October 1, 1935, p. 24.
44. John Landesco *Organized Crime in Chicago* (Chicago: University of Chicago Press, 1968), p. 231.
45. Joe Kraus, *The Kosher Capones: A History of*

Chicago's Jewish Gangsters (Ithaca: Cornell University Press, 2019), p. 49.

46. Britt R. Travis, "Jews Not Admitted, Anti-Semitism, Civil Rights, and Public Accommodation Laws," *American History* 107, Issue 4 (March 2021), pp. 847–870.

47. Edward C. Halperin, "The Rise and Fall of the Jewish American Hospital," *Academic Medicine* 97, no. 5 (2012), pp. 610–614.

48. Marie Syrkin, *Gold Meir: Woman with a Cause* (New York: G.P. Putnam's Sons, 1966), pp. 1–45.

49. Michael Brown, "The American Element in the Rise of Golda Meir, 1906–1929," *Jewish History* 6, no. 1 (1992), pp. 36–50.

50. Hadar Alon, "Interview with David Ben Gurion April 1968 at Sde Boker, when he was 82-years-old," Ynet News, online, July 25, 2016.

Chapter 9

1. Edmund J. James, *The Immigrant Jew in America* (New York: Buck & Company, 1908), pp. 173–220.

2. *Handbook of the Central High School of Philadelphia* (Philadelphia: Barwell Foundation, 1926).

3. *Harvard Crimson*, November 8, 1929.

4. *Catalogue of Graduates of the Public Latin School in Boston, 1816–1917* (Boston, 1918).

5. Jerome Karabel, *The Chosen: Admission and Exclusion at Harvard, Yale, and Princeton* (Boston: Houghton Mifflin, 2005).

6. Stephen Steinberg, *The Academic Melting Pot: Catholics and Jew in America's Higher Education* (New Brunswick Transaction Books, 1971).

7. Amy Wallace, *Prodigy: A Biography of William James Sidis, America's Greatest Child Prodigy* (New York: Dutton, 1988).

8. Fred M. Hechinger, The Trouble with Quotas," *New York Times*, February 10, 1987, Section 3, p. 1.

9. *Harvard Class of 1895* (Cambridge: Cambridge University Press, 1905), p. 38.

10. Morris Raphael Cohen, *New York Times*, January 31, 1947, p. 22.

11. *Harvard Crimson*, December 20, 1907.

12. "President Eliot Says that the Jewish Race Is Physically Inferior to Others," *New York Times*, December 21, 1907.

13. William Z. Ripley, *The Races of Europe: A Sociological Study* (New York: Appleton, 1899).

14. Jerome Karabel, *The Chosen: The Hidden History of Admission and Exclusion from Harvard, Yale, and Princeton* (Boston: Houghton Mifflin, 2005).

15. *Harvard Class of 1920—Twenty-fifth Anniversary Report* (Cambridge: Printed by the Class, 1945).

16. "Dr. Leo Davidoff, Surgeon, Dies," *New York Times*, December 25, 1975.

17. *Harvard Crimson*, March 3, 1919.

18. Zvi Zeff, *Dyed in Crimson* (Urbana: University of Illinois Press, 2023).

19. *Report of the Harvard Class of 1920*, p. 396.

20. "A.M. Sonnebend Is Dead: Boston Industrialist-Financier," *New York Times*, February 12, 1964.

21. "Lowell Tells Jews Limit at Colleges Might Help Them Combat Increasing Tendency to Anti-Semitism," *New York Times*, June 17, 1922.

22. David Brooks, *New York Times*, November 8, 2005; Jerome Karabel, *The Chosen: The Hidden Story of Admission and Exclusion at Harvard, Yale, and Princeton* (Boston: Houghton Mifflin, 2005), p. 106.

23. Stephen Thernstrom, "Poor but Hopeful Students," in Bernard Bailyn, ed., *Glimpses of Harvard Past* (Cambridge: Harvard University Press, 1986), pp. 127–128.

24. Nathan Glazer and Patrick Moynihan, *Beyond the Melting Pot* (Cambridge: MIT Press, 1963), p. 156.

Chapter 10

1. Steven A. Riess, *Sports and the American Jew* (Syracuse: Syracuse University Press, 1998), pp. 2, 14.

2. Educational Alliance Fifth Annual Report, 1897, p. 28.

3. Educational Alliance Eleventh Annual Report, 1903, p. 62.

4. Mike Silver, *Stars in the Ring: Jewish Champions in the Golden Age of Boxing* (New York: Lyons Press, 2016).

5. Arthur J. Daley, *New York Times*, November 29, 1934, p. 23.

6. *New York Times*, July 28, 1922.

7. "Leonard Retains Title. 60,000 See Him Beat Tendler. Champion Gives Brilliant Exhibition, Outfighting Rival in 15-Round Battle," *New York Times*, July 24, 1923, front page.

8. "Boxing's Unique Nobleman," *New York Times*, March 9, 1994, p. 11.

9. "Attendance at McLarnin-Ross Fight exceeded only by Heavyweights," *New York Times*, November 29, 1934, p. 23.

10. "Killed 22 Japanese in Defending Comrades. Guadalcanal Hero," *New York Times*, February 26, 1943, p. 25.

11. *New York Times*, March 9, 1994, p. 11.

12. Phil Berger, "Ray Arcel, Trainer Who Handled Many Boxing Stars, Is Dead at 94," *New York Times*, March 8, 1994, p. 8.

13. "Nat Fleischer, 84, Died. Was 'Mr. Boxing,'" *New York Times*, June 26, 1972, p. 36.

14. Allen Barbe, *The Atlantic Magazine*, March 27, 2012.

15. Bruce Weber, "Bert Sugar, Boxing Writer and Commentator, Is Dead at 75," *New York Times*, March 26, 2012, p. 18.

16. "Jacob Golomb, 58, a Manufacturer," *New York Times*, August 25, 1951.

17. "Eddie Gottlieb Dies: A Pioneer of NBA Pro-Basketball," *New York Times*, December 8, 1978, p. 46.

18. Arnold "Red" Auerbach and Joe Fitzgerald, *Red Auerbach: An Autobiography* (New York: G.P. Putnam's Sons, 1977), pp. 21–29.

19. "Red Auerbach, 89, Who Built a Basketball Dynasty," *New York Times*, October 30, 2006, p. 8.

20. "Red Holzman, Hall of Fame Coach, Dies at 78," *New York Times*, November 15, 1998, p. 46.

21. Richard Goldstein, "Red Klotz, Beloved Foil for the Harlem Globetrotters, Dies at 93," *New York Times*, July 14, 2014, p. 21.

22. Vincent Mallozzi, Lou Bender, Columbia Star Who Helped Popularize Basketball in New York, Dies at 99," *New York Times*, September 17, 2008.

23. Vincent Mallozzi, "Ralph Kaplowitz, 89, Dies," *New York Times*, February 14, 2009.

24. "Andy Cohen Keeps His Name," *New York Times*, July 22, 1928, p. 106.

25. Hank Greenberg with Ira Berkow, *Hank Greenberg: The Story of My Life* (Chicago: Ivan R. Dee, 1989), pp. 1–4.

26. Greenberg with Berkow, p. 138.

27. *New York Times*, January 4, 1879.

28. Marnie Eisenstadt and Johnathan Croyle, "The Untold Story of the Syracuse Olympic Gold Medalist You've Never Heard Of," *Empire Magazine*, August 4, 2016.

29. "Abel Kiviat, Runner, Dies at 99. Held World 1,500-meter Record," *New York Times*, August 26, 1991, p. 7.

30. "Lillian Copeland Dies at 59," *New York Times*, July 8, 1964.

31. "Marty Glickman, Announcer and Blocked Olympian, 83," *New York Times*, January 4, 2001. Also, Arthur Pincus, "50 Years Later, Bitter Memories of the Berlin Games," *New York Times*, August 10, 1986, p. 9.

32. Stanley B. Frank, *Jews in Sports* (New York: Miles, 1936).

33. "Michigan Defeats Wisconsin, 21 to 0: Friedman's Passing and Running Lead to Three Touchdowns by Wolverines; 45,000 Witness Contest," *New York Times*, October 26, 1924.

34. *The Guardian*, January 6, 2023.

35. Richard Goldstein, "Dick Savitt Dies at 95; Won Australian and Wimbledon Titles in 1951," *New York Times*, January 6, 2023.

Chapter 11

1. Howard Pollack, *George Gershwin: His Life and Work* (Berkeley: University of California Press, 2007), p. 8.

2. "George Gershwin, Composer, Is Dead," *New York Times*, July 12, 1937, front page.

3. Howard Pollack, *Aaron Copland: The Life and Work of an Uncommon Man* (New York: Henry Holt, 1999), p.18.

4. Pollack, *Aaron Copland*, p. 24.

5. Pollack, *Aaron Copland*, p. 32.

6. Carol J. Oja and Judith Tuck, editors, *Aaron Copland and His World* (Princeton: Princeton University Press, 2005), quoting Leon Botstein, p. 442.

7. Leonard Bernstein and Neil Simeone, *The Leonard Bernstein Letters* (New Haven: Yale University Press, 2013). Allen Shaw, *Leonard Bernstein: An American Musician* (New Haven: Yale University Press, 2014), pp. 22–24.

8. Bernstein and Simeone, *The Leonard Bernstein Letters*.

9. Donal Henahan, "Leonard Bernstein, 72, Music's Monarch, Dies," *New York Times*, October 15, 1990.

10. Philip Glass, *Words Without Music: A Memoir* (New York: Norton, 2016), p. 17.

11. Bob Dylan, *Chronicles*, Volume One (New York: Simon & Schuster, 2004).

12. Meryle Secrest, *Stephen Sondheim: A Life* (New York: Knopf, 2011).

13. "The Promised Land by Mary Antin," *New York Times*, April 14, 1912. "Mary Antin Wrote Noted Book: Russian Jewish Immigrant Won Acclaim Here with Her Promised Land; Dies at 67," *New York Times*, May 18, 1949.

14. Dinitia Smith, Harold Bloom, Critic Who Championed Western Canon, Dies at 89," *New York Times*, October 14, 2019, p. 29.

15. Marie Brenner, "Mailer Goes Egyptian," *New York Magazine*, March 28, 1983, pp. 28–38.

16. David Denby, The Making of Norman Mailer," *New Yorker*, December 19, 2022.

17. William Grimes, "Herman Wouk, Best-Selling Novelist with a Realist's Touch, Dies at 103," *New York Times*, May 17, 2019, p. 27.

18. Herman Wouk, *Sailor and Fiddler: Reflections of a 100-Year-Old Author* (New York: Simon & Schuster, 2016), p. 12.

19. Rachel Gordon, "Herman Wouk the Legendary Author Who Brought Judaism into the Mainstream," *Times of Israel*, March 17, 2019.

20. Christoph Lehmann-Haupt, "Leon Uris, Author of Exodus, Dies at 78," *New York Times*, June 24, 2003, p. 20.

21. Tracy Daugherty, *Just One Catch: A Biography of Joseph Heller* (New York: St. Martin's Press, 2011), pp. 25–30.

22. Richard Severo and Herbert Mitgang, Joseph Heller, Author of 'Catch-22,' Dies at 76," *New York Times*, December 13, 1999.

23. Mel Gussow and Charles McGrath, "Saul Bellow, Who Breathed Life into American Novel Dies at 89," *New York Times*, April 6, 2005, front page.

24. Eric Pace, Isaac Bashevis Singer, Nobel Laureate for His Yiddish Stories, Dead at 87," *New York Times*, July 26, 1991, p. 5.

25. Joseph Berger, "Elie Wiesel, Auschwitz Survivor and Nobel Prize Winner, Dies at 87," *New York Times*, July 20, 2016, p. 17.

26. Margalit Fox, "Chaim Potok, 73, Dies. Novelist Illuminates World of Chasidic Judaism," *New York Times*, June 24, 2002, p. 17.

27. Mervyn Rothstein, "Bernard Malamud, Author, Dies at 71," *New York Times*, March 20, 1988, p. 26.

28. Charles McGrath, "Philip Roth, Towering Novelist Explored Lust, Jewish Life and America, Dies at 85," *New York Times*, May 22, 2018, p. 28.

29. Jennifer Burns, *Goddess of the Markets: Ayn Rand and the American Right* (New York: Oxford University Press, 2009), pp. 9–10.

30. Wolfgang Saxon, Ayn Rand, Fountainhead Author, Dies," *New York Times*, March 7, 1982.

Chapter 12

1. "Broadway and Thomashefsky," *New York Times*, March 10, 1918, p. X.13. John Corbin, "How the Other Half Laughs," *Harper's Magazine* 98, 1898, p. 47.

2. "Thomashefsky, 71, Yiddish Actor Dies. He Introduced the Theater to His People on the East Side, Delighted Packed Houses," *New York Times*, July 10, 1939, p. 23. Also, "30,000 Pay Tribute to Thomashefsky. Yiddish Actor is Honored by East Side," *New York Times*, July 12, 1939, p. 26.

3. Alan L. Gansberg, *Little Caesar: A Biography of Edward G. Robinson* (Lanham, MD: Scarecrow, 2004).

4. "Edward G. Robinson, 79, Dies. His Little Caesar Set a Style. Appeared in 100 Films," *New York Times*, January 27, 1973, front page.

5. "Paul Muni, Actor, Dies at Coast, Won Fame in Biographical Roles, Portrayed Darrow, Pasteur, Zola Juarez, and Gangster Roles in Stage and Film Career," *New York Times*, August 26, 1967, front page.

6. "Walter Matthau, 79, Rumpled Star and Comic Icon, Dies," *New York Times*, July 20, 2000, p. 20. Also, Rob Edelman and Audrey Kupferberg, *Matthau: A Life* (Lanham, MD: Rowman & Littlefield, 2002).

7. "Eddie Cantor Dead. Comedy Star Was 72," *New York Times*, October 11, 1964, front page. David Weinstein, *The Eddie Cantor Story: A Jewish Life in Performance and Politics* (Waltham, MA: Brandeis University Press, 2018).

8. "Walker Sees Molly Picon," *New York Times*, March 17, 1930, p. 19.

9. "Molly Picon Delights Again," *New York Times*, November 17, 1934, p. 13.

10. "Sophie Tucker Dies in Her Home, 79," *New York Times*, February 10, 1966, front page.

11. "Mrs. B. Thomashefsky," *New York Times*, July 8, 1962, p. 65.

12. Shawn Levy, *King of Comedy: The Life and Art of Jerrie Lewis* (New York: St. Martin's Press, 1996).

13. "Analyzing Jewish Comics," *Time Magazine*, October 2, 1978. Also, Samuel S. Janus, "The Great Jewish-American Comedian's Identity Crisis," *American Journal of Psychoanalysis* 40 (September 1980), pp. 259–265.

14. Amanda Vaill, *Somewhere: The Life of Jerry Robbins* (New York: Broadway Books, 2006), pp. 7–10.

15. Lawrence Epstein, *George Burns: An American Life* (Jefferson, NC: McFarland, 2011).

16. Max Marx, "Ninety-Eight-Year-Old George Burns Shares Memories of His Life," *Cigar Aficionado*, March 7, 2010.

17. Shawn Levy, *King of Comedy: The Life and Art of Jerry Lewis* (New York: St. Martin's Press, 1999).

18. David Lehr, Jerry Lewis, a Jester Both Silly and Stormy, Dies at 91," *New York Times*, August 20, 2017, front page.

19. Kenneth Tynan, "Frolics and Detours of a Short Hebrew Man. Mel Brooks' Indestructible Comedy," *New Yorker*, October 22, 1978.

20. "John Garfield, Actor 39, Famed for Tough Roles in Stage and Screen, Had Cardiac Ailment," *New York Times*, May 22, 1952, p. 21.

21. Robert Berkvist, Eli Wallach, Multifaceted Actor on Stage and Screen, Dies at 98," *New York Times*, June 25, 201, p. 16.

22. David Kehr, Tony Curtis, Hollywood Leading Man, Dies at 85," *New York Times*, September 30, 2010, p. 22.

23. "James Caan, Actor Who Won Fame in 'The Godfather,' Dies at 82," *New York Times*, August 5, 2022, p. 22. *The Guardian*, July 8, 2022.

24. Bruce Weber, "Peter Falk 'Columbo' Actor Dies at 83," *New York Times*, June 24, 2011, p. 7.

25. John T. McQuiston, "Lee J. Cobb, the Actor, is Dead at 69," *New York Times*, February 17, 1976, p. 33.

26. Virginia Heffernan, "Leonard Nimoy, Spock of 'Star Trek,' Dies at 83," *New York Times*, February 27, 2015, front page.

27. Alan Arkin, *An Improvised Life* (New York: Da Capo, 2011), p. 5.

28. Robert Berkvist and Peter Keepnews, "Alan Arkin, Comic Actor with a Serious Side, Dies at 89," *New York Times*, July 5, 2023, p. 10.

29. Leslie Ledbetter, "Lillian Roth, Actress and Singer, Dies," *New York Times*, May 13, 1980, p. C20.

30. Lauren Bacall, *Lauren Bacall, By Myself and Then Some* (New York: Harper, 2005), pp. 1–2.

31. Enid Nemy, "Lauren Bacall Dies at 89; In a Bygone Hollywood, She Purred Every Word," *New York Times*, August 12, 2014.

32. William J. Mann, *Hello! Gorgeous: Becoming Barbra Streisand* (Boston: Houghton Mifflin, 2012), pp. 23–24.

33. Charles Champlin, "The Founding Fathers of Hollywood," *Los Angeles Times*, September 25, 1988.

34. Neal Gabler, *An Empire of Their Own: How Jews Invented Hollywood* (New York: Anchor, 1988).

35. Ben Hecht, *A Child of the Century* (New Haven: Yale University Press, 1954), p. 538.

36. Adolph Zukor and Dale Kramer, *The Public Is Never Wrong: The Autobiography of Adolph Zukor* (New York: G.P. Putnam's Sons, 1953), pp. 29–31, 38.

37. Scott Eyman, *Lion of Hollywood: The Life and Legend of Louis B. Mayer* (New York: Simon & Schuster, 2005).

38. "Louis B. Mayer, Film Maker Dies; Former

Production Chief of M-G-M, 72," *New York Times*, October 30, 1957, p. 29.

39. Robert Berkvist, "Sidney Lumet, Director of Serpico, Dies at 86," *New York Times*, April 9, 2011, front page.

40. Neil Genzlinger, "The Wit of Ernest Lubitsch," *New York Times*, May 24, 2017.

41. "Stanley Kramer, Director and Producer, Dies at 87," *New York Times*, February 20, 2001.

42. James Steingold, "Alan J. Pakula, Film Director, Dies at 70," *New York Times*, November 20, 1998.

43. William Friedkin, *The Friedkin Connection: A Memoir* (New York: Harper, 2014).

44. Stephen Holden, "Stanley Kubrick: Film Director with a Bleak Vision Dies at 70," *New York Times*, March 8, 1999, front page.

45. "Ben Hecht, Novelist and Playwright, Dies," *New York Times*, April 19, 1964, front page. Also, Ben Hecht, *A Child of the Century* (New York: Simon & Schuster, 1954).

46. "Clifford Odets, Playwright Dies, Author of Broadway Dramas and Movie Scripts," *New York Times*, August 16, 1963, p. 27.

47. Marilyn Berger, "Arthur Miller, Moral Voice of the American Stage, Dies at 89," *New York Times*, February 12, 2005, front page.

48. Arthur Miller, *Timebends: A Life* (New York: Grove, 2013).

49. Marilyn Berger, "Arthur Miller, Moral Voice of the American Stage, Dies at 89," *New York Times*, February 12, 2005, front page.

50. Arthur Miller, "A Boy Grew Up in Brooklyn," *Holiday Magazine*, February 1955.

51. Charles Isherwood, "Neil Simon, Broadway Master of Comedy, Is Dead at 91," *New York Times*, August 26, 2018, front page.

52. Susan Koprince, *Understanding Neil Simon* (Columbia: University of South Carolina Press, 2002).

53. Colin Campbell, "Paddy Chayefsky, Dead 58, Playwright," *New York Times*, August 2, 1981, front page.

54. "David T. Nederlander, 81, Dies; Head of Theater-Owning Family," *New York Times*, October 17, 1967, p. 44.

55. "Joseph Papp, Theater's Champion, Dies," *New York Times*, November 1, 1991, front page.

56. Elia Kazan named as communists Clifford Odets, Joseph Edward Bromberg, Lewis Leverett, Morris Carnovsky, Phoebe Brand, Tony Kraber, Ted Wellman, and Pearl Miller (second wife of Lee Strasberg).

57. Mel Gussow," Lee Strasberg of Actors Studio Dead," *New York Times*, February 18, 1982, p. 20.

58. John Curry, "Harold Clurman, Stage Director Critic and Author, Is Dead at 78," *New York Times*, September 10, 1980, front page.

59. Bruce Weber, "Mike Nichols, Urbane Director Loved by Crowds and Critics, Dies at 83," *New York Times*, November 20, 2014.

60. "Top Director George S. Kaufman, Dies at 71," *New York Times*, June 3, 1961, front page.

61. Richard Severo and Peter Keepnews, "Norman Lear, Whose Comedies Changed the Face of TV, Is Dead," *New York Times*, December 6, 2023.

62. Jesse Green, "Let Us Tell You a Story: How Jewish People Built the American Theater as We Know It," *New York Times*, November 29, 2023.

Chapter 13

1. William McDougall, *Is America Safe for Democracy?* (New York: Charles Scribner, 1921). William McDougall, *National Welfare and National Decay* (London: Methuen, 1921), p. 167.

2. Wolfgang Saxon, "Melvin Calvin Dies at 85; Biochemist Won Nobel Prize," *New York Times*, January 10, 1997, p. 6.

3. Don R. Hecker, "Paul Berg, Nobel-Winning Pioneer of Genetic Engineering, Is Dead at 96," *New York Times*, February 23, 2023.

4. Victor K. McElheny, "Selman Waksman, Nobel Winner, Dies," *New York Times*, August 17, 1973, front page.

5. William S. Broad, "Joshua Lederberg, 82, A Nobel Winner, Dies," *New York Times*, February 5, 2008.

6. Eric Pace, "George Wald, Nobel Biologist, Dies at 90," *New York Times*, April 14, 1997, p. 9.

7. Nicholas Wade, "Marshall Nirenberg, Biochemist Who Untangled Genetic Code, Dies at 82," *New York Times*, January 21, 201, p. 30.

8. David Tuller, "Julius Axelrod Dies at 92, Won Nobel in Medicine," *New York Times*, December 31, 2004, p. 24.

9. H. Roger Segelken, "Baruch S. Blumberg Discovered and Tackled Hepatitis B, Dies at 85," *New York Times*, April 7, 2011, p. 26.

10. Denis Gellene, "Rosalyn S. Yalow, Nobel Medical Physicist, Dies at 89," *New York Times*, June 1, 2011, p. 18.

11. Marilyn Berger, "Isidor Isaac Rabi, A Pioneer in Atomic Physics, Dies at 89," *New York Times*, January 12, 1988, front page.

12. Tina Levitan, *The Laureates: Jewish Winners of the Nobel Prize* (New York: Twayne, 1960), p. 90.

13. Kenneth Chang, "Donald Glazer Nobel Winner in Physics, Dies at 86," *New York Times*, March 4, 2013, p. 19.

14. James Gleick, "Richard Feynman Dead at 69; Leading Theoretical Physicist," *New York Times*, February 17, 1988, front page.

15. James Gleick, *Genius: The Life and Science of Richard Feynman* (New York: Vintage, 1993).

16. Michael M. Weinstein, "Paul A. Samuelson, Economist, Dies at 94," *New York Times*, December 13, 2009, front page.

17. Nicholas D. Kristof, "Simon Kuznets is Dead at 84," *New York Times*, July 11, 1985, p. 6.

18. Simon Kuznets, Stephanie Lo, and E. Glen Weyl, editors, *Jewish Economies: Development and Migration in America and Beyond* (New York: Routledge, 2012).

19. Holcolm B. Noble, "Milton Friedman, Free

Market Theorist, Dies at 94," *New York Times*, November 16, 2006. Also, Milton Friedman and Rose Friedman, *Two Lucky People: Milton and Rose Friedman, Memoirs* (Chicago: University of Chicago Press, 1981), p. 17.

20. David Oshinsky, *Polio: An American Story* (New York: Oxford University Press, 2005).

21. Stuart Anderson, *Forbes Magazine*, January 19, 2018.

22. Gilbert King, "Salk, Sabin and the Race Against Polio," *Smithsonian Magazine*, April 3, 2012.

23. Harold M. Schmeck, Jr., "Dr. Jonas Salk, Whose Vaccine Turned Tide on Polio, Dies at 80," *New York Times*, June 24, 1995, front page.

24. Charlotte DeCroes Jacobs, *Jonas Salk: A Life* (New York: Oxford University Press, 2015), pp. 7–15.

25. Harold M. Schmeck, Jr., "Albert Sabin, Polio Researcher, 86, Dies," *New York Times*, May 4, 1993, p. 8.

26. "Dr. Pincus, Developer of Birth-Control Pill, Dies. Worcester Foundation Chief Worked with Chang and Rock on Contraceptive," *New York Times*, August 23, 1967, p. 45.

27. Leonard G. Robinson, *The Agricultural Activities of Jews in America* (New York: American Jewish Committee, 1912), pp. 53–54.

28. *The Berkshire Eagle*, Pittsfield, Massachusetts, April 24, 1943, p. 7.

Chapter 14

1. S.B. Goodkin, *Prominent Jews of America: A Collection of Biographical Sketches of Jews Who Have Distinguished Themselves in Commerce, Professional and Religious Endeavors* (Toledo: American Hebrew Publication Society, 1919).

2. Clay Risen, "Aaron Feuerstein, Mill Owner who Refused to Leave, Dies at 95," *New York Times*, November 5, 2021, p. A19.

3. "Helena Rubenstein, Beauty Expert, Died Here at 94," *New York Times*, April 2, 1965, front page.

4. Richard Severo, "Estée Lauder, Pursuer of Beauty and Cosmetics Titan, Dies at 97," *New York Times*, April 26, 2004, front page. Leonard A. Lauder, *The Company I Keep: My Life in Beauty* (New York: Harper, 2020).

5. Fred E. Basten, *Max Factor: The Man Who Changed the Faces of the World* (New York: Arcade, 2008).

6. Sheila Muto, Max Factor, Jr., 91, Dies; Popularized Makeup," *New York Times*, July 14, 1996, p. 31.

7. Enid Nemy, "Charles Revson of the Revlon Empire Dies," *New York Times*, August 25, 1975, p. 30.

8. Enid Nemy, "Charles Revson of the Revlon Empire Dies," *New York Times*, August 25, 1975, https://www.nytimes.com/1975/08/25/archives/charles-revson-of-the-revlon-empire-dies.html.

9. Barbara Campbell, "Samuel Rubin Dies: Arts Patron was 77," *New York Times*, December 23, 1978, p. 26.

10. M.A. Farber, "Lawrence Gelb Dies, Founder of Clairol," *New York Times*, September 28, 1989, p. 44.

11. Laura Manischewitz Alpern, *Manischewitz: The Matzah Family: The Making of an American Icon* (Jersey City: Ktav, 2000).

12. Morris Mirkin, "Founder of Rental Car Company Dies," *Los Angeles Times*, June 30, 1985.

13. Sharon R. King, Jules W. Lederer, 81, Salesman and Budget-Rent-A-Car," *New York Times*, January 23, 1999, p. A17.

14. Dennis Hevesi, "Samuel Glazer Dies at 89; Popularized Drip Coffee," *New York Times*, March 23, 2012, p. B15.

15. Dennis Hevesi, "Irvine Robbins, Ice Cream Entrepreneur and a Maestro of 31 Flavors, Dies at 90," *New York Times*, May 7, 2008.

16. Richard D. Lyons, "Reuben Mattus, 81, Founder of Haagen-Dazs," *New York Times*, January 29, 1994, p. 26.

17. "Handwerker of Nathan's Famous, Dies," *New York Times*, March 25, 1974, p. 34.

18. "Ida Rosenthal, Co-Founder of Maidenform Dies," *New York Times*, March 30, 1973, p. 42.

19. "Lane Bryant Firm Founder is Dead," *The Philadelphia Inquirer*, September 28, 1951.

20. Bruce Weber, "Don Fisher, 81, Founder of The Gap, Dies," *New York Times*, September 28, 2009, p. A37. Top of Form

21. Michael Gross, *Genuine Authentic: The Real Life of Ralph Lauren* (New York: Harper, 2003).

22. Matt W. Cody, *Calvin Klein* (New York: Chelsea House, 2013).

23. Glen Rifkin, "Ralph Roberts, Cable TV Pioneer, Who Built Comcast, Dies at 95," *New York Times*, June 19, 2015, p. A20.

24. Jonathan Kandell, "Laurence A. Tisch, Investor Known for Saving CBS Inc. Dies at 80," *New York Times*, November 16, 2003, p. 43.

25. Peter Goldin, *Quiet Diplomat: A Biography of Max M. Fisher* (New York: Cornwall Books, 1992).

26. "Max Fisher, 96, Philanthropist and Adviser to Presidents, Dies," *New York Times*, March 4, 2005, p. 19.

27. Joan Cook, "Henry Crown, Industrialist, Dies, Billionaire, 94: Rose from Poverty," *New York Times*, August 16, 1990, p. B14.

28. "Samuel I. Newhouse, Builder of an Empire in Newspapers and Broadcasting, Is Dead at 84," *New York Times*, August 30, 1979, front page.

29. "S.I. Newhouse Jr. Who Turned Condé Nest into a Magazine Powerhouse, Dies at 89," *New York Times*, October 1, 2017.Bottom of Form

30. David W. Dunlap, "Irwin Chanin, Builder of Theaters and Art Deco Towers, Dies at 96," *New York Times*, February 26, 1988, p. D17. Deborah Dash Moore, "Who Built New York? Jewish Builders in the Interwar Decades," *American Jewish History* 101, no. 3, July 2017, pp. 311–335.

31. "A.E. Lefcourt Dies Suddenly," *New York Times*, November 14, 1932, p. 17.

32. Glenn Fowler, "Henry H. Minskoff, 73, Head Major Building Company," *New York Times*, August 15, 1984. p. B24.

33. Eric Rice, William J. Levitt, 86, Pioneer of Suburbs, Dies," *New York Times*, January 29, 1994, front page.

34. Wolfgang Saxon, Sam Goldstein, Real Estate Investor, Dead," *New York Times*, October 19, 1987, p. B10.

35. Jack Houston and Stanley Ziemba, Arthur Rubloff, 83, Colossus of Real Estate Development," *Chicago Tribune*, May 25, 1986. "Arthur Rubloff is Dead at 83," *New York Times*, May 25, 1986, p. 32.

36. "A.N. Pritzker, 90, Hyatt Hotel Chain Owner," *New York Times*, February 9, 1986, p. 44.

37. Jack Buncher, *New York Times*, December 6, 2001, p. A3.

38. Bruce Weber, "Matthew Bucksbaum, Mall Developer, Dead at 87," *New York Times*, November 29, 2013, p. A14.

39. *Kansas City Star*, December 5, 2007.

40. "Sam Eig, Montgomery Builder and Philanthropist, Dies at 93," *Washington Post*, December 26, 1982.

41. "Morris Cafritz, Builder, Dead; Developed Properties in Capital; Financier," *New York Times*, June 13, 1964, p. 23.

42. Richard Goldstein, Malcolm Glazer, Owner Buccaneers and Manchester United, Is Dead at 85," *New York Times*, May 29, 2014, p. B18.

43. Clair Poole, "Moore of the Same," *Texas Monthly*, October 1988.

Chapter 15

1. Christopher M. Sterba, *Good Americans: Italian and Jewish Immigrants During the First World War* (New York: Oxford University Press, 2002), p. 61.

2. Marsha L. Rosenblit and Jonathan Karp, editors, *World War I and the Jews* (New York: Berghahn, 2017), p. 295.

3. Emma Goldman, *Anarchism and Other Essays* (New York: Mother Earth Publication Association, 1910), p. 56.

4. *Anarchism on Trial: Speeches of Alexander Beckman and Emma Goldman before the District Court of the City of New York, July 1917*, p. 60.

5. *The War Record of American Jews: First Report* (New York: American Jewish Committee, 1919).

6. Samuel W. McCall, *Patriotism of the American Jew* (New York: Plymouth Press, 1924), pp. 126–127.

7. Sterba, *Good Americans*, p. 70.

8. *History of the Seventy-Seventh Division: August 25, 1917 to November 11, 1918* (New York: 77th Division Association, 1919).

9. Jewish Telegraph Agency, May 26, 2017. Jacob R. Marcus, *The Jew in the American World: A Source Book* (Detroit: Wayne State University Press, 1986), p. 308.

10. Harry P. Singer, *Heroes All* (Washington, D.C.: Fassett, 1919), p. 21.

11. "Praises Jews as Soldiers," *New York Times*, January 22, 1919.

12. Lee J. Levinger, "The Jew as Soldier," *The American Hebrew*, vol. 110, no. 2, November 25, 1921, p. 116.

13. Estelle F. Ward, *The Story of Northwestern University* (New York: Dodd, Mead, 1924), p. 77.

14. Levinger, "The Jew as Soldier," p. 33.

15. Lee J. Levinger, *A Jewish Chaplain in France* (New York: Macmillan, 1921), pp. 114–132.

16. Lee J. Levinger, *A History of the Jews in the United States* (New York: Union of American Hebrew Congregations. Nineteenth Edition, 1959).

17. *Harvard Class of 1918. Twenty-Fifth Anniversary Report* (Cambridge: Printed for the Class, 1943).

18. *Harvard Class of 1920. Twenty-Fifth Anniversary Report* (Cambridge: Printed for the Class, 1945).

19. Richard Gid Powers, *Not Without Honor: The History of American Anti-Communism* (New Haven: Yale University Press, 1998), pp. 46–47.

20. "General Pershing Urges Abolition of Race Prejudice," *The Sentinel*, December 17, 1926, p. 21.

Chapter 16

1. Israel Friedlaender, *The Jews of Russia and Poland* (New York: G.P. Putnam's Sons, 1915), p. 208.

2. Barry R. Chiswick, "The Occupational Attainment and Earnings of American Jewry, 1890–1900," *Contemporary Jewry* 20 (1999): 68–98.

3. Ilan Stavans, editor, *The Oxford Book of Jewish Stories* (New York: Oxford University Press, 1998), pp. 68–77.

4. Nathan Glazer, *Social Characteristics of American Jews; 1654–1954* (New York: American Jewish Committee, 1955), p. 15.

5. Eli Lederhendler, *American Jewry: A History* (Cambridge: Cambridge University Press, 2017), p. 90.

6. William Zebina Ripley, *The Races of Europe: A Sociological Study* (New York: Appleton, 1898), pp. 368–400.

7. Stephen Birmingham, *The Rest of Us: The Rise of America's Eastern European Jews* (Boston: Little, Brown, 1984).

8. Hutchings Hopgood, *The Spirit of the Ghetto: Studies of the Jewish Quarter of New York* (New York: Funk & Wagnalls, 1902), pp. 36–37.

9. Edward J. James, editor, *The Immigrant Jew in America* (New York: Burk, 1907), p. 135.

10. Paul H. Douglass, "Is the New Immigrant More Unskilled Than the Old?" *Journal of the American Statistical Association* 16 (June 1919): 393.

11. Deborah Dash Moore, *At Home in America:*

Second Generation New York Jews (New York: Columbia University Press, 1981), p. 103.

12. Steven Pearse, *The Golden Age of Jewish Achievement: The Compendium of Culture, People and Their Stunning Performance* (Deucation, 2009), p. 300.

13. Barry R. Chiswick, *Explorations in Economic History* 28, no. 1 (January 1991): 64–86.

14. Barry R. Chiswick and Nicholas Larsen, "Russian Jewish Immigrants in the United States: The Adjustment of English Language Proficiency and Earnings," *Contemporary Jewry* 35, no. 3 (2015): 191–209.

15. "Lowell tells Jews Limit at Colleges Might Help Them Combat Increasing Tendency to anti-Semitism," *New York Times*, June 22, 1922.

16. Simon Kuznets, *Economic Structure of U.S. Jewry: Recent Trends* (The Institute of Contemporary Jewry, Hebrew University of Jerusalem, 1972), pp. 1–17.

17. Werner Sombart, *The Jews and Modern Capitalism* (London: Fisher Unwin, 1913), pp. 258,261, 272. During the 1930s Werner Sombart adopted Nazi ideology, and no longer complimented Jews for their positive contributions to modern capitalism.

18. Norman Lebrecht, *Genius & Anxiety: How Jews Changed the World* (New York: Scribner's, 2020).

19. Richard Lynn and Satoshi Kanazawa, "How to Explain High Jewish Achievement: The Role of Intelligence and Values," *Personality and Individual Differences* 44, no. 4 (March 2008): 801–808.

20. Robert Eisen, *Judaism and Success: How Religion Paved the Way to Modern Jewish Achievement* (Toronto: University of Toronto Press, 2023).

21. Maristella Botticini and Zvi Ekstein, *The Chosen Few: How Education Shaped Jewish History: 70-1492* (Princeton: Princeton University Press, 2012).

22. Eli Lederhendler, *Jewish Immigration and American Capitalism, 1889–1920* (New York: Cambridge University Press, 2009).

23. Hans Eysenck, *Genius: The Natural History of Creativity* (Cambridge: Cambridge University Press, 1975), p. 159.

24. Gregory Cochran, Jason Hardy, and Henry Harpending, "Natural History of Ashkenazi Intelligence," *Journal of Biosocial Science* 38, no. 5 (September 2006): 659–693.

25. "God Bless America; The Story Behind the Song," *New York Times*, July 20, 1940. Sheryl Koskowitz, "God Bless America: 100 Years of an Immigrant's Anthem," *New York Times*, July 2, 2018, p. C1.

26. J.X. Cohen, *Toward Fair Play for Jewish Workers: Third Report on Jewish Non-Employment* (New York: American Jewish Congress, 1938), pp. 6, 28.

27. *Jewish America in 2020*, Pew Research Center, May 11, 2021.

28. David Reed, America of the Melting Pot Comes to an End," *New York Times*, April 27, 1924, Section XX, p. 3.

Bibliography

Alpern, Laura M. *Manischewitz: The Matzah Family: The Making of an American Icon.* Jersey City: Ktav, 2000

Antin, Mary. *The Promised Land.* Boston: Houghton Mifflin, 1912.

Arkin, Alan. *An Improvised Life.* New York: Da Capo, 2011.

Auerbach, Arnold "Red," and Joe Fitzgerald. *Red Auerbach: An Autobiography.* New York: G.P. Putnam's Sons, 1977.

Bacall, Lauren. *By Myself and Then Some.* New York: Harper, 2005.

Basten, Fred E. *Max Factor: The Man Who Changed the Faces of the World.* New York: Arcade, 2008.

Bergreen, Laurence. *As Thousands Cheer: The Life of Irving Berlin.* New York: Da Capo, 1996.

Bernheimer, Charles E., editor. *The Russian Jew in the United States: Studies of Social Conditions in New York, Philadelphia and Chicago.* Philadelphia: Winston, 1905.

Bernstein, Leonard, and Neil Simeone, editor. *The Leonard Bernstein Letters.* New Haven: Yale University Press, 2013.

Birmingham, Stephen. *The Rest of Us: The Rise of America's Eastern European Jews.* Boston: Little, Brown, 1984.

Bogen, Boris. *Jewish Philanthropy.* New York: Macmillan, 1917.

Botticini, Maristella, and Zvi Ekstein. *The Chosen Few: How Education Shaped Jewish History: 70–1492.* Princeton: Princeton University Press, 2012.

Breck, Allen D. *The Centennial History of the Jews of Colorado; 1859–1959.* Denver: University of Denver Press, 1960.

Burns, Jennifer. *Goddess of the Markets: Ayn Rand and the American Right.* New York: Oxford University Press, 2009.

Burroughs, Harry E. *Boys in Men's Shoes: A World of Working Children.* New York: Macmillan, 1944.

Campbell, Susan. *Frog Hollow.* Middletown, CT: Wesleyan University Press, 2010.

Cody, Matt W. *Calvin Klein.* New York: Chelsea House, 2013.

Cohen, J.X. *Toward Fair Play for Jewish Workers: Third Report on Jewish Non-Employment.* New York: American Jewish Congress, 1938.

Cohen, Morris Raphael. *A Dreamer's Journey.* Boston: Beacon Press, 1949.

Cohen, Rose. *Out of the Shadow: A Russian-Jewish Childhood in the Lower East Side.* New York: Doran, 1918.

Consumers' League. *The Sweatshops: Blight of the Tenements.* New York, 1904.

Cutler, Irving. *The Jews of Chicago: From Shtetl to Suburb.* Urbana: University of Illinois Press, 1996.

Daugherty, Tracy. *Just One Catch: A Biography of Joseph Heller.* New York: St. Martin's Press, 2011.

DiGirolamo, V,incent. *Shouting the News: A History of America's Newsboys.* New York: Oxford University Press, 2019.

Dillon, Phyllis, and Andrew Godley. "The Evolution of the Jewish Garment Industry, 1840–1940." In *Chosen Capital: The Jewish Encounter with American Capitalism,* edited by Rebecca Kubrin. New Brunswick: Rutgers University Press, 2012.

Dolkart, Andrew S. "From the Rag Trade to Riches." In *Chosen Capital: The Jewish Encounter with American Capitalism,* edited by Rebecca Kubrin. New Brunswick: Rutgers University Press, 2012.

Dubnow, Simon. *History of the Jews of Russia and Poland, Volume III.* Philadelphia: Jewish Publication Society, 1920.

Dushkin, Alexander M. *Jewish Education in New York City.* New York: New York Bureau of Jewish Education, 1915.

Dylan, Bob. *Chronicles, Volume One.* New York: Simon & Schuster, 2004.

Edelman, Rob, and Audrey Kupferberg. *Matthau: A Life.* Lanham, MD: Rowman & Littlefield, 2000.

Eisen, Robert. *Judaism and Success: How Religion Paved the Way to Modern Jewish Achievement.* Toronto: University of Toronto Press, 2023.

Elshtain, Jean B. *The Jane Addams Reader.* New York: Basic Books, 2020.

Epstein, Lawrence. *George Burns: An American Life.* Jefferson, NC: McFarland, 2011.

Eyman, Scott. *Lion of Hollywood: The Life and Legend of Louis B. Mayer.* New York: Simon & Schuster, 2005.

Eysenck, Hans. *Genius: The Natural History of Creativity.* Cambridge: Cambridge University Press, 1975.

Ford, Henry. *The International Jew: The World's

Foremost Problem. Reprint of a Series of Articles Appearing in the Dearborn Independent from May 22 to October 2, 1920. Dearborn, Michigan, 1920.

Fraser, Steven. *Labor Will Rule: Sidney Hillman and the Rise of American Labor.* New York: Free Press, 1991.

Fried, Albert. *The Rise and Fall of the Jewish Gangster.* New York: Columbia University Press, 1993.

Friedkin, William. *The Friedkin Connection: A Memoir.* New York: Harper, 2014.

Friedlander, Israel. *The Jews of Russia and Poland.* New York: G.P. Putnam's Sons, 1915.

Friedman, Milton, and Rose Friedman. *Two Lucky People: Milton and Rose Friedman, Memoirs.* Chicago: University of Chicago Press, 1981.

Gabler, Neal. *An Empire of Their Own: How Jews Invented Hollywood.* New York: Anchor, 1988.

Gansberg, Alan L. *Little Caesar: A Biography of Edward G. Robinson.* Lanham, MD: Scarecrow, 2004.

Garraty, John A. *Henry Cabot Lodge: Biography.* New York: Knopf, 1953.

Glass, Philip. *Words Without Music: A Memoir.* New York: Norton, 2016.

Glazer, Nathan. *Social Characteristics of American Jews; 1654–1954.* New York: American Jewish Committee, 1955.

Glazer, Nathan, and Patrick Moynihan. *Beyond the Melting Pot.* Cambridge: MIT Press, 1963.

Gleick, James. *Genius: The Life and Science of Richard Feynman.* New York: Vintage, 1993.

Goldin, Peter. *Quiet Diplomat: A Biography of Max M. Fisher.* New York: Cornwall Books, 1992.

Goldman, Emma. *Anarchism and Other Essays.* New York: Mother Earth Publication Association, 1910.

Gompers, Samuel. *Seventy Years of Life and Labor: An Autobiography.* New York: Dutton, 1925.

Goodkin, S.B. *Prominent Jews of America: A Collection of Biographical Sketches of Jews who have Distinguished themselves in Commerce, Professional and Religious Endeavors.* Toledo: American Hebrew Publication Society, 1919.

Grant, Madison. *The Passing of the Great Race.* New York: Charles Scribner's Sons, 1916.

Greenberg, Hank. *The Story of My Life.* Edited by Ira Berkow. Chicago: Ivan Dee, 1989.

Gross, Michael. *Genuine Authentic: The Real Life of Ralph Lauren.* New York: Harper, 2003.

Hecht, Ben. *A Child of the Century.* New Haven: Yale University Press, 1954.

Hillquit, Morris. *History of Socialism in the United States.* New York: Funk & Wagnalls, 1903.

Hopgood, Hutchings. *The Spirit of the Ghetto: Studies of the Jewish Quarter of New York.* New York: Funk & Wagnalls, 1902.

Jacobs, Charlotte D. *Jonas Salk: A Life.* New York: Oxford University Press, 2015.

James, Edmund. *The Immigrant Jew in America.* New York: Buck, 1907.

Kaplan, James. *Irving Berlin: New York Genius.* New Haven: Yale University Press, 2019.

Karabel, Jerome. *The Chosen: The Hidden History of Admission and Exclusion from Harvard, Yale, and Princeton.* Boston: Houghton Mifflin, 2005.

Katz, Daniel. *All Together Different: Yiddish Socialists, Garment Workers, and the Labor Roots of Multiculturalism.* New York: New York University Press, 2011.

Kelly, Florence. *The Sweating System Hull House Maps and Papers.* 1895.

Koprince, Susan. *Understanding Neil Simon.* Columbia: University of South Carolina Press, 2002.

Kramer, Judith B., and Seymour Leventman. *Children of the Gilded Ghetto: Conflict Resolution of Three Generations of American Jews.* New Haven: Yale University Press, 1961.

Kraus, Joe. *The Kosher Capones: A History of Chicago's Jewish Gangsters.* Ithaca: Cornell University Press, 2019.

Kuznets, Simon, Stephanie Lo, and Glen Weyl, editors. *Jewish Economies: Development and Migration in America and Beyond.* New York: Routledge, 2012.

Kvoraceus, William. *Juvenile Delinquency and School.* New York: World Books, 1945.

Landesco, John. *Organized Crime in Chicago.* Chicago: University of Chicago Press, 1968.

Lauder, Leonard A. *The Company I Keep: My Life in Beauty.* New York: Harper, 2020.

Lebrecht, Norman. *Genius & Anxiety: How Jews Changed the World.* New York: Scribner's, 2020.

Lederhendler, Eli. *American Jewry: A New History.* Cambridge: Cambridge University Press, 2017.

Lederhendler, Eli. *Jewish Immigrants and American Capitalism 1880–1920.* New York: Cambridge University Press, 2009.

Levine, Louis. *The Ladies Garment Workers Union.* New York: Huesch, 1924.

Levinger, Lee J. *A History of the Jews in the United States.* New York: Union of American Hebrew Congregations, Nineteenth Edition, 1959.

Levinger, Lee J. *A Jewish Chaplain in France.* New York: Macmillan, 1921.

Levitan, Tina. *The Laureates: Jewish Winners of the Nobel Prize.* New York: Twayne, 1960.

Levy, Shawn. *King of Comedy: The Life and Art of Jerrie Lewis.* New York: St. Martin's Press, 1996.

Linfield, H.S. *The Jewish Population in the United States, 1927.* American Jewish Year Book, 1928.

Lyons, Eugene. *David Sarnoff—A Biography.* New York: Harper & Row, 1980.

Mann, William J. *Hello! Gorgeous: Becoming Barbra Streisand.* Boston: Houghton Mifflin, 2012.

Markham, Edwin. *Children in Bondage.* New York: Hearst, 1907.

McCall, Samuel W. *Patriotism of the American Jew.* New York: Plymouth Press, 1924.

McDougall, William. *Is America Safe for Democracy?* New York: Charles Scribner, 1921.

McDougall, William. *National Welfare and National Decay.* London: Methuen, 1921.

McGill, Nettie P. *Children in Street Work.* U.S. Children's Bureau, Publication #183. Washington, D.C.: U.S. Government Printing Office, 1928.

Miller, Arthur. *Timebends: A Life*. New York: Grove, 2013.
Moore, Deborah D. *At Home in America*. New York: Columbia University Press, 1981.
Oja, Carol J., and Judith Tuck, editors. *Aaron Copland and His World*. Princeton: Princeton University Press, 2000.
Oshinsky, David. *Polio: An American Story*. New York: Oxford University Press, 2005.
Pearse, Steven. *The Golden Age of Jewish Achievement: The Compendium of Culture, People and Their Stunning Performance*. Deucation, 2009.
Polacheck, Hilda S. *I Came a Stranger: The Story of a Hull-House Girl*. Urbana: University of Illinois Press, 1989.
Pollack, Howard. *Aaron Copland: The Life and Work of an Uncommon Man*. New York: Henry Holt, 1999.
Pollack, Howard. *George Gershwin: His Life and Work*. Berkeley: University of California Press, 2007.
Powers, Richard G. *Not Without Honor: The History of American Anti-Communism*. New Haven: Yale University Press, 1998.
Pratt, Norma. *Morris Hillquit: A Political History of an American Jewish Socialist*. Westport, CT: Greenwood Press, 1979.
Proskauer, Bertha R. *Julia Richman; Appreciation of a Great Teacher*. 1912.
Rabinowitz, Matilda. *Immigrant Girl, Radical Woman: A Memoir from the Early Twentieth Century*. Ithaca: Cornell University Press, 2017.
Riess, Steven A. *Sports and the American Jew*. Syracuse: Syracuse University Press, 1998.
Riis, Jacob A. *How the Other Half Lives: Studies Among the Tenements of New York*. New York: Charles Scribner's Sons, 1890.
Ripley, William Z. *The Races of Europe: A Sociological Study*. New York: Appleton, 1899.
Robinson, Leonard G. *The Agricultural Activities of Jews in America*. New York: American Jewish Committee, 1912.
Rogoff, Abraham. *The Founding of the Jewish Trade Unions in the United States: 1880–1900*. New York, 1945.
Rogoff, Leonard. *Homelands: Southern Jewish Identity in Durham and Chapel Hill, North Carolina*. Tuscaloosa: University of Alabama Press, 2001.
Rosenblit, Marsha L., and Jonathan Karp, editors. *World War I and the Jews*. New York: Berghahn, 2017.
Sachar, Howard. *A History of Jews in America*. New York: Vintage, 1993.
Secrest, Meryle. *Stephen Sondheim: A Life*. New York: Knopf, 2011.
Shaw, Allen. *Leonard Bernstein: An American Musician*. New Haven: Yale University Press, 2014.
Shnayerson, Michael. *Bugsy Siegel: The Dark Side of the American Dream*. New Haven: Yale University Press, 2020.
Silver, Mike. *Stars in the Ring: Jewish Champions in the Golden Age of Boxing*. New York: Lyons Press, 2016.
Singer, Harry P. *Heroes All*. Washington, D.C: Fassett, 1919.
Solomon, Barbara A. *Pioneers in Service: A History of the Associated Jewish Philanthropies of Boston*. Boston, 1956.
Sombert, Werner. *The Jews and Modern Capitalism*. London: Fisher Unwin, 1913.
Sorin, Gerald. *A Time for Building: The Third Migration, 1880–1920*. Baltimore: John Hopkins University Press, 1992.
Steinberg, Stephen. *The Academic Melting Pot: Catholics and Jew in America's Higher Education*. New Brunswick: Transaction Books, 1971.
Sterba, Christopher M. *Good Americans: Italian and Jewish Immigrants During the First World War*. New York: Oxford University Press, 2002.
Syrkin, Marie. *Gold Meir: Woman with a Cause*. New York: G.P. Putnam's Sons, 1966.
Thernstrom, Stephen. *Poor but Hopeful Students*. Edited by Bernard Bailyn. *Glimpses of Harvard Past*. Cambridge: Harvard University Press, 1986.
Vaill, Amanda. *Somewhere: The Life of Jerry Robbins*. New York: Broadway Books, 2006.
Wald, Lillian. *The House on Henry Street*. New York: Henry Holt, 1924.
Ward, Estelle F. *The Story of Northwestern University*. New York: Dodd, Mead, 1924.
Ware, Louise. *Jacob A. Riis: Police Reporter, Reporter, Useful Citizen*. New York: Appleton, 1938.
Weinstein, David. *The Eddie Cantor Story: A Jewish Life in Performance and Politics*. Waltham, MA: Brandeis University Press, 2018.
Weizmann, Chaim. *Trial and Error: The Autobiography of Chaim Weizmann, Book One*. Lexington, MA: Plunkett Lake Press, 2013.
Wouk, Herman. *Sailor and Fiddler: Reflections of a 100-Year-Old Author*. New York: Simon & Schuster, 2016.
Zukor, Adolph, and Dale Kramer. *The Public Is Never Wrong: The Autobiography of Adolph Zukor*. New York: G.P. Putnam's Sons, 1953.

Index

www.ingramcontent.com/pod-product-compliance
Lightning Source LLC
Chambersburg PA
CBHW080553270326
41929CB00019B/3286
* 9 7 8 1 4 7 6 6 9 5 4 7 1 *